12·95

Regional Policy in the European Community

Regional Policy in the European Community

THE ROLE OF REGIONAL INCENTIVES

Edited by
Douglas Yuill, Kevin Allen and Chris Hull

CROOM HELM LONDON

© 1980 Centre for the Study of Public Policy
Croom Helm Ltd, 2–10 St John's Road, London SW11

British Library Cataloguing in Publication Data

Regional policy in the European Community.
    1. Subsidies – European Economic Community
    countries
    2. Regional planning – European Economic
    Community countries   3. European Economic
    Community countries – Economic policy
    I. Yuill, Douglas   II. Allen, Kevin
    III. Hull, Chris
    338.91'4   HC240.9.S9

    ISBN 0–85664–904–X

Reproduced from copy supplied
printed and bound in Great Britain
by Billing and Sons Limited
Guildford, London, Oxford, Worcester

CONTENTS

PREFACE

Between 1975 and 1977 we, and the other contributors to this book, were engaged on a study of regional incentives in the European Community financed by the European Commission, the Federal German Ministry of Economics, the *Land* of Hesse and the International Institute of Management, Berlin, and based at the International Institute of Management. This study culminated in the presentation of a report to the sponsoring bodies in October 1977, a report which is to be published by the European Commission in August 1979 as *Regional Incentives in the European Community: A Comparative Study*. One spin-off from the study was a two-volume bibliography, *Regional Problems and Policies in the European Community*, edited by Kevin Allen and published by Saxon House; another is this book.

This current volume is, however, far more than simply a spin-off from the October 1977 report. Rather, it both complements that report and develops on it. For example, this book not only describes current policy but sets it in the context of the regional problem in each country and also the development of policy in that country. It therefore has far more of a story to tell at the individual-country level than the October 1977 report (which concerned itself solely with contemporary incentive policy) — a story, moreover, which is taken up until summer 1979. Second, this book is aimed at a general readership and not at particular sponsors. As a result it is far less technical. In particular, it avoids a detailed discussion of the concept of effective value (i.e. the value of an incentive in net-grant-equivalent terms after taking tax treatment, the timing and phasing of incentive payment and eligible items of expenditure into account), as well as omitting precise numerical effective values. Instead, broad effective-value rankings are used. In contrast, at least one-quarter of the October 1977 report is given over to the effective-value concept — the methodology used, the assumptions made in respect of each country's incentive package and the results obtained. Third, and something not found in the October 1977 report, each country chapter in this book compares regional incentives and policy in that country with incentives and policy elsewhere in the European Community. There is also a substantial final chapter drawing together the lessons of each country chapter, and making detailed comparisons for the Community as a whole.

This book, written in the 18 months since the completion of the October 1977 study, has not been easy to produce. One problem has been the difficulty of providing detailed and structured information — essential to any publication which aspires to be comparative — while at the same time maintaining an interesting storyline. Another has been that the country-chapter authors have, of course, had commitments elsewhere. The difficulties would, however, have been greater were it not for their goodwill and patience in responding to what, at times, must have seemed unending requests for extra pieces of highly detailed information, information perhaps only of peripheral interest in their own country but essential to complete the picture for the Community as a whole. To them, therefore, our thanks.

Between October 1977 and October 1978 the greater part of the work on this book was done from the International Institute of Management, Berlin, and from then onwards at the Centre for the Study of Public Policy, at the University of Strathclyde. We are grateful to both institutes for the facilities they provided and to colleagues for their advice and encouragement. We are also extremely grateful to our secretary at the Centre for the Study of Public Policy, Mrs Moira Lowe, who quickly, efficiently and with good humour typed what must have seemed like endless drafts. Finally, we must thank Silke, Kirsten and Danni for their patience and understanding. They, even more so than ourselves, must at times have wondered whether this book would ever be finished.

Douglas Yuill (CSPP)
Kevin Allen (CSPP)
Chris Hull (IIM)

ACKNOWLEDGEMENTS

In January 1978 the editors of this book, together with Silvio Ronzani and Ullrich Casper, participated in the Atlantic Conference on Balanced National Growth at Racine, Wisconsin. For this conference, background notes on regional incentive policy in Britain, France, Germany and Italy were prepared. These notes, together with the other conference papers, will be published by Lexington in Summer 1979 under the title *Balanced National Growth* (edited by Kevin Allen). The chapters on France, Germany, Italy and the United Kingdom in this book are based to some degree on these background notes and we are grateful to Lexington for allowing us to make use of this material in the preparation of this book.

EDITORS' NOTE

At the start of January 1979, £1 sterling was worth approximately the following in the currencies of the European Community countries:

Belgium:	FB 58.40
Denmark:	DKr 10.25
France:	FF 8.47
Germany:	DM 3.71
Ireland:	£1.00
Italy:	Lire 1,675
Luxembourg:	FLx 58.40
Netherlands:	Fl 3.99

1 INTRODUCTION

Throughout the 1960s and in the early 1970s regional policy was given a high priority in most European countries. The period was one of much innovation and experimentation, and one, too, where expenditure on regional policy increased significantly. There was, however, good reason for the interest and enthusiasm towards regional policy in what was, throughout Europe, a period of comparative economic 'boom'. While some regions enjoyed rapid economic growth, and indeed growth which led to overheating in many instances, others did not share in the rising prosperity. With an economic structure heavily dependent on declining activities like agriculture, coal, mining, iron and steel and textiles, unemployment in these problem regions was high, activity rates were low, out-migration was substantial (adding further to the problems of congestion facing the prosperous regions) and *per capita* income levels were below the national average. Given these circumstances, the economic justification for regional policy — that by redistributing economic activity from the pressured to the problem regions unemployed and underemployed resources could be taken up, thus adding to national growth — was strong; and it was complemented by political, social and egalitarian forces, particularly towards the end of the 1960s when distributional issues became of increasing importance throughout Europe. As a result, and as already noted, the period was one of very active regional policy in most countries.

There were, however, significant differences between countries in terms of policy emphasis, and the forms of policy adopted; this is not surprising in view of the variety of economic, political, social and institutional features found in Europe. Nevertheless, looking at the countries of the European Community, four main elements of policy can be isolated.

In the first place there was infrastructure investment — an attempt to bring the standard of infrastructure in the problem regions up to the national level or beyond. This element of policy was especially important in rural and sparsely populated regions where it was often viewed as an essential prerequisite for modern economic development; but in all areas it made for the more effective operation of the other components of policy.

The second element of policy involved the use of state-owned or

13

state-controlled firms to help develop the problem regions. The setting of investment targets for state industry in the problem areas was of particular significance in the Italian *Mezzogiorno*, but government pressures on state industry to locate or invest in the problem regions, and to take on other 'social obligations, were also evident in a number of other countries.

The third component of policy concerned the use of disincentives or controls in the pressured regions, the aim being to divert investment to the more depressed areas. This element of policy was particularly attractive since, in many countries, there were serious worries about congestion and general living conditions in the major urban centres. For most of the period up until 1973-4 control policies operated relatively stringently in France (in the Paris region) and the United Kingdom (in London and the south-east); and in the early 1970s controls were also introduced in Italy and the Netherlands.

Finally, and present in all countries of the European Community, there were regional incentives – perhaps the key element of regional policy. While infrastructure investment was largely 'permissive' of development, disincentives and controls were operated in fewer than half the Community countries and normally depended on the provision of incentives to help 'sugar the pill' for those firms forced to relocate. For its part, state industry played a major role only in Italy, and even here was compensated by the payment of incentives. Certainly, regional-incentive expenditures grew massively during the 1960s and early 1970s – increasing more than twenty-fold in the British case, for example. And in addition there was a rapid growth in the variety of incentive types on offer. By the start of the 1970s, the regional-incentive armoury was well stocked in almost every Community country, the incentives on offer ranging from capital grants to interest-subsidised loans, from accelerated-depreciation allowances to direct tax concessions, from employment premia to rent subsidies, from concessions on electricity prices to labour-training aids, and from removal-cost assistance to transport subsidies.

Truly, the period spanning the 1960s and taking in, too, the start of the 1970s was the heyday of regional policy and regional-incentive policy in particular. Although regional policy has not been dismantled in more recent years, it has certainly been operating in a more difficult, even hostile, environment. Conditions of widespread high levels of unemployment, inflation, industrial overcapacity, low levels of investment, increasing competition from low-labour-cost countries and public-expenditure curtailment are obviously not conducive to a major regional-policy effort. Rather, since the oil-crisis years of 1973-4, the emphasis throughout Europe has been on the need for national growth and development. Given this, a questioning of regional policy has begun in many countries, as part of which there has been a keen interest in the policies followed in other countries, especially in the incentive field.

This book is intended to give a structured overview of regional incentives and policy in the European Community countries, set in the context of the regional problem in those countries. To allow for ready inter-country comparison, the nine country chapters which follow this introduction adhere to a common format. Each begins with a brief description of the nature and severity of the regional problem. There then follows a section on the development of regional policy, concentrating in particular on changes within the regional-incentive system, before moving on to a broad description of the current regional-incentive package. The penultimate section in each chapter then 'homes in' on the major incentives. In treating these incentives, particular attention is paid to two key features, eligibility conditions and award levels — features which obviously determine the availability and value of the incentives. Moreover, it is not only nominal rates of award which are considered (although these can obviously be important as a 'first impression' of the attractiveness of any given package) but also *effective* values: that is, the value of an incentive after taking account of tax treatment, the timing and phasing of award and eligible items of expenditure. It is, after all, likely to be the effective value of an incentive — in effect, its net present value after tax as a percentage of total project capital costs — which, rather than its nominal value, will tend to influence the investment/location decision of applicant firms.

Each country chapter finishes with a section comparing and contrasting the regional-incentive package in that country with those on offer elsewhere in the European Community. The main comparative work, however, is left until the final concluding chapter. This chapter not only summarises and brings together the main points made in the country chapters but also highlights and draws out implications from the main differences and similarities between the various Community countries. In addition, it sets the policies of the individual countries in the context of Commission regional policy. It ends by considering possible future developments in the regional-policy field — a topic of particular interest given the current atmosphere of reappraisal and questioning.

2   REGIONAL INCENTIVES IN BELGIUM

The Nature of the Problem

There are two senses in which one can talk of 'the regional problem' in Belgium. In common with the situation found in other European Community countries, there is the problem posed by particularly depressed or underdeveloped pockets of the country, and reflected in high unemployment rates, low income levels and heavy out-migration. But in addition there is the Belgium-specific regional problem of trying to balance the needs and expectations of two major linguistic communities — the Flemish-speaking north and French-speaking Wallonia in the south (with the predominantly bilingual Brussels conurbation within the province of Brabant in the centre). For Belgium as a whole, the latter problem is obviously more important, and it has also had a major influence on the perception of, and policy reaction to, the former problem. It is useful, therefore, to begin with a brief review of the north-south differences in Belgium in the post-war period.

Immediately after the war, Wallonia was more industrialised than Flanders, but it was an industrialisation based on an out-dated economic structure and stagnating labour force. Since the early 1930s Wallonia's population has remained virtually unchanged. In contrast, the population in Flanders has grown by about one million, such that the Flemish-speaking community now accounts for over 55 per cent of the total national population (of almost 10 million) compared to 32 per cent in the French-speaking areas and some 11 per cent in the bilingual Brussels conurbation. Wallonia's main industries have also changed comparatively little since the war, although coal mining has undergone a major decline in the last 15 years (from a workforce of well over 100,000 to one of just over 25,000). The iron and steel industries and metal manufacturing have remained the key industries throughout the post-war period, and still account for over 20 per cent of Wallonia's gross value added. In contrast, the Flemish north has made fairly dynamic progress since the war. As already noted, population has grown rapidly[1] and there has also been marked success in encouraging industrial development in the area. Indeed, according to one estimate, 'in recent years 75-90 per cent of foreign industrial investment in Belgium has been devoted to Flanders'.[2]

It is, of course, far too simple to speak of a dynamic Flanders and

16

stagnating Wallonia. Both communities have their prosperous and their problem regions. Limburg in the north and Luxembourg in Wallonia, for example, are the two poorest provinces in Belgium while, after Brabant, Antwerp in the north and Liège in Wallonia are the two richest.[3] Interestingly enough, since it is not true of most other countries in the European Community, regional disparities in Belgium show themselves perhaps most clearly in respect of *per capita* income levels (even though they have tended to be narrowing in terms of this indicator over the years). Viewing this country in terms of its nine constituent provinces (Antwerp, West Flanders, East Flanders and Limburg in the north; Liège, Hainaut, Namur and Luxembourg in Wallonia; and Brabant, centred on Brussels) *per capita* income levels in 1972 were above average (100) only in Brabant (123.4), Antwerp (105.3) and Liège (100.1) and were as low as 78 per cent of the national average in Luxembourg and Limburg. These, the poorest provinces, therefore had *per capita* income levels of just over 60 per cent of the Brabant level.

Although income levels are perhaps the clearest indicators of the existence of a regional problem in Belgium, there are other indicators which also show significant inter-regional variations. Unemployment rates, for example, differ considerably between different parts of the country — even at province level. In 1977, monthly average unemployment was no less than 15.1 per cent in Liège, 14.6 per cent in Limburg and 12.7 per cent in Hainaut (all older industrial regions) compared with 9.2 per cent in Brabant, 8.6 per cent in West Flanders, and only 7.6 per cent in Luxembourg.

Despite the fact that the problem of certain areas in Belgium is obvious from such standard economic indicators as income per head and unemployment, the designation of these areas as problem areas has proven to be especially difficult. This, however, is perhaps not surprising, given the political sensitivity of any spatial policy in the Belgian context. That area designation has been possible at all can probably be traced back to two factors — the principle of broadly equal treatment of the two major communities and, less important, the fact that, as we shall see, the regional differential in the Belgian incentive package is not major.

Problem areas were first designated in Belgium as part of the Regional Expansion Law of 1959. Under this law the designated regions (called Development Zones) had to have one or more of the following characteristics: high permanent unemployment (together with a clear lack of job opportunities); heavy out-migration; large socially or economically unsettling commuting movements; and an actual or impending decline of important economic activities. The areas designated held about 15 per cent of the population and were perhaps most notable for the extent to which they were scattered about the country. As we shall see in the next section, they were not, however, treated very much more favourably than the rest of the country (the interest-subsidy differential in favour of the problem regions, for example, was a mere two percentage points per annum), with the result that new measures had to be introduced in an attempt to stimulate regional development in 1966. These measures were concentrated, in particular, on areas threatened by the closure of coal mines or the rundown of other industries, especially textiles. The west of West Flanders, south of East Flanders, north of Hainaut and the area around Liège, together with much of north-east Belgium, were all designated (as Zones of Economic Reconversion and Development). In total, some 26 per cent of the surface area of the country was covered, holding about 35 per cent of the population — more than double the population contained in the 1959 Development Zones.

In 1970 further regional-incentive legislation was introduced. As part of this legislation, new criteria for the delineation of problem areas were laid down — serious structural unemployment and related labour-market problems, current or foreseeable decline of important economic activities, abnormally low standards of living and slow economic growth. The areas actually designated, however, remained as before. The so-called Category I Development Zones in 1970 consisted simply of those Reconversion and Development Zones favoured under the 1966 law, while Category II Development Zones were the (mainly agricultural) areas designated in 1959 but then dropped in 1966. The former, as already noted, covered 26 per cent of the country and held 35 per cent of the national population, while the latter accounted for 7 per cent of the land mass and 7 per cent of the population. The Category I and Category II Development Zones are shown on the map in Figure 2.1.

In September 1971, new assisted areas were proposed but, since they related to no fewer than 41 of the 44 administrative districts in Belgium, they were viewed as too wide-ranging for regional-policy purposes by the European Commission. The Commission's counter-suggestion (made in April 1972) of Development Zones within 28 administrative districts is still under discussion and, in the meantime, the Category I and II Zones noted above remain in force. That the discussion has lasted so long (and that the areas initially suggested had

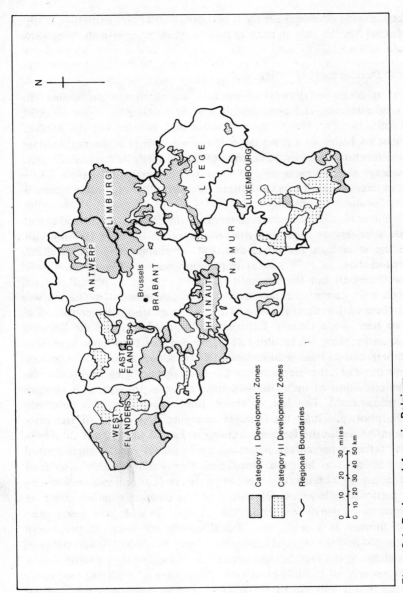

Figure 2.1: Designated Areas in Belgium

LIMBURG

LIEGE

LUXEMBOURG

ANTWERP

NAMUR

Brussels

BRABANT

HAINAUT

EAST FLANDERS

WEST FLANDERS

N

Category I Development Zones

Category II Development Zones

Regional Boundaries

0   10   20   30 miles
0 10 20 30 40 50 km

such a wide coverage) simply reinforces a point made earlier – namely, that within the Belgian context area designation is particularly sensitive and difficult.

The Development of Policy

In the course of the previous section, we mentioned, in passing, the three main regional-development laws in Belgium – those of 1959, 1966 and 1970. Within this section we wish to trace out the development of policy in a more detailed fashion before, in the two sections which follow, going on to describe the current Belgian regional-incentive package and the main regional incentives in turn. A final section then compares and contrasts the Belgian aids with other regional measures in the European Community.

Up until 1959 the main concern of the Belgian policy-maker was the economy at large, and the few incentives on offer (interest subsidies, state loan guarantees and land-tax exemptions) were available nation-wide. In 1959 new attempts were made to stimulate industrial development, but the emphasis remained very much on the national economy, despite the fact that regional-development legislation was introduced for the first time. The 1959 measures were contained in two laws – the General Expansion Law of 17 July and the Regional Expansion Law of 18 July. The joint aims of these laws have been summarised as 'the maintenance of an adequate level of domestic employment, the importation of new technological methods, the modernisation of industrial structure, and the promotion of regional development'.[4] The last objective, however, was given a relatively low priority. Thus, for example, the subsidy element of the main incentive under the Regional Expansion Law – the interest subsidy – was (at four percentage points on up to 50 per cent of eligible fixed investment for between three and five years) exactly the same as could be obtained by 'special' projects (i.e. projects undertaking a particularly large capital outlay with a clear stimulating effect on economic activity) throughout the country. Indeed, even for projects not deemed as 'special', the national subsidy was – at two percentage points – half the regional concession. True, there was also a capital grant available in the regions (and not in the nation at large) covering up to 20 per cent of building costs and 7.5 per cent of plant and machinery costs – but only up to a maximum of FB 1 million. On the whole, therefore, the regional advantage within the incentive package was slight.

Continuing problems in the regions and, in particular, the difficulties facing those areas heavily reliant on coal mining and textiles led to further regional-development legislation in 1966. Under this legislation, as already noted, the coverage of the assisted areas was significantly extended. At the same time the regional differential within existing incentive measures was increased. Within the newly designated areas, for example, the interest subsidy could be as high as five percentage points on up to two-thirds of eligible fixed investment for up to five years. Moreover, projects which were particularly attractive in terms of both employment impact and technological content qualified for an interest-free period during the first two years of the five years of the subsidy. In addition, a new capital grant was introduced as an alternative to the interest subsidy, together with a whole variety of fiscal concessions — accelerated depreciation at a maximum rate of twice the standard linear rate, tax exemption from the non-inflationary element of capital gains, exemption from the registration tax levied at the incorporation of companies and exemption from the payment of tax on any capital grant received. Further, various elements of the 1959 law were continued, including state loan guarantees and exemption from the advance levy which had to be paid on income from immovable property.

The main 1966 incentives — the interest subsidy, the (alternative) capital grant, the state loan guarantees and the various fiscal concessions noted above — also formed the core of the 1970 package. The 1970 law did, however, represent a new departure in certain respects. In particular, it put forward new criteria for the determination of problem areas even though, as we have seen, these criteria were not in fact used in the designation of the Category I and II Zones (reflecting both the political problems attached to area designation in Belgium and the fact that the European Commission was unwilling to have assisted areas relating to all but three of the 44 administrative districts in the country). A further new departure was that the sectoral coverage of the incentives on offer was extended beyond industrial and handicraft activities to include certain service activities — trade, tourism, management and engineering techniques and research and development. As for the incentives themselves, the main change was that the interest subsidy was increased to a maximum five percentage points on 75 per cent of eligible fixed investment for up to five years, with a further one-percentage-point subsidy being available for advanced-technology projects and so-called 'Progress Contracts'. Subsidies were also offered in respect of certain infrastructure investment and both training and labour aids were also made available.

The 1970 incentive package (and the one which is still current) is discussed in more detail in the next section. Before that, we should, however, briefly mention a number of other aspects of regional policy beyond the award of incentives. Seen very much as a complement to incentive policy are measures to stimulate infrastructure investment, both general and specific. At a general level much emphasis has been on canal and road building, although it is worth noting that most of the early motorways were in the Flemish part of the country. As far as specific infrastructure is concerned, industrial estates have always been given high priority and there are also incentives to aid the acquisition and preparation of industrial sites and to render more attractive those Development Zones which are less privileged from the infrastructural point of view (through subsidising drainage, water purification and other infrastructure investment). But, away from infrastructure measures, other arms of regional policy which are important in some countries are not found in Belgium. There is, for example, no disincentive or control policy along the lines of the British and French measures and relatively little attention has been devoted to decentralising office jobs, public or private. Moreover, although Regional Development Companies have been established, with the aim of actively participating in the financing of interesting regional projects, their status has been the subject of intense debate and, in keeping with this, their activity has been modest (being limited generally to project evaluation and advice). So far, seven such companies have been set up — five in Flanders and one each in Wallonia and Brussels.

The Current Incentive Package

A key feature of the financial incentives on offer in Belgium is that, for reasons already explained, there is little or no regional component to many of them. State guarantees, for example, covering the whole or partial redemption of public-credit-institute loans are national aids, as is financial assistance payable to encourage the geographical mobility of unemployed workers. Similarly, interest-free advances for management consultancy and research and development, as well as the provision of equity finance, are available on a country-wide basis. Interest subsidies, grants and loan guarantees for the purchase and equipping of industrial sites by public bodies are also national, as is the government purchase or construction of factory buildings for subsequent sale or letting (a provision which has not so far been used). Aid for advanced technical labour training (with grants, generally at some 25 per cent of the combined wages and social-security costs of the labour undergoing training) is also available nation-wide, although the rate of award is slightly higher in the Development Zones.

More specifically regional are labour grants. These were first introduced in 1970 and amount to FB 15,000 per annum per additional adult worker recruited, payable in the Category I Development Zones for five years and in the Category II Zones for three years. Additional employment is identified by comparing average employment in the year preceding the quarter of application with average employment in the following year. As a result the subsidy is paid with a year's delay. Moreover, the grant must be repaid if, without the agreement of the competent Minister, employment decreases within two years of the last payment of the premium. The crucial point to note about these labour grants, however, is that they are at present limited to very small enterprises – of not more than ten employees. They cannot, therefore, be viewed as a major incentive instrument in the regions – at least in their current form.

Far more important are the interest subsidy and the capital grant available under the 1970 Economic Expansion Law. Both are project-based, discretionary and are closely inter-related one with the other, since capital grants can partly or totally replace interest subsidies, and moreover are calculated largely on the basis of interest-subsidy values. These, the two main regional financial incentives, are discussed in detail in the next section.

Turning now to the fiscal concessions on offer in the Development Zones, these are: a five-year exemption from real-estate income tax; tax exemption from the non-inflationary element of capital gains; exemption from the registration tax levied at the incorporation of companies; and an accelerated-depreciation allowance. Although no hard information is available on expenditure on any of these fiscal incentives the three tax exemptions are certainly not of major significance. For example, the most important, the exemption from real-estate income tax, is (assuming a 'typical' project and discounting to take account of the timing and phasing of 'payment') worth less than 1 per cent of project fixed-capital costs after tax. Far more valuable to investors is the accelerated-depreciation allowance. This is a discretionary, project-related concession on the cost price of plant, equipment and industrial buildings and involves a doubling, for three consecutive years, of the normal national straight-line depreciation allowance (calculated on the basis of a 20-year fiscal life for industrial buildings and a 10-year life for plant). Like the interest subsidy and the capital grant, the accelerated-depreciation allowance is considered in more detail below.

The Main Incentives

For each of the main Belgian regional aids — the interest subsidy, the capital grant and the accelerated-depreciation allowance — we concentrate in this section on two key aspects: eligibility conditions and award levels. We begin, however, by considering the system of incentive administration in Belgium, together with the general scale of the incentives on offer.

Incentive administration is particularly interesting in the Belgian context given the linguistic (and other) divisions within the country. For the financial measures, applications are made through approved credit institutions (normally banks) to the appropriate State Secretary for Regional Economy — in the Flemish north, in Wallonia or in the Brussels region. Each State Secretary then decides on the awards to be made in his region (for projects up to a certain size limit), following detailed administrative directives laid down by his region's Ministerial Committee for Regional Affairs. There is one such committee in each of the regions, made up of members of the central government with particular regional responsibilities. In general, each Regional Affairs Committee concerns itself with the distribution, in its region, of that part of the national budget which has been regionalised. As far as financial incentives are concerned the committee not only lays down the rules for the State Secretary to follow but is also involved in the detailed administration of some of the larger cases. The *implementation* of the various incentive schemes is therefore at least to a degree regionalised. This is, however, not to say that *control* lies at the regional level. A central-government committee, the Ministerial Committee for Economic and Social Co-ordination, both fixes the basic principles of the government's economic, financial and social policy, and co-ordinates its execution. In the field of regional-incentive policy this committee determines the *maximum amount* of public support that can be given within the framework of the Economic Expansion Laws, as well as undertaking the detailed examination of the most important projects. Therefore, despite a move towards regionalisation in Belgium based on the Flemish, Walloon and Brussels regions (including regionalised budget appropriation amounting, in 1976, to 7 per cent of the national budget) the financial incentive schemes on offer in the regions remain — for the present at least — firmly within central-government control.

Control of the accelerated-depreciation allowance also lies with central government. Applications are made through the Ministry of Economic Affairs and the decision whether or not to make an award is taken by the appropriate State Secretary for Regional Economy following guidelines similar to those laid down for the capital grant and interest subsidy. Indeed, the decision on what aid to award any given project will normally be made at the same time for all incentives, the measures on offer being viewed as a package. Once it has been agreed to award an accelerated-depreciation allowance (and normally this incentive will only go to projects also in receipt of an interest subsidy and/or capital grant) claims relating to particular items of project expenditure are then made along with the tax return for the year in which the expenditure is made. Quite clearly, the accelerated-depreciation allowance is very much an integral part of the Belgian regional-incentive package. Indeed, it is far more integrated than similar measures elsewhere in the European Community, the standard practice elsewhere being for fiscal aids to be administered by the tax authorities quite independently of the remaining regional incentives on offer.

While administrative questions are particularly interesting in Belgium, questions concerning the scale of the incentive package are particularly difficult. There are two basic reasons for this. First, in common with the position in most other countries there is virtually no relevant information available on the accelerated-depreciation allowance; and second, financial statistics cover all incentive awards under the Economic Expansion Laws (which are, of course, both national *and* regional in character) and not simply those made in the problem regions. Between 1972 and 1977, some 540 projects on average were awarded an interest subsidy annually under these laws (just under one-quarter of these cases also being in receipt of a loan guarantee) while, on average, 162 projects annually obtained a capital grant. In the same period, annual capital-grant expenditure averaged FB 1822 million, while interest-subsidy costs were estimated at a further FB 3556 million annually for the period 1972-6. No information is available on jobs associated with the interest subsidy alone, but the interest subsidy and capital grant together are estimated to have been associated with projects involving almost 130,000 jobs in the same period. The investment associated with these two aids is estimated to have been some FB 54,920 million annually between 1972 and 1976.[5]

Eligibility Conditions

Our prime concern here is with the main conditions of award laid down for the various incentives — and especially with the eligibility of particular activities, particular areas and particular project-type and size groups. We have already made the point that the interest subsidy and the capital grant are, in large measure, *alternative* financial incentives. It is therefore sensible to treat them together in this discussion, since they face very similar conditions of award and of eligibility. Indeed, as we shall see, there is really only one major difference between them, and this is that, to obtain a capital grant, a project must be at least 50 per cent internally financed. No such condition applies to the award of an interest subsidy.

Under the Economic Expansion Law of 1970 all industrial activities (including mining, and also construction in as far as it deals with construction materials and pre-fabrication) and artisan activities, as well as enterprises in the service sector involved in commerce, tourism, management and engineering techniques, and research and development, are eligible for both the interest subsidy and the capital grant. As noted earlier, the eligibility of service-sector activities was new to the 1970 legislation. Previously, only industrial and artisan activities had been eligible. But although the service sector is certainly 'better off' under the 1970 law it is still relatively poorly treated. The so-called 'priority sectors' of the Belgian economy are composed entirely of manufacturing activities, with the result that, although services are eligible for assistance, they qualify for only moderate rates of award (while priority 1 sectors may receive the maximum-percentage-point subsidy, this maximum is reduced by one percentage point for priority 2 sectors and by two percentage points for non-priority sectors, including services). Certainly manufacturing and construction together have accounted for well over 90 per cent of regional-incentive expenditure in recent years, most of the aid being concentrated on only three sectors — iron and steel, metal manufacturing and chemicals.

For the accelerated depreciation allowance the position in respect of eligible activities and especially in respect of service eligibility is possibly even more restrictive than for the interest subsidy and capital grant. Although in theory the same activities are eligible as qualify for the main financial incentives, in practice awards tend to be restricted to the priority 1 and 2 sectors, i.e. basically to manufacturing. As far as the service sector is concerned, therefore, the position with respect to the Belgian regional-incentive package is similar to that found in most other European Community countries, services as a whole being poorly treated despite the changes made in 1970.

Turning now to spatial eligibility, we have already seen that new criteria for identifying the problem regions were evolved in 1970, but that areas designated by the 1966 and 1959 Regional Expansion Laws remained in force (as Category I and Category II Development Zones, respectively). The interest subsidy and the capital grant are available in both zones, and indeed are available at the same rates in both zones. For the accelerated-depreciation allowance, too, no practical distinction is drawn between the two types of Development Zone, although in principle it is restricted to Category I Zones. No information is available on the distribution of awards — fiscal or financial — by type of problem area, but it is known that the main financial incentives are split between Flanders and Wallonia roughly in the ratio 50:50 — reflecting the principle noted earlier of broadly equal treatment of the two main linguistic communities.[6]

Other factors determining eligibility for the main regional incentives in Belgium are project type and project size. The accelerated-depreciation allowance, for example, is available only where a minimum of 20 new jobs are created, and thus tends in practice to be limited to setting-up projects and major extensions. There is no equivalent explicit job condition attached to the financial incentives but projects of less than FB 500,000 (a small sum by any standards) are normally excluded while projects of more than FB 100 million may be required to transfer convertible bonds to the state in return for the assistance received. Otherwise all project types qualify for the interest subsidy and capital grant as long as there is a 'reasonable' increase in fixed-capital investment, although in the case of a transfer only the net investment increase qualifies for assistance. In the period 1959-76 more than one-third of assisted projects were setting-up projects, the remainder being projects relating to already existing plants.

In addition to activity eligibility, spatial eligibility and size and project-type eligibility, there are a number of more general criteria taken into account in the award of incentives. These include the creation of employment, the effect on economic structure, the financial soundness of the applicant, the degree of conformity with national environmental-protection and anti-inflation policies and the goods to be produced (energy-saving products, products of socio-economic importance and products exported to countries outside the European Community are favoured). For the most part, however, these additional criteria are not quantified and, indeed, tend to be somewhat vague. One exception to this we have already noted — that for the accelerated-depreciation allowance a minimum of 20 new jobs must be created. Another exception, also noted previously, is that at least 50 per cent of project investment must be internally financed before a project can qualify for the capital grant. Otherwise, however, the conditions tend to be less than precise, in keeping with the general discretionary nature of the Belgian regional-incentive package. Not surprisingly, perhaps, some 18 per cent of interest-subsidy applications were turned down between 1959 and 1977, although it should be noted that a number of these were almost certainly later accepted on submission of a revised application.

Award Levels

In this sub-section we want to treat each of the three main incentives separately. We begin by considering the interest subsidy. In many respects this is the most important Belgian subsidy, although its significance has been reduced somewhat since the introduction of the (alternative) capital grant in 1966. In the period 1971-5 expenditure on interest subsidies accounted for just under two-thirds of all Belgian financial-incentive assistance. Within the European Community it is unusual for such emphasis to be given to interest subsidies within incentive packages. For this reason, the Belgian interest subsidy is especially interesting.

Two other features distinguish the Belgian subsidy from those found elsewhere in Europe. First, it is very much part and parcel of a *national* incentive system. While the maximum regional subsidy is five percentage points (six percentage points for advanced-technology projects and 'Progress Contracts' and seven percentage points under special cyclical conditions) on up to 75 per cent of eligible investment over a maximum of five years, the standard national maxima are three percentage points (four percentage points for advanced-technology projects), 50 per cent and three years (five years under special cyclical conditions). And, second, the concessionary element is not available over the full life of the loan being assisted (loans are usually of ten years' duration) but rather, as noted above, is normally limited to between three and five years. In most other respects, however, the Belgian interest subsidy reflects standard European practice. Repayment of the loan is, for example, on a straight-line basis with a principal-repayment holiday of up to two years; and there is no interest-free period available (although such a concession did exist under the 1966 legislation).

Because of the discretionary nature of interest-subsidy awards it is not easy to identify the average regional concession. What can be said is that it certainly lies below the regional maxima noted above and probably is about four percentage points on two-thirds of eligible investment over four years. That the average award falls below the possible maximum is one factor reducing the real or effective value of the subsidy on recipient projects. A further such factor is that, like all interest subsidies and soft loans, the Belgian concession is taxed whenever profits are made since, by reducing debt-servicing charges, it leads to an increase in taxable profits. Yet another factor which could reduce the effective value of the subsidy is the timing and phasing of its award. In practice, however, there are no significant extra delays in the Belgian system in this respect. True, the application for assistance must have been made, and (unusual for such an incentive) a decision on that application must have been received, before the start of project construction, but the application-processing period is relatively short by European standards — about two months on average — so that any delay here is minimal. Once a positive decision has been made, the interest subsidy is paid direct to the approved credit institution supplying the loan being subsidised, and this institution then passes on the benefit to the applicant firm in the form of reduced interest charges.

We mentioned above that the loan being subsidised could, at the regional level, cover up to 75 per cent of eligible investment, but did not enlarge on just what investment is considered eligible. Clearly, this is an important topic, with obvious implications for the effective value of any subsidy award made. In fact, the list of eligible items is fairly standard in the European context. All direct investment in the acquisition or construction of buildings, plant and equipment (including site purchase) is eligible, as are ancillary buildings like canteens and offices where they form a constituent part of the project. The main ineligible item is working capital, and vehicles are also generally ineligible. Ineligible, too, are most short-life assets, since the life of any asset subsidised must be at least that of the subsidy period — a rule found often among concessionary loan schemes in Europe. One area where the Belgian scheme is perhaps more generous than others is in its encouragement of market and organisational studies and of research on the development of prototypes, new products and new manufacturing processes — investment in all such activities being treated as eligible for assistance.

Finally, we should note that the interest subsidy can be combined with other incentives, and in particular with capital grants, state loan guarantees and the various fiscal concessions on offer. However, when combined with a state guarantee (and this is the case for something under one-quarter of all loans awarded) the maximum value of the interest subsidy is reduced by one percentage point, while when combined with a capital grant the maximum interest-subsidy coverage of eligible investment costs is reduced by the coverage of the capital grant. Since the capital grant can have such an important bearing on the value of any interest-subsidy award made and, in any case, is itself an important element of the Belgian regional-incentive package, we now turn to consider it in more detail.

The Belgian capital grant is often put forward as being the capital-grant equivalent of the interest subsidy. Indeed this was the idea behind it. It was meant to give the same subsidy to those firms financing a project from internal means (and at least 50 per cent of the project had to be 'own-financed' to obtain the grant) as was paid to other projects in the form of an interest-subsidised loan. But the interesting feature of the capital grant is in fact the extent to which it differs from the interest subsidy.

In the first place, the level of assistance is calculated by summing the undiscounted annual-interest subsidies which would have been due had the project's 'own finance' been in the form of a ten-year interest-subsidised loan repaid annually on a straight-line basis, with neither principal-repayment holiday nor interest-free periods. The subsidy period is therefore ten years, and not three to five years as with the interest subsidy — thus making the capital grant the more valuable concession, at least in nominal terms.

Secondly, the capital grant is not 'paid' over a three- to five-year period as is the interest subsidy, but rather is awarded in three equal annual instalments. The first of these instalments is paid not less than one year after the decision to award a capital grant, and is on condition that a specific part of the investment being assisted has indeed been carried out; the second follows one year later provided that the investment programme has been completed — except where the project has a particularly long construction period (of over 18 months), in which case at least 75 per cent of the programme must have been completed; the third and last instalment is made after a further year, subject to the attainment of the project objectives (such as the creation of new jobs). The capital grant is therefore treated more favourably then the interest subsidy in terms of timing and phasing of award, unless of course the project faces extreme delays in construction or does not meet the targets set for it.

A final area where the capital grant differs from the interest subsidy is in respect of tax treatment. While, as we have seen, the interest subsidy is taxed 'in full' wherever taxable profits are being made, the capital grant is taxed only indirectly since grant-aided assets must be depreciated for tax purposes net of any grant received. In this way the impact of taxation on the effective value of the capital grant is considerably reduced so that, in respect of tax treatment too, the capital grant is dealt with more favourably than the interest subsidy.[7] This contrasts sharply with the position in the United Kingdom (the only other country offering a grant alternative to an interest-subsidised loan), where the interest-relief grants available under the selective-financial-assistance scheme are treated as income for tax purposes, and thus taxed directly and 'in full', simply to keep them in line with the tax treatment of the concessionary element of selective-financial-assistance soft loans.

Indeed, it is really only in terms of eligible items of expenditure that the capital grant and interest subsidy are similarly treated. In all other important respects — nominal award values, the timing and phasing of the award and tax treatment — the capital grant is treated more favourably then the interest subsidy.

Like the interest subsidy, the capital grant can be combined with other regional incentives. However, where awarded in conjunction with the interest subsidy, the combined incentives must not exceed the interest-subsidy maxima noted earlier. Moreover, when added to the accelerated-depreciation allowance the effective value of the capital grant is reduced, since the net present value of the tax to be paid on it increases.

For its part, the accelerated-depreciation allowance, as we have seen, consists of a doubling of the standard straight-line depreciation rate (of 5 per cent for industrial buildings and 10 per cent for plant) over three consecutive years. Although the decision whether or not to make an award is discretionary, the award itself is at fixed rates. Eligible items include industrial buildings and plant and equipment (as long as it has a minimum life of five years — thus excluding, for example, vehicles). Also not covered are a number of items which qualify for even more favourable national fiscal aids — ships and scientific research equipment, to name but two. In common with other accelerated-depreciation allowances in Europe, leasing is not an eligible form of expenditure, but items purchased with cash (whether in one payment or through a series of phased payments) as well as those bought under hire-purchase agreements do qualify.

Comparative Conclusions

In comparison with regional-incentive policy in the other countries of the European Community, regional-incentive policy in Belgium has a relatively low profile. For example, alone among the regional-incentive packages of the Community countries, the Belgian incentive scheme contains no direct capital grant — perhaps the most visible incentive type that can be put on offer. Rather, as we have seen, the emphasis is on subsidising interest rates — either in the form of a direct interest subsidy (sometimes with the addition of a loan guarantee), or in the form of the grant equivalent of an interest subsidy in those cases where project funds are (at least 50 per cent) internally provided. In no other regional-incentive scheme does subsidised interest, or its equivalent, play such an important role.

The rather low-profile nature of regional-incentive policy in Belgium is reflected also in the value of the available incentives. In effective-value terms, the three main incentives all have 'medium-to-low' maximum values, so that the maximum value of the regional-incentive package as a whole is also relatively low. For example, the interest subsidy is on a par with the Danish and German interest-related aids in effective-value terms but is less valuable than UK selective financial assistance and very much less valuable than the Italian national soft loan. In many ways this is surprising since, as already noted, the interest subsidy in Belgium is a central element of the package, whereas in most other countries interest subsidies simply represent an extra subsidy on top of a basic capital grant. The reason for the 'only average' effective value lies not so much in the percentage subsidy on offer (at five percentage points per annum the Belgian subsidy is higher than that found in the United Kingdom, Denmark and Germany, and lower only than that available in Italy) but rather in the fact that the subsidy is of only a maximum of five years' duration. In all other similar schemes in the European Community the subsidy is available over the full life of the loan to which it is attached — in most cases, 15 years or more.

We noted above that the capital grant in Belgium is not a direct capital grant but rather is offered as a (broadly equivalent) alternative to the interest subsidy in those cases where more than 50 per cent of project funds are internally financed. As such, it is a rare type of subsidy in Europe; its only close relation, as we have seen, is the interest-relief grant available as part of the selective-financial-assistance scheme in the United Kingdom. The fact that the capital grant is offered as an alternative to the interest subsidy is particularly interesting and novel, especially since the option of which incentive to take lies solely with the applicant firm. This is at least one factor which may increase the attractiveness of the interest subsidy/capital grant to firms beyond their arithmetic effective values. It is certainly rare in the

European Community for firms to be given an explicit choice (free of administrative pressures) of which incentive instrument to take.

Like the interest subsidy, the accelerated-depreciation allowance in Belgium is also only average in effective-value terms, even though it is available on both buildings and plant and machinery. Of the other regional accelerated-depreciation allowances in the European Community (minor as well as major), only in Germany is there a similar wide coverage of eligible items. Where the Belgian scheme falls down is in the degree of acceleration — a mere doubling of standard straight-line depreciation for three years being all that is available. In contrast the other regional accelerated-depreciation allowances in the Community offer first-year allowances of between 20 and 50 per cent. Two further features of the Belgian allowance make it stand out from others in Europe. First, there is administrative discretion in the decision whether or not to make an award. Every other regional accelerated-depreciation allowance (and this is true, too, of most tax concessions) is awarded more or less automatically if the conditions of award are met. Second, there are very tough job conditions attached to the allowance, there being a requirement that 20 new jobs be created. In no other country is such a stringent side condition attached to a regional accelerated-depreciation allowance, a fact which must considerably reduce the scale of its impact.

A key theme up until now has been that Belgian regional-incentive policy is a low-profile policy. This can be seen not only in the form and value of the incentives on offer but also, for example, in the fact that the basic concession, the interest subsidy, is simply a generous version of a nationally available aid. More so than in other countries, regional incentives in Belgium tend to have national counterparts. A further point is that, at least as presented to applicant firms, the Belgian regional-incentive package is among the most discretionary in the Community. As we have seen, even the decision whether or not to award an accelerated-depreciation allowance is discretionary; and it is very rare indeed for fiscal incentives to be discretionary.

But the reason for such a low-profile approach to explicitly *regional* incentives is not difficult to find. It is a consequence not only of the highly centralised approach to economic policy followed in Belgium (under which national-incentive measures are given the most prominence) but also of the basic division of the country into the Flemish north and Wallonian south. In addition to the points already made, this division most obviously explains the administrative set-up of the incentive system and the extreme sensitivity attached to the question of area delineation. Perhaps more so than in any other country in Europe at the present time (with the possible exception of Italy), the regional problem in Belgium is a problem of truly national importance.

Notes

1. It may, however, be doubted whether this trend will continue since, recently, the birth rate has fallen to the Wallonian level.
2. F.J. Gay, 'Benelux' in H.D. Clout (ed.), *Regional Development in Western Europe* (John Wiley and Sons, London, 1975), p. 146.
3. Measured in terms of average *per capita* taxable income. See OECD, *Regional Problems and Policies in OECD Countries* (OECD, Paris, 1976), vol. 2, p. 50. The index figures below are also taken from this source.
4. G.R. Thoman, *Foreign Investment and Regional Development: The Theory and Practice of Investment Incentives with a Case Study of Belgium* (Praeger, London, 1973), p. 19.
5. As already noted, these figures are national and not regional. Some indication of the regional component can, however, be gauged from the fact that, between 1962 and 1975, some 85 per cent of national assistance was in fact devoted to the problem regions. See OECD, *Regional Problems and Policies*, p. 59.
6. In fact, over the period 1962-76 the Flemish north has received 51 per cent of the total assistance made available, the Wallonian south 48.15 per cent and the Brussels region the remainder.
7. The capital grant was even more favourably treated under the 1966 legislation, since this legislation included a tax exemption on the direct taxation of the capital grant.

3 REGIONAL INCENTIVES IN DENMARK

The Nature of the Problem

Over the post-war period, Denmark, like most other western European countries, has undergone a very rapid and marked industrial development. The development has not, however, been uniform throughout the country but, rather, has tended to be concentrated in the big towns (Aalborg, Aarhus, Odense) and, above all, in Copenhagen. At the same time, there has been a major shift of employment out of the agricultural sector. Accounting for over one-quarter of national employment in 1950, agricultural employment had declined to less than 10 per cent of the national total by the mid-1970s. In absolute terms, more than a quarter of a million primary-sector jobs were lost in the period 1950-70, while in the same period overall employment increased by 470,000. The employment decline within agriculture was, in part, due to technological progress, but there was also a 'pull' element from other sectors of the economy and, in recent years, especially from the tertiary sector. Indeed, by 1977, tertiary employment accounted for no less than 56 per cent of the national total, having been 51 per cent in 1970 and a mere 35.4 per cent in 1950.[1]

The various structural changes have obviously had an impact on the distribution of the Danish population. Generally speaking, the predominantly rural north and west of Jutland, together with the smaller islands, have lost population over the post-war period while, up until recently, the Copenhagen area and, from 1960 onwards, Aarhus have been experiencing migratory inflows. But not only the distribution of population has been affected by the structural changes. As would be expected, employment opportunities have also been unevenly spread throughout the country. In the late 1950s, for example, unemployment rates in rural districts were well over double those in the Copenhagen area.

To remedy these various spatial inequalities a regional-development policy was introduced in 1958,[2] development being encouraged in the west and north of the Jutland peninsula, as well as on many of the larger islands. As we shall see, these areas remain the current focus of policy although there are signs that the nature of the problem may be changing. Since 1973, Copenhagen has actually been losing population; there has been a trend towards more equality in the distribution of unemployment; and designated problem areas have been amongst those parts of the country which have been growing most rapidly.

The Development of Policy

Since first coming into force in June 1958, the Regional Development Act (the main Danish legislation in the regional-policy field) has undergone frequent modification — in 1962, in 1967, in 1969 and again in 1972. The general trend has been towards trying to make the incentives on offer more efficient and towards limiting the areas where support can be obtained, while, at the same time, enlarging the firms eligible for assistance. Despite obvious differences of emphasis over time, the broad objectives of industrial-development policy have remained unchanged — to obtain a more equal development in the different parts of the country; to prevent excessive concentration of industry in the metropolitan areas and big towns; to make the development of the general structure of Danish industry more rational; and, finally, to improve export performance.

The 1958 Act was, in many ways, a pilot act. In terms of assistance, it was restricted to the granting of government guarantees on investment loans to industrial concerns (within a limit of DKr 50 million annually) on condition that the capital required to carry through the project could not be raised without government support (the so-called 'criterion of need'). Geographical coverage was not specified within the Act itself, but in practice aid was limited to areas outside the more industrialised centres.

The main change in 1962 was the introduction of government loans for municipalities and non-profit organisations to help cover some of the expenses of buying up industrial sites and, in some cases, of constructing factory buildings with the object of selling or letting them. This incentive was reserved for especially backward areas and areas facing acute financial difficulties, in particular North, West and South Jutland and Lolland-Falster. The annual budget was DKr 10 million in 1963/4 and DKr 15 million from 1964/5 up until 1967/8. Also as part of the 1962 measures, the funds available for government loan guarantees were increased to DKr 100 million annually, and the guarantees were extended to cover not only industrial concerns but also, under certain conditions, trade and service industries.

In 1967 the administration of the Regional Development Act was transferred to Silkeborg, a town in Jutland of about 30,000 inhabitants. At the same time a Regional Development Board (to be described in detail below) was set up and invested with the general administration

of the Act — work which, up until then, had been carried out within
the Ministry of Commerce. In addition to this administrative change,
1967 also saw a change in the Regional Development Act itself with, of
particular note, regional development areas being explicitly delineated
for the first time. Under powers given to him by the Act, and using
a wide range of criteria (including low level of industrialisation, skewed
economic structure, low income levels, high out-migration and low
population growth, small and scattered townships, serious unemployment problems and limited occupational and educational opportunities)
the Minister of Commerce (on the recommendations of the Regional
Development Board) designated North, West and South Jutland,
together with a number of the larger islands including Lolland-Falster,
Bornholm and Langeland, as General Development Regions.

On the incentive front, loan guarantees remained the prime means of
assistance in the 1967 legislation and, indeed, were extended to cover,
on a limited scale, loans to working capital. In certain special cases,
grants were also made available to firms which found themselves in
difficulty as a result of a problem-area location. Loans to municipalities
continued to be offered in respect of factory-building costs, but non-
profit organisations no longer qualified and site purchase was no longer
viewed as an eligible item of expenditure.

In 1969 the Regional Development Act was further modified. The
criterion of need, which had been part of the incentive system since
1958, was abolished so that economically strong companies could, for
the first time, be aided. Of similar significance, a new capital grant was
introduced (the investment grant) covering up to 25 per cent of initial
project capital costs. This grant scheme was restricted to so-called
Special Development Regions — especially backward areas within the
previously identified General Development Regions. The Special
Development Regions were designated by the Minister of Commerce
(on the recommendation of the Regional Development Board) as North
Jutland, South-West Jutland and the already-designated islands.

The most recent amendments to the Regional Development Act
occurred in 1972. The loan-guarantee system which had been part and
parcel of the incentive package since its inception was withdrawn, to
be replaced by a concessionary-loan scheme. In addition, it became
possible to award grants and loans to firms in respect of certain special
infrastructure investment and to offer grants towards the removal
expenses of both firms and key staff. These new incentives, together
with the other components of the current regional-incentive package,
are described in more detail in the next section. But before that,

attention should be drawn to two interesting points which arise from the chronology just presented.

First, compared to policy in many other European countries, regional-incentive policy in Denmark is still relatively young; and a regional-incentive policy of any significance is younger still since, in many respects, regional incentives in Denmark did not 'take off' until 1969, with the abandonment of the criterion of need and the introduction of the investment grant. The fact that official problem areas were not designated until 1967 is a further indication of the late development of policy. But this is not altogether surprising since 'in Denmark, sectoral and regional imbalances have been less important than in many other countries'.[3]

Second, there is virtually no mention in the above chronology of other possible policy instruments — infrastructure provision, government-office dispersal, disincentives. There has, in fact, been significant infrastructural investment in the problem areas in recent years, one of the most major developments being the opening of a new university in Aalborg. Moreover, it is widely recognised that the difficulties facing many of the smaller islands simply cannot be solved by industrial investment (whether or not aided by incentives) but can be alleviated through, for example, improved ferry services. All such infrastructural investment, however, tends to fall within the sphere of regional planning, which, being the responsibility of the Environment Ministry, has tended in Denmark to be treated somewhat separately from regional development *per se* (the responsibility of the Ministry of Commerce, at least as far as incentive policy is concerned).[4] Like infrastructure provision, government-office dispersal has also played a role in developing the problem regions, if a minor one. We have already noted that the administration of the Regional Development Act moved to Silkeborg in 1967. In addition, the national organisation handling trade between Greenland and Denmark decentralised to Aalborg. Finally, it should be noted that, while there has been no disincentive or control policy up until now, there has at least been discussion of the possibility of firms being forced to supply information in cases of relocation and expansion. For the moment, however, this proposal has not been developed further.

The Current Incentive Package

It will be apparent from our description of the development of regional-incentive policy that, by 1972, a not unimpressive array of policy instruments had been asssembled — on paper at least. The purpose of this section is to describe these instruments in somewhat more detail, before going on in the next section to a more detailed study of the three measures which in practice have proved to be of most importance — the company soft loan, the municipality loan and the investment grant. In a final section we then compare the Danish incentives with other regional incentives in the European Community.

With the enactment of the 1972 Regional Development Act no fewer than ten separate incentive instruments were available in Denmark — soft loans to companies; soft loans to municipalities; investment grants; operational grants; removal grants for firms; removal grants for staff; loans and grants for infrastructure projects; guarantees on loans for working capital; and guarantees for pre-rationalisation studies. Let us look briefly at each of these in turn.

The company soft loan is at a fixed 7.5 per cent rate of interest (the rate in force since 1972), some 3 per cent below the current market rate for medium-term loans. The loan is available towards eligible project fixed-capital costs and has a duration of up to 20 years for buildings and up to 10 years for plant. In law, principal-repayment holidays of up to five years can be obtained but in practice a maximum of two years that are free of principal repayment is standard.

The municipality soft loan is on offer only to municipalities to allow them to build industrial buildings for specified clients; the buildings are then normally rented, but can be bought. The loan is at a fixed 7 per cent rate of interest and is for a standard 25 years. Although only 75 per cent of building costs are covered by the loan, municipalities are obliged to subsidise the remaining 25 per cent on the same terms when calculating the appropriate rental or selling price. The annual rent is therefore 4 per cent (i.e. one-twenty-fifth) of total building costs plus 7 per cent of the outstanding loan plus general running expenses.

As we have already seen, the investment grant was originally introduced into the Danish regional-incentive system in 1969. It is a project-related grant, available on up to 25 per cent of eligible fixed-capital costs. Unlike all the other incentives, which are available throughout the so-called General Development Regions, the investment grant is limited to those areas facing especially severe problems — the Special Development Regions.

The operational grant (which can only be awarded after consultation with the European Commission) is aimed at industrial companies whose results suffer subsequent to setting up a new project or carrying out an extension in the Development Regions. To be eligible, the companies must either have been in receipt of a company soft loan or have moved into an industrial building part-financed by a municipality soft loan. The grant is payable within three years of the signing of the company-soft-loan contract or of the move into the municipal industrial building. No rates of award are specified, but funds are limited and are very much reserved for special cases.

Removal grants are available towards the costs of moving both firms and key staff to the Development Regions. Removals of both industrial and service enterprises can be aided by the company-removal grant where the costs of moving are substantial. The staff-removal grant assists the transfer of staff essential to the satisfactory operation of the company in its new site through an award of DKr 4,000 per head to those moving.

There are two further grants within the current Danish regional-incentive package. One is awarded to essential infrastructure projects where these safeguard or attract industrial activities (loans are also available for this purpose), while the other is aimed primarily at assisting the drafting of plans and feasibility studies for projects of general importance to the industrial development of a region. This latter grant has also been used to aid the operation of so-called Regional Development Committees. Five of these committees have been supported (to the tune of DKr 100,000 each) from public funds — one each in Southern Jutland, West Jutland, North Jutland, Lolland-Falster and Bornholm. Their objective is to promote the development of their regions by collecting information of interest to firms wishing to locate there, by advising existing firms and by arranging campaigns both to attract new firms and to promote the products of their regions. All the committees have been established on local initiative, are locally staffed and receive — in addition to regional assistance — financial support through local municipalities and, to a limited extent, local private firms.

In addition to the various grants and loans noted above, guarantees are available on both working-capital loans and loans for pre-rationalisation studies. Like the operational grant, the guarantee on working-capital loans is restricted to companies which have received a company soft loan or occupy an industrial building part-financed by a municipality soft loan. The guarantee cannot be awarded more than three years after receipt of the company soft loan or occupation of the municipality-leased building and may only be granted if it would otherwise be impossible to procure sufficient working capital. The guarantee on loans for pre-rationalisation studies is constrained by a similar condition, since it is required that it must otherwise be impossible to finance such studies. Both forms of guarantee are of five years' duration; the amount guaranteed reduces during the period.

The Danes thus have a wide range of incentives on offer under the Regional Development Act 1972. On the other hand, many of the incentives listed above are only rarely used (which is not wholly surprising, given the restrictive nature of some of the conditions of award) or involve only minimal expenditure. The operational grant, for example, has been awarded just once since 1972/3. Grants towards feasibility studies totalled less than DKr 2.5 million over the period 1972/3 to 1975/6, while loans and grants on infrastructure projects amounted to a mere DKr 3.5 million over the same timespan (although a further DKr 4.5 million was paid out in 1976/7). Between 1972 and 1976 the 95 staff-removal grants awarded cost DKr 380,000 in total, while expenditure on company-removal grants was some 1.5 million. No awards were made in respect of the working-capital-loan-guarantee scheme and no applications were received for guarantees on pre-rationalisation studies. In total, then, well under DKr 10 million was paid out on seven of the ten listed incentives over the period 1972 to 1976 — an annual average of less than DKr 2.5 million. In contrast the company soft loan, the investment grant and the municipality soft loan involve current expenditure of the order of DKr 140 million, DKr 40 million and DKr 20 million per annum, respectively. Clearly, these three incentives are of central importance within the present Danish regional-incentive package. They are therefore considered in more detail in the following section.

The Main Incentives

In describing the company-soft-loan, the investment-grant and the municipality-soft-loan schemes we concentrate on those conditions of award which determine the eligibility or otherwise of applicant projects and on those factors which determine the effective level of award. But before doing this, it is worthwhile to examine two more general features — the system of incentive administration and the scale of the incentives on offer.

The administration of the Regional Development Act is the responsibility of the Regional Development Board; the day-to-day work and implementation of the Board's decisions is carried out by the Regional Development Directorate located, as already noted, in Silkeborg.[5] The Board is composed of ten ordinary members and a chairman, all appointed by the Minister of Commerce and representing the 'interested' government ministries (Commerce, Finance, Labour, Environment,

Interior), the Federation of Danish Industries, the Economic Council of the Labour Unions, the National Federation of Local Councils, the Federation of County Councils and the Regional Development Committees. A key feature of the Danish incentive system is the degree of administrative discretion inherent within it. Because of this a small Executive Committee, composed of a maximum of six members and drawn from the ranks of the Board, has been set up to make award decisions at the individual-project level following rules of procedure laid down by the Minister of Commerce. As a result, decisions can be speedily made (within six to eight weeks).

Turning now to the scale of the main incentives, 461 company-soft-loan offers were made in the period 1972/3 to 1976/7, together with 207 investment-grant awards and 60 municipality soft loans. Over this five-year period, company-soft-loan expenditure amounted to DKr 566.8 million (annual average DKr 113.4 million), with DKr 139 million being awarded in the most recent year for which information is available — 1976/7. Over the same period, investment-grant expenditure averaged DKr 31 million (DKr 41 million being paid out in 1976/7), while just under DKr 20 million annually took the shape of municipality soft loans (1976/7: DKr 19 million). In total, then, just under DKr 200 million was paid out in the form of company soft loans, investment grants and municipality soft loans in 1976/7, making the Danish regional-incentive package relatively small-scale by European Community standards — especially when it is borne in mind that the above loan figures refer to the principal value of the loans offered, and not to their subsidy element.

Eligibility Conditions

As already noted, the Danish regional-incentive system is both highly discretionary and — not unrelated to this — highly centralised (despite not being administered from Copenhagen). All applications for project aid are channelled through the Executive Committee of the Regional Development Board, which decides on the award of one or more incentives on the basis of a 'total evaluation' of the project under consideration. As part of this evaluation, four main requirements have to be met — the project must be on a reasonable commercial basis (and there should, for example, be sufficient 'own finance'), the project must be managed with the necessary technical and administrative skills; the project must be well founded and be profitable; and the project must make a significant impact on the Development Regions. In short, the project must be viable — technically, financially and commercially

– and must be expected to make its mark on the designated problem areas.

We saw earlier that there are two levels of designated problem area in Denmark, the General Development Regions and (within these) the Special Development Regions. Until 1978 the former accounted for just under one-third of the Danish population (and some 58 per cent of the surface area of Denmark), while the latter held 16 per cent of the population (and covered just under 30 per cent of the country's surface area). In 1978 various adjustments were made to the designated areas, as a result of which the General Development Regions were cut back to 52 per cent of the surface area (holding 27 per cent of the population), while the Special Development Regions were extended to cover 33 per cent of the surface area (17 per cent of the population). The new designated areas (which came into full force on 1 January 1979) are shown on the map in Figure 3.1.

It can be seen that the Special Development Regions are found primarily in North Jutland, in North-West Jutland (the result of the recent changes) and in the south-west of Jutland, as well as on the larger islands including Lolland-Falster, Bornholm, Langeland and the Faroes. In addition to these areas, the General Development Regions cover much of the remaining western part of Jutland (a significant section of West Jutland having been de-designated as part of the 1978 changes), South-East Jutland, a small area north-east of Aarhus and (new in 1978) part of Zeeland. Both the company soft loan and the municipality soft loan are available throughout the General Development Regions. The investment grant, in contrast, is limited to the Special Development Regions. These regions are further favoured by the tendency, on the part of the Regional Development Board, to accept more risk and give more support to projects locating there rather than in the rest of the General Development Regions.

Apart from the viability and location conditions, there are few other general conditions of award attached to the main Danish regional incentives. Most economic activities, for example, are eligible *a priori*. Agriculture and construction, however, do not qualify unless industrialised. The service and hotel sectors are also ineligible for the municipality soft loan (since only industrial buildings can be aided) and in practice tend to be relatively poorly catered for by the other schemes. Only 21 hotel and service projects received a company soft loan between June 1972 and March 1976 (out of a total of 335 projects aided in that period), while fewer than 5 per cent of investment-grant awards have gone to the hotel and service sectors. In practice, most aid

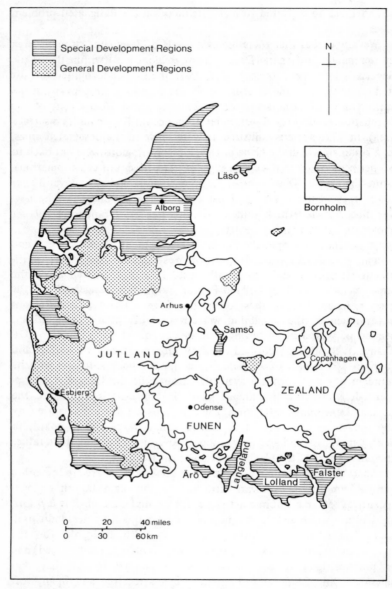

Figure 3.1: Designated Areas in Denmark

has gone to the manufacturing sector, with the iron and metal industries and food processing receiving around 40 per cent of company-soft-loan/investment-grant expenditure in the period up until March 1976.

As with economic activity, project-type eligibility is not explicitly covered within the general conditions of incentive award. We have, however, already noted that the project should have a significant impact on the recipient region. For this reason, setting-up projects and extensions are the main project types assisted although rationalisations, re-organisations, modernisations and transfers do in theory also qualify (except, of course, for the municipality soft loan, which, by its nature, tends to be limited to setting-up projects).[6] In recent years, more than 70 per cent of aided projects have been extensions of local companies, while the remainder have been overwhelmingly new 'setting-up' projects (as distinct from transfers from outside of the Development Regions). Only a handful of projects have involved moves to the Development Regions from outside.

One final area where conditions are imposed — in practice if not in theory — is in respect of project size. Company soft loans are not normally awarded to projects involving fixed investment of less than DKr 500,000 or more than DKr 40 million,[7] while investment grants usually go only to projects with fixed-investment costs of more than DKr 1 million.

As a result of these various conditions of award and practical constraints, but also as a very strong reflection of the highly discretionary nature of the Danish regional-incentive system, just over 35 per cent of company-soft-loan applications and some 43 per cent of municipality-soft-loan applications were rejected in the period 1972/3 to 1976/7. For the even more selectively awarded investment grant, turndown over the same period was even higher — almost 50 per cent of applications were rejected.

Award Levels

This topic can be covered with relative ease for the municipality soft loan since, although there is discretion in the decision whether or not to make an award, the terms of any award are by and large fixed. As we have seen, the municipality-soft-loan scheme makes loans available to General Development Region municipalities at a fixed 7 per cent rate of interest to allow them to construct industrial buildings for specified clients. The assisted project will normally be a setting-up project, although local industries starting new production as part of an expansion tend to be viewed sympathetically. As well as construction costs (including the costs of constructing office accommodation within the building), the loan covers site purchase and the provision of infra- structure connections. It does not, however, extend to the cost of equipping the building with, for example, plant and machinery, al- though 'usual installations' in respect of heating, light, power and water are eligible.

As noted earlier, only 12 municipality soft loans have been awarded annually in recent years – the average award between April 1974 and April 1977 being about DKr 1.7 million. Repayment is six-monthly on a straight-line basis normally over 25 years (even though the maximum repayment period in law is 30 years). The loan covers a standard 75 per cent of eligible building costs, but municipalities are obliged to subsidise the remaining 25 per cent on the same terms when calculating the appropriate rental or selling price so that, as far as the recipient firm is concerned, the subsidy is available on all eligible building costs. The buildings normally range in size from 600 m^2 to 10,000 m^2 and are usually rented, although purchase is also possible. Reflecting the terms and conditions of the loan, the annual rent is 4 per cent (i.e. one- twenty-fifth) of total building costs plus 7 per cent of the outstanding loan plus general running expenses. The leaseholder can buy the build- ing at any time during the course of the lease, at a purchase price which similarly takes account of the subsidy element of the loan.[8]

Before leaving the municipality soft loan one final feature should be mentioned, since it has a bearing on the effective value of the loan subsidy to the recipient firms – namely, that the subsidy may, in practice, be liable for tax. By reducing rental charges on the purchase price of the building to the client, the concessionary element of the loans leads to an increase in taxable profits (or a reduction in losses). To the extent the taxable profits are being made, the subsidy is there- fore taxed, a fact which can significantly reduce its value to the recipient.

For the company soft loan it is not quite so easy to identify 'typical' award levels, since there is a significant element of discretion with respect to the level of award offered. Although the loan itself is at a fixed 7.5 per cent rate of interest, repayable six-monthly on a straight-line basis, it has a duration of *up to* 20 years for buildings and *up to* 10 years for plant, a principal-repayment-holiday concession of *up to* 5 years and a coverage of *up to* 90 per cent of eligible project costs. Actual awards are varied by the regional-incentive authorities within these maxima so as to tailor the loan to the needs and desir- ability of each project and the recipient location.

In practice, average loan duration is 18 years for buildings and 8 years for plant, while the standard principal-repayment holiday is one or two years. A norm in terms of loan coverage is less easy to identify. Eligible items of expenditure, it is true, are standardised and include plant and machinery, buildings (including offices on the premises), site purchase and preliminary investigations. However, not all expenditure on these items is taken into account for company-soft-loan purposes. First, that proportion of eligible expenditure which can be covered by a so-called mortgage-credit loan is excluded.[9] The mortgage-credit-loan system is peculiarly Danish. In return for the deposit of mortgage deeds, special mortgage-credit institutions issue bearer bonds with a nominal value equal to the loan awarded. The borrower must then sell these bonds for what they will fetch on the Stock Exchange. Normally, a mortgage-credit loan covers between 40 and 60 per cent of eligible project expenditure. Second, the value of any investment grant awarded must also be subtracted from eligible project costs. Where, for example, an investment grant covers 25 per cent of eligible investment and a mortgage-credit loan takes account of a further 50 per cent, then only the remaining 25 per cent is eligible for the company soft loan. Thus, although the company soft loan nominally covers up to 90 per cent of eligible-project fixed-capital costs, these are so constrained in practice that, in the above case, a maximum of only 22.5 per cent (i.e. 90 per cent of 25 per cent) of project fixed-capital costs would be eligible for the loan. This is one of the reasons why the average company soft loan is normally less than DKr 1.5 million (i.e. is smaller than the municipality soft loan even though a municipality soft loan is limited to 75 per cent of building costs alone); but another reason is that less than the maximum 90 per cent loan is often awarded.

The various restrictions on eligible items of expenditure obviously reduce the effective value of the company soft loan, as does the fact that not all forms of expenditure are eligible — assets bought on hire purchase or leased, for example, are not eligible. A further factor reducing the loan's effective value is that the subsidy element within it is taxed whenever profits are made, since the subsidy reduces tax-deductible debt-servicing charges. Finally, it should be noted that the loan can be drawn down only on completion of project construction. There are therefore inevitable delays between incurring expenditure and receipt of the loan, which further reduce the effective value of this incentive.

The final major incentive weapon in the Danish armoury is the investment grant. Like the company soft loan, it is highly discretionary, both in terms of award level and the decision whether or not to make an award (indeed, almost one-half of all formal applications are turned down). The maximum grant is 25 per cent of eligible-project fixed-capital costs less the difference (but only the difference, so it is not the same as within the company-soft-loan scheme) between the nominal value and the market price of the mortgage deeds issued in respect of the project by the mortgage-credit institution which is part-financing the project. Actual awards (averaging, in absolute terms, DKr 700,000 per award between 1972 and 1977) tend, however, to be considerably below this maximum. Indeed, in practice, the 25 per cent maximum applies only to eligible building costs incurred by setting-up projects. For plant and machinery setting-up costs the maximum is 20 per cent. Moreover, the normal award for extensions is only 15 per cent. Obviously it is difficult to identify an average award and, in fact, no hard information is available on this. It should, however, be recalled that 70 per cent of aided projects would in fact be extensions of local firms.

There are a number of additional points to be considered in calculating the effective value of the investment grant. Beyond the fact that the difference between the nominal value and market price of the mortgage deeds issued by the mortgage-credit institution must be taken into account, it must also be noted that not all capital costs are eligible for the grant. Plant and machinery, buildings and site purchase are the main eligible items of expenditure, while working capital is the main ineligible item. The position in respect of eligible items of expenditure is therefore similar to that for the company soft loan. Eligible forms of expenditure are also similarly treated, leased assets and assets bought on hire purchase being ineligible. As far as tax treatment is concerned the investment grant is regarded as income and is therefore taxed to the extent that it leads to increased profits. However, it can be brought into income at any time within ten years after it is received, and can thus be fed into income earlier when losses are being made or in the tenth year. In this way the effective value of the investment grant is not greatly reduced by its tax treatment. A final factor reducing the effective value of the grant is that there tends to be a delay between project expenditure and grant receipt, since the grant is paid out in a lump sum only on completion of project construction.

Comparative Conclusions

Perhaps the most outstanding feature of the Danish regional-incentive package from a comparative European point of view is its highly discretionary nature — both in terms of the decision whether or not to make an award and the level of that award. In probably no other country in the European Community (with the possible exception of Luxembourg) is there so much doubt at the time an application is submitted about whether or not that application will be accepted and, if accepted, about the level of assistance which will then ensue. Certainly it is rare in Europe for there to be no virtually automatic subsidy on offer — a basic award representing at least the minimum which firms investing in the problem regions can expect. It is also rare for formal turndown rates to be quite as high as they are in Denmark, especially when it is borne in mind that, in the Danish case, firms presumably make informal approaches to the Regional Development Board to 'test the water' before submitting formal applications.

The reasons for the high level of administrative discretion in Danish regional-incentive policy are not hard to find, however. First, the relatively small number of cases processed annually makes a discretionary approach feasible. The fact that it has proved possible for all interested parties to be represented on the decision-making body and that that body is concerned with the administration of *all* regional incentives in the country has further eased the problems of setting up a wholly discretionary system. Finally, the relatively limited funds available for regional-incentive policy anyway ruled out the introduction of an effective automatic aid. In perhaps no other country in the European Community do budget constraints have such an impact on policy as in Denmark.

One consequence of discretion in the Danish system is that there is far less overt discrimination within the available incentive schemes than in the other countries of the European Community. There is not even a distinction in terms of rates of award between the Special and General Development Regions, although the investment grant is of course only available in the former. Rather, differences in the treatment of areas, industries, project types or whatever take place within the discretion offered by a uniform maximum award.

Of the three main regional incentives in Denmark the investment grant is without doubt the most interesting. Different from most other capital grants in Europe, it does not form the base of the incentive package but rather is restricted to those areas where the problem is seen to be at its most serious, and within those areas to projects which will have the most impact. Its main function, in short, is to 'top up' the company soft loan (and, if awarded, the municipality soft loan) in particularly deserving cases. At its maximum level, the investment grant has an effective value which is in line with most other district capital grants in the Community countries. As we have seen, however, the level of grant awarded is highly discretionary, the maximum rarely being offered. Indeed, in what might be called the 'standard' case (i.e. extension projects) the grant tends to have a nominal value of only about two-thirds the possible maximum. At this level, it obviously compares much less favourably with others in Europe.

Despite this, the investment grant is far and away the most valuable regional incentive in Denmark in effective-value terms, both the company soft loan and the municipality soft loan being worth only about one-third of its maximum value. At this level, these loans are on a par with the Belgian interest subsidy and the ERP regional soft loan in Germany, are slightly less valuable than British selective financial assistance and are significantly less valuable than the national-soft-loan scheme in Italy. The basic reason for this lies not so much in the level of interest subsidy offered (the percentage-point concession, principal-repayment holidays and loan duration are all fairly standard from a European Community viewpoint) as in the fact that such a small proportion of project costs tends to be eligible for the loan — little over 20 per cent, as we have seen, in the case of the company soft loan.

The low effective value of both the company soft loan and the municipality soft loan, and the relatively high effective value of the investment grant mean that the value of the Danish regional-incentive package as a whole is very much determined by the level of investment grant awarded. Only when an investment-grant award is made (and only when the amount offered is close to the maximum) is the Danish package comparable in effective-value terms with 'standard' regional-incentive schemes in Europe. Where no investment grant is available (and the grant, to repeat once again, is limited to the Special Development Regions and is offered only selectively in these areas) then the Danish incentive package has a low effective value by European Community standards. But this situation of an attractive incentive package in the Special Development Regions and much less valuable incentives elsewhere in the General Development Regions is surely only to be expected. It is, after all, in the Special Development Regions that the most serious problems are to be found. In the remainder of the General Development Regions the regional problem is not of major importance, certainly not when measured on a European Community scale.

Notes

1. See OECD, *Regional Problems and Policies in OECD Countries* (OECD, Paris, 1976), vol. 1, p. 79.

2. According to one commentator, 'dislodging some of the well-being of Copenhagen to the benefit of the country' has been the main aim of policy. C. Elbo, 'Denmark' in H.D. Clout (ed.), *Regional Development in Western Europe* (John Wiley and Sons, London, 1975), p. 233.

3. OECD, *Regional Problems and Policies*, p. 80.

4. With the passing of the National and Regional Planning Act, 1974, this separate treatment of regional planning and regional policies may change.

5. The Directorate of Regional Development is also authorised to administer other schemes of financial aid to trade and industry, which are not exclusively aimed at regional development. Compared with the specific regional-development-support schemes, however, these schemes are very small.

6. Municipality soft loans may, however, on occasion also be awarded to local industries starting new production.

7. Projects of more than DKr 40 million tend, rather, to apply for European Investment Bank loans. Such loans have become increasingly important in recent years.

8. The standard price would be total building costs less the subsidy less any rental instalments already paid.

9. Whether a mortgage-credit loan is actually raised is, however, immaterial.

4 REGIONAL INCENTIVES IN FRANCE

The Nature of the Problem

The regional problem in France has three principal aspects: the dominance of Paris over the rest of the country; the regional effects of agricultural change and the regional effects of industrial change.

The Paris region (*Ile-de-France*) accounts for only 2.2 per cent of the surface area of France but 18.8 per cent of its total population and 22.1 per cent of its employed population.[1] More important than the capital region's quantitative dominance over the rest of the country, however, is its qualitative dominance. For example, the Paris region's 18.8 per cent of total population accounted for 28.3 per cent of those employed nationally in service-sector occupations in 1976. Moreover, for certain categories of tertiary employment, the figure is much higher: some 40 per cent of the country's senior management and members of the liberal professions are to be found in the capital and its region, as are about half of its engineers and almost two-thirds of its pure and applied researchers.[2] On another measure, average annual salaries in the Paris region in 1973 were 128.5 per cent of the national average annual salary; or again, of the five hundred largest French firms and company groups, over 75 per cent had their registered offices in the Paris region in 1976, while less than 4 per cent had their registered offices in the west, south-west, *Massif Central*, *Languedoc* and Corsica.[3]

While the dominance of Paris is clearly a key element of the French regional problem so, too, is the virtual agricultural and social revolution which has taken place in rural France over the last three decades — a revolution which has brought with it enormous problems of depopulation, unemployment and out-migration. Whereas 36 per cent of the employed population were still engaged in agriculture in 1946, this figure had dropped to 21 per cent by 1962 and to less than 10 per cent by 1975.[4] The areas most affected by this agricultural outflow have been almost the whole of western and south-western France, together with the *Massif Central*.

But it has not only been structural changes within agriculture which have brought regional problems in their wake. Structural changes within industry have also contributed to the French regional problem. The industries principally affected have been traditional ones such as coal mining, iron and steel making and textiles.[5] Between 1945 and 1960 coal-mining employment declined from 260,000 to 190,000, largely as a result of rationalisation. This decline continued in the 1960s because of energy substitution and price competition from imported coal. Policies of planned manpower depletion were introduced and there was a further rapid reduction in the labour force in the early 1970s. Despite a certain respite given by the energy crisis, the main affected areas in the north (*Nord*) and in Lorraine continue to lose jobs in the industry. Employment in iron and steelmaking similarly declined during the sixties and early seventies. Equally important, however, has been the relocation of the industry away from traditional ore-mining areas (notably Lorraine) towards the coast (Dunkirk in the north and Fos in the south). Finally, in the textile industry, employment dropped by 30 per cent between 1955 and 1972 and continues to decline in the face of competitive pressures from abroad. The regions principally affected have been the north, the Vosges and those other parts of Alsace which traditionally rely on the textile industry for employment.

The Development of Policy

Recognition of regional problems as a legitimate object of public policy dates in France from the late 1940s, debate about the existence of regional problems and the need for regional policy having been stimulated by an important book by Gravier.[6] It was not, however, until the mid-1950s that the first package of regional-policy measures was introduced.

As part of this package the problem areas were delineated in a rather *ad hoc* fashion according to the criterion of relatively high levels of actual or potential unemployment. No hard and fast area-designation rules were established, however, so that it proved impossible, for political reasons, not to keep adding localities to the list of Assisted Areas.[7] In an attempt to emasculate these local political pressures, policy was essentially reversed in 1960 with the introduction of a totally discretionary system in which no areas were designated *a priori*. Discretion was intended to give the administration a free hand to channel incentive assistance to those areas which it felt to be most in need. In practice, however, the very absence of any definition of the problem areas made the new scheme even more susceptible to political pressures than the old one. As a consequence, yet another approach was adopted in 1964.

Under this approach the Assisted Areas were explicitly designated and in a much more systematic fashion than in the mid-1950s. The criteria employed were demographic trends, levels of economic development and both actual and potential disequilibria in the labour market. Essentially the same criteria are employed today, although it is difficult to be any more explicit about the delineation methodology, because the analyses which underlie area delineation are never made public. While local political pressures doubtless continue to be of importance in drawing the map of the Assisted Areas, their influence is probably less dramatic than in the mid-1950s.

Since 1964 the Assisted Areas have not changed substantially (although there have been certain shifts in priority within them). The areas where France's regional-development grant is currently available may be viewed as France's principal problem regions (see Figure 4.1 below). They cover the whole of western and south-western France (where the regional problem is characterised by falling agricultural employment, low industrialisation and demographic decline/instability) together with a number of areas along the northern and north-eastern borders (where the regional problem results in large part from industrial structural change, the problems of providing alternative industrial or tertiary employment and, particularly in recent years, net out-migration).[8]

But of course changes in area-designation methodologies and in the delineation of the problem regions are only one aspect of the development of policy. There are at least three other components of regional policy in France which must also be discussed — urban-development policy and, in particular, those policies designed to contain the growth of Paris; policies intended to improve infrastructural provision in the problem regions; and incentive policies intended to attract industrial and tertiary investment into the problem regions. These last form the main subject-matter of this chapter and are thus held over until the next two sections, where we consider, first, the broad incentive package and then the main regional incentives. Within the remainder of this section we wish to discuss the other two components of policy — urban-development policy and infrastructure policy.

Urban-development Policy

Controls to contain the growth of the Paris region were among the first regional-policy initiatives of the mid-1950s. At that time, they were applied only to industrial establishments wishing to expand *in situ* in the Paris region and took the form of making such expansion subject to special administrative permission (in addition to the usual planning permission for new construction). Today, controls relate to both industrial and tertiary establishments and involve both special permission (*agrément*) and penalty taxes (*redevance*). Special permission is required for any new establishment or expansion of an existing establishment in excess of 1,500 m² of industrial floor space and in excess of 1,000 m² of office floor space. The penalty tax, paid only once, ranges from FF 25 to FF 150 per m² for industrial establishments and from FF 100 to FF 400 per m² for service establishments. Generally speaking, the rate of tax is higher the closer the establishment is located to the centre of Paris.

Critics of the control policy argue that it has led to the deindustrialisation of parts of the Paris region (causing severe local unemployment) and that the penalty tax only adds to existing inflationary pressures in the region. Its advocates, in contrast, contend that the policy is not necessarily as restrictive as is often implied, since the rigidity of its application can be modulated as circumstances require. Perhaps more important, all major projected industrial and tertiary developments in the region come to the notice of the authorities such that negotiations can be undertaken with investors to seek to encourage them to locate at least part of their projected development outside the capital and in the problem regions. In the case of larger firms, this kind of 'trading' is common – and has latterly been institutionalised and generalised in that 'location contracts' are now made between the administration and major firms in a bid to ensure that investment is located in line with regional-policy priorities.[9]

France's urban-development policy is not, however, limited only to the Paris region. As part of a strategic design elaborated in the late 1950s and early 1960s which sought to relate national economic policy more closely to regional economic policy (in particular in response to increased competition from abroad as the Common Market was established) there was a shift in policy emphasis towards the 'growth-pole' concept. The intention was that by promoting a small number of 'countervailing capitals' it would be possible to mobilise the resources of the nation as a whole to maximise economic output while at the same time containing and reducing spatial imbalances. Eight such growth poles scattered throughout France were designated (Lille-Tourcoing-Roubaix, Metz-Nancy, Strasbourg, Lyons-St Etienne-Grenoble, Marseilles, Toulouse, Bordeaux and Nantes-St Nazare). Incentive and infrastructure assistance was to be concentrated on these centres.

In more recent years, however, there has been something of a retreat from the growth-pole strategy, mainly because of the fear of undesirable 'backwash' effects. The retreat has been in two stages.

First came a policy for 'medium-size' towns (*villes moyennes*). Viewed in relation to the designated growth poles, this policy can be seen as an attempt to stabilise the hinterlands of the growth poles with the designated medium-size towns qualifying for the maximum rates of regional-development grant and for special central-government assistance for infrastructural improvement. The second stage of the retreat came more recently with the introduction of a policy to favour 'natural' local regions (*politique des pays*), a policy which bears witness to the continuing problems of rural depopulation.

A final and important element in France's urban-development policy has been the creation of a number of new towns intended to relieve the development pressures on the major urban centres. Nine new towns have been developed around the capital as well as adjacent to Lyons, Lille, Rouen and Marseilles.[10]

Infrastructure Policy

The link between national and economic planning and regional policy reflected in the growth-pole concept is apparent, too, in the field of infrastructure policy. Since the early 1960s each of France's five-year economic and social development plans has sought to identify the infrastructural requirements of the 22 regions into which the country is divided for planning purposes. Infrastructure is understood here in the broad sense of state capital expenditure. The annual state budget is also regionalised in an attempt to ensure that each government department's spending is in line with regional-development priorities. In the seventh plan (1976-80) the departmental and spatial distribution of state capital expenditure has been taken an important step forward by inviting government departments and agencies to tie portions of their quinquennial budgetary allocations to specific priority programmes.

In addition to the above-described regional component in the general budgetary process, there are a number of more specific infrastructural policies. In the mid-1950s, for example, legislation was passed to permit the creation of 'mixed-economy companies' − joint public-sector/private-sector initiatives to undertake major infrastructural programmes in particular regions. Such companies have been established to carry out major regional irrigation and drainage projects in many areas of southern and south-western France. In addition, since the mid-1960s, France has pursued a policy of rural renewal (*rénovation rurale*) to promote social and physical infrastructure as well as to encourage the modernisation of agriculture and of small and medium-sized industry. This policy is pursued in areas totalling some 27 per cent of the surface area of the country (including Brittany, the *Massif Central*, the Pyrenees, Corsica, the Alps, the Vosges and the Jura). Finally, with regard to infrastructure policy, mention should be made of the role of DATAR (*Délégation à l'Aménagement du Territoire et à l'Action Régionale*), the co-ordinating agency charged with the execution of France's regional policy, and traditionally having a considerable influence in determining France's regional-policy priorities. In terms of infrastructure policy, DATAR makes a number of specific contributions in addition to generally seeking to influence the policies and programmes pursued by individual government departments. It has, for example, recently undertaken long-term studies of projected regional infrastructural requirements in roads, air-line traffic, telecommunications and waterways. DATAR has funds at its disposal which, even if limited to about only 1 per cent of annual national capital expenditure, can be used in conjunction with departmental budgets to encourage particular projects. DATAR also has a budget to help develop infrastructure on a more confined scale at the local level, and in particular industrial estates.

The Current Incentive Package

As already noted, regional incentives are the third main component of French regional policy. By and large, all the major incentive types currently on offer were introduced in the first regional policy package in the mid-1950s. Perhaps the main incentive innovation since then has been the introduction of specific schemes for the tertiary sector (to which we return below) but there have been other interesting trends over the years. In particular, capital grants, which have been the key incentive instrument throughout the period, have tended to become less discretionary; soft loans, never of any major significance, have steadily decreased in importance; and incentive award-making, initially highly centralised, has been devolved first to the 22 regions and, more recently, to the 95 *départements*.

At present, the two main regional incentives in France are the regional-development grant (*prime de développement régional*) and the local-business-tax concession (*exonération de la taxe professionelle*). Together, they account for some 80 per cent of annual regional-incentive expenditure. The regional-development grant is a project-related grant payable principally to manufacturing industry. It is largely automatic in terms of both conditions and rates of award, although these vary spatially and by project type. The local-business-tax concession is similarly project-related. It involves a concession for a period of

up to five years on all or part of a firm's liability to the business tax
raised by each *département*. Being the main French regional incentives,
the regional-development grant and the local-business-tax concession
are considered further in the next section.

Of the remaining regional aids, two schemes aimed directly at service
activities (i.e. at both tertiary firms and at tertiary functions with
manufacturing firms) are of particular interest, specific service-industry
schemes being found only rarely in the European Community. The
service-activities grant (*prime de localisation de certaines activités
tertiaires*) is project-related and is given for the setting-up, extension
or transfer from the Paris region of management, administration,
consultancy and data-processing activities. To be eligible, a project must
involve 30 new jobs (reduced to 20 if the registered offices of the
company set up in the aided areas), these jobs representing an increase
of at least 50 per cent in the original 'tertiary' labour force in the case
of an extension (or simply 100 new jobs where the extension involves
the creation of a new service function or the decentralisation of a
service activity previously carried out in the Paris region). The service-
activities grant is available throughout the country other than in the
Paris Basin – although only qualitatively significant projects (*activités
ou services de haut nouveau*) may be assisted in the Lyons region –
and is awarded at the rate of FF 20,000 per job in areas where the
regional-development grant is available and at FF 10,000 per job in the
other Designated Areas.

The second tertiary grant is the research-activities grant (*prime de
localisation d'activités de recherche*). This incentive is also project-
related and is available for the setting-up, extension and transfer of
pure and applied research activities. Ten new research-related jobs
are required, which in the case of an extension must normally represent
an increase of at least 30 per cent in the original research-related labour
force (or 50 new jobs with no stipulated percentage increase for extension by transfer from the Paris region; extension by the creation of a
new activity; and a first extension following the setting-up of qualifying
activities). As with the service-activities grant, the research-activities
grant is available throughout France, excluding the Paris Basin (but,
unlike the service-activities grant, there is no qualification as regards
the eligibility of the Lyons region). Awards vary according to the value
of associated investment and location. For projects with fixed capital
investment of less than FF 10 million, awards are FF 25,000 per job
created, but may not exceed (other than exceptionally) 15 per cent of
investment except in certain towns (designated *pôles de recherche*),

where the limit is 25 per cent of investment. For larger projects awards are discretionary up to the maxima of FF 25,000 per job and 25 per cent of investment.

Away from grants for the tertiary sector, but still on incentives to encourage moves out of the Paris region, a so-called 'decentralisation grant' (*indemnité de décentralisation*) is available to industrial firms partially to reimburse them for the cost of transferring all or part of their production from the Paris region (including the five southernmost *cantons* of the *département* of Oise) to a location outside the Paris Basin. The firm must vacate at least 500 m² of industrial floor space, and the award comprises 90 per cent of the incurred cost of dismantling plant and equipment plus 60 per cent of the cost of transporting the same to the new location.

A final grant within the French regional-incentive package (apart from those mentioned below in relation to aid for small-scale artisan firms) is the land grant (*bonification des terrains par le fonds d'aide à la décentralisation et par les collectivités locales*). This is a project-related grant available for investment which fulfils the requirements for the regional-development grant (or for either of the tertiary grants). In practice, land grants almost invariably go to projects which actually receive a regional-development grant. The award is payable on the cost price of the developed site acquired for the project, on condition that it is located on a designated industrial estate. Awards are up to one-half of the price of the site, as long as certain minimum 'own-contribution' requirements are met, and are usually also conditional upon 30 new jobs per hectare being created (although a proportionally reduced award may be given for fewer jobs).

Next in importance to grants within the regional-incentive system in France are fiscal aids. In addition to the already-mentioned local-business-tax concession, there are two other regional fiscal aids on offer. The first of these is the special depreciation allowance (*amortissement exceptionnel*), a fixed 25 per cent first-year allowance additional to standard depreciation and limited strictly to project-related buildings in those areas of southern and south-western France where the regional-development grant is available (see Figure 4.1 below). Within these areas eligibility is restricted to setting-up projects and extensions as well as to certain internal-reorganisation and take-over projects. In addition, various job conditions – identical to those applied to the local-business-tax concession and discussed in detail in the next section – must be met.

The remaining fiscal incentive in the French regional package relates to the transfer tax (*droit de mutation*) applicable to the sale of certain intangible assets and, more importantly, of used industrial buildings (at least five years old). This incentive is available for setting-up and extension projects (in Zones A and B of Figure 4.2) and, again, the job conditions of award for these project types are the same as for the local-business-tax concession. For projects transferring out of either the Paris or Lyons regions (the incentive can then be awarded also in Zone C on Figure 4.2) the job conditions of award are at least ten new jobs for projects located in areas with a population of less than 15,000 inhabitants and 30 new jobs in all other cases. The incentive is also available for regrouping on to an industrial estate or transfer to an industrial estate from a location in a residential area — and for a restricted number of modernisation projects. For regrouping, transfer and modernisation, the maintenance of existing jobs is required. The award takes the form of a reduction in the normal rate of transfer tax, from 13.8 to 2 per cent for buildings and from 17.2 to 2 per cent for intangibles.

We mentioned earlier that soft loans have declined in importance within the regional-incentive package over the years. Although soft-loan facilities are still available in theory for regional industrial development through the central government's *fonds de développement économique et social* (FDES), the relevant FDES committee, the *Comité un ter*, has in recent years tended to make awards according to sectoral rather than regional criteria.

Since 1974 four new grant schemes have been added to the regional-incentive packages — all aimed at providing incentives for small-scale artisan firms. The first of these (*indemnité particulière de décentralisation en faveur d'entreprises artisanales de sous-traitance*) is a decentralisation grant for artisan sub-contractors in the Paris region who follow the relocated firms for which they normally work. Rates of award are 100 per cent of the first FF 20,000 of incurred removal costs (dismantling, transport, reassembly of plant and equipment), 75 per cent of the next FF 30,000 and 60 per cent of any amount exceeding FF 50,000.

The *prime à l'installation d'entreprises artisanales* is intended to encourage the setting-up of artisan firms in rural areas (and some selected urban locations). Awards are available in all localities outside the Paris region with populations not exceeding 5,000 (not exceeding 20,000 inhabitants in the designated Upland and Rural Areas). There is a minimum capital-investment requirement of FF 50,000 and rates of award vary according to location — with higher awards in the *Massif Central* — and size of investment. The maximum award is 30 per cent of investment in the *Massif* and 16 per cent elsewhere.

The *prime de développement artisanal* was brought in to complement the scheme just described, but only in the *Massif Central*, by
making assistance available there for extension projects in places with
a population of less than 50,000 inhabitants. At least three new
permanent jobs must be created within three years and a minimum of
FF 150,000 must be invested in premises and plant and equipment.
The rates of award are identical to those offered under the regional-
development-grant scheme.

The last of the four artisan schemes (*aide spéciale rurale*) is the most
general small-project scheme yet introduced. It is a grant scheme which
in general terms applies to all *cantons* within the problem regions with a
population density of less than ten inhabitants per square kilometre.
Aid is available for both industrial and service projects as well as for
'artisanal' trades, tourism and hotels. Awards vary according to the
number of jobs created and project type. For setting up, the amount
paid per job created is FF 20,000 for the first ten jobs, FF 15,000 for
the next ten and FF 8,000 for a final ten. No aid is given for any job
above the thirtieth. For extension projects, account is taken of the
existing labour force when calculating the award so that, for example,
an establishment with 18 employees which created three new jobs
would receive FF 15,000 for each of the first two jobs and FF 8,000
for the third.

These, then, are the regional incentives of any significance offered
by national government in France. In addition to these national
schemes, there are a number of aids available from sub-national government. In the past, sub-national financial aid has principally featured
the sale and preparation of sites at concessionary prices, the supply of
temporary factory premises (*usines relais*) and job-creation grants. New
legislation, however, allows the regions (*Etablissements Publics
Régionaux*) to make awards of their own for setting-up projects, which
may be obtained in addition to central-government assistance. Although
the powers which this legislation confers on the regions are limited,
it will be interesting to see how they are used and how they develop
over the next few years.

The Major Incentives

Having provided an overview of the complete package of regional
incentives on offer in France, we wish in this section to take a more
detailed look at the two principal incentives, the regional-development
grant and the local-business-tax concession (concentrating, in particular,

on eligibility conditions and award levels). It will be recalled that these two incentives account for some 80 per cent of annual incentive spending in France. The more important of them, accounting for almost one-half of the annual incentive spending, is the regional-development grant.

The Regional-development Grant

The regional-development grant is the latter-day name of the project-related grant which has been the centre-piece of French regional-incentive policy since its beginnings in the mid-1950s. Between 1975 and 1977, 1,851 regional-development-grant applications were approved to the value of just over FF 1,400 million. Associated with this outlay was investment of some FF 11,700 million and over 104,500 jobs (according to estimates based on targets agreed between applicant firms and the awarding authorities).

Applications are submitted to the *préfet* of the *département* where the project is located in the case of qualifying investment totalling less than FF 10 million, and the award decision is taken by the *préfet* on the advice of the advisory committee comprising local representatives of several 'interested' government departments and public agencies. Projects involving eligible investment of FF 10 million or more (and a certain number of special cases which may be of a smaller size) are dealt with in Paris and the award decision is taken by the Minister of Economics upon the advice of an advisory committee — again comprising representatives of several 'interested' government departments and public agencies. In line with the position in most other countries in the European Community, aid cannot be given to projects which have started before the submission of an application for assistance. However, in contrast to the position of most other countries, an applicant — by submitting a so-called 'letter of intent' in which the project is briefly outlined — may go ahead with the project without prejudice as long as the full application follows within six months.

Eligibility Conditions. The broad parameters of eligibility for the regional-development grant are defined according to spatial, activity and project-type criteria. There are then a number of other conditions, and in particular job and investment conditions, which must be fulfilled before an award can be made. We look first at spatial, activity and project-type coverage.

As Figure 4.1 shows, the regional-development grant is available in about half of France, comprising the entire western and south-western parts of the country as well as certain areas on the northern and north-eastern borders. Within the eligible areas there is variation in the conditions of award regarding both minimum levels of investment and minimum job-creation/maintenance requirements. Although we describe these job and investment conditions in detail shortly, it should be noted here that, generally speaking, they are less demanding in the Upland and Rural Areas and in Corsica than elsewhere in the Designated Areas and, in addition, are less stringent the smaller the locality in which the project is situated. By and large, only the Designated Areas shown in Figure 4.1 qualify for regional-development-grant aid, but there is some discretion to extend eligibility to projects located just outside these areas where it is likely that, by virtue of their size and proximity, such projects will have a significant impact on the Designated Areas. However, in practice, only limited use is made of this provision.

Regarding activity coverage, the regional-development grant is intended first and foremost for the manufacturing sector. Even though there is no formal list of eligible and ineligible activities, in practice the following activities are generally excluded: the extraction of natural resources, construction, haulage, tourism and agriculture (except for the food-processing industry). In addition, while certain service-sector projects are eligible, they are more likely to apply for assistance under one or other of the service-specific schemes noted earlier. Consequently, virtually all awards go to manufacturing projects.

As far as project-type coverage is concerned, the main qualifying project types are setting-up projects and extensions. However 'setting-up' refers not only to the creation of a new establishment 'from scratch' but also includes the take-over of establishments in difficulty, although stringent rules requiring that the establishment being taken over be independent of the firm effecting the take-over are applied in order to preclude abuse of this provision by multi-establishment firms (notably holding companies). Similarly, extension projects are defined such as to include not only the expansion of existing establishments but also certain re-organisation projects, where the establishment being re-organised is in a declining sector and where there is a complete change of product. However, rationalisation, modernisation and other similar forms of internal re-organisation are not eligible.

Beyond these broad parameters of spatial, activity and project-type eligibility, there are a number of other conditions of award. Chief among these, as already noted, are minimum investment and minimum job requirements. These are set out in full in Table 4.1. From the table, it can be seen that, in terms of both job and investment conditions, there

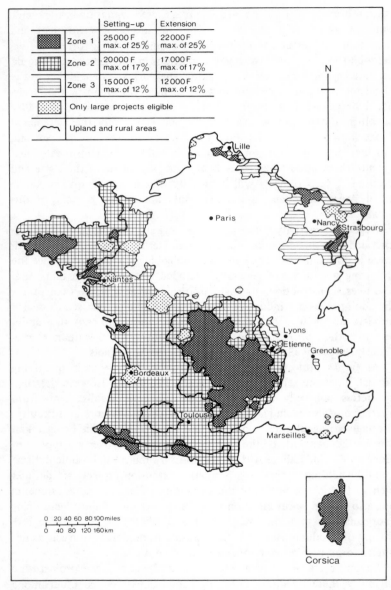

		Setting–up	Extension
▓	Zone 1	25000 F max. of 25%	22000 F max. of 25%
▦	Zone 2	20000 F max. of 17%	17000 F max. of 17%
▤	Zone 3	15000 F max. of 12%	12000 F max. of 12%
▒	Only large projects eligible		
〜	Upland and rural areas		

N

Lille

Paris

Nancy

Strasbourg

Nantes

Lyons

St.Etienne

Grenoble

Bordeaux

Toulouse

Marseilles

0   20 40 60 80 100 miles
0   40 80 120 160 km

Corsica

Figure 4.1: Designated Areas in France (Regional-development Grant)

Table 4.1: Regional-development Grant: Job and Investment Conditions of Award

Size of locality:	General Case		Upland and Rural Areas and Corsica		
	< 15,000	15,000+	< 15,000	15,000–49,999	50,000+
Setting-up projects					
Minimum investment (FF):	300,000	800,000	300,000	500,000	800,000
Minimum jobs:	10	30	6	15	30
Extensions					
Minimum investment (FF):	300,000	800,000	300,000	500,000	800,000
Minimum jobs:	10 & 25% increase	30 & 25% increase	6 & 20% increase	15 & 20% increase	30 & 25% increase
	or	*or*	*or*	*or*	*or*
	50 & 10% increase	120	50 & 10% increase	50 & 10% increase	120
	or		*or*	*or*	
	120		120	120	

Note: In those areas in Figure 4.1 where only large projects are eligible, at least 100 jobs must be created and FF 10 million invested. Extension projects are not eligible.

is discrimination between, on the one hand, the Upland and Rural Areas and Corsica and, on the other, the remaining Designated Areas (with the former, in general, facing less stringent award conditions); and also between different sizes of locality (with areas of less than 15,000 being favoured over those of 15,000 or more). While not wishing to discuss Table 4.1 in detail, it should be noted that for setting-up projects the minimum job requirement ranges from six new jobs in localities of less than 15,000 in the Upland and Rural Areas and Corsica to 30 new jobs in localities of over 50,000 (15,000 in the general case), while the minimum-investment requirement ranges from FF 300,000 to FF 800,000. For extension projects the picture is rather more complicated, at least as far as minimum job conditions are concerned. Linked to each minimum job condition is a requirement to increase the original labour force by a set percentage. However, where this percentage increase cannot be met, then a lesser percentage increase is acceptable as long as a greater absolute number of jobs is created — culminating in the situation that if 120 jobs are created no percentage increase is stipulated. Nevertheless, even with these complications, the general picture is the same as for setting-up projects; and indeed those absolute job conditions demanding the highest percentage increase are identical to those for setting-up projects.

We noted earlier that the definition of setting-up projects includes take-overs and that the definition of extensions includes internal re-organisation. In the case of both the internal re-organisation and the take-over of establishments in difficulties it is clearly unlikely that jobs will be created; rather, they will be maintained. For such projects the minimum number of jobs which must be maintained is the minimum number stipulated for setting-up projects in the locality in question (as set out in Table 4.1).

Before leaving Table 4.1, we should mention a number of requirements attached to those jobs to be created or maintained. Only permanent jobs qualify. Jobs normally performed by temporary or seasonal workers or by outworkers (i.e. those working for the firm from their homes) or by apprentices are usually not taken into account; nor are jobs occupied by illegal immigrants or induced elsewhere in or outside the firm. Part-time jobs *are* counted (where permanent), but only after converting them into full-time equivalents. Finally, firms may be required to give hiring priority to the local registered unemployed, although this condition is particularly ineffective when the applicant is seeking quite specific skills which are not locally available among the unemployed.

In addition to the minimum job and investment conditions noted above, every project in receipt of a regional-development grant must, within a maximum period of three years, fulfil investment targets and job-creation targets agreed between the administration and the applicant firm. These targets may be higher than the minima set for the particular location and the particular project type. A certain period of grace may be allowed, however, if non-fulfilment of the job/investment conditions within three years is due to *force majeure*. Certainly, the granting of a period of grace has become less infrequent in recent years owing to the difficult economic conditions which firms have had to face.

A final condition of award which must be mentioned — and this condition is found within all project-related incentive schemes in the European Community — is that the projects to be aided be viable. In the case of the regional-development grant this viability assessment covers commercial, technical and financial viability. It is generally the financial-viability assessment (i.e. an assessment of the firm's short-term-liquidity position) which is most likely to affect a firm's chances of receiving aid. This condition of award is of particular importance because it gives the administration a certain scope for discretion in whether or not to assist particular projects, although it would be wrong to imply that the condition is systematically used to this end. It is, however, not unusual for an award to be made conditional upon a stipulated improvement in liquidity.

These then are the main conditions of award. One could list a large number of other conditions, but they tend to be of minor importance except in very specific instances. The regional-development-grant scheme is an essentially automatic scheme in terms of its eligibility requirements — at least within the matrix of spatial, activity, project-type, job, investment, and project-viability requirements set out above.

Award Levels. The value of the regional-development grant is related to the number of jobs created/maintained and the amount of qualifying investment associated with the project. Each of these quantities is an estimate made on the basis of forecasts provided by the applicant and vetted by the authorities. The value of the award is calculated as an absolute sum of money per job created/maintained, subject to the constraint that the resultant total is not higher than a stipulated percentage of qualifying-project expenditure. For example, the maximum possible award under the scheme is FF 25,000 up to a ceiling of 25 per cent of eligible project expenditure. The full matrix of award rates is shown in Figure 4.1, from which it can be seen that rates of award normally vary according to location (the Designated Areas being divided into three zones for award purposes) and project type (setting-up projects being favoured over extensions in terms of the amount per job offered). There are, however, four circumstances in which the rates of award in Figure 4.1 do not necessarily or directly apply.

First, in the case of large projects (involving qualifying investment of FF 10 million or more) there is a provision whereby the authorities may award up to 25 per cent of eligible expenditure, irrespective of location and project type and unrelated to the number of jobs created. Similarly, there is a provision allowing the job-determined award limit to be ignored, although the award is still subject to the investment-related limit for the particular location. Both of these provisions are used only sparingly, but they do give the administration some 'bargaining capacity'. Third, in the case of extension projects only, if the original labour force in the establishment is already 800 or more, then every job beyond the 800th is subject to a limit of FF 10,000 per job, irrespective of location. Fourth, for projects located just outside the Designated Areas but deemed to be eligible for aid because of their impact on the proximate Designated Areas, the rates of award are FF 15,000 per job for setting-up and FF 12,000 per job for extension, subject in both cases to an investment-related ceiling of 12 per cent of qualifying expenditure.

We turn now from how awards are calculated to the value of awards actually made. The figures which follow relate to 1977, the most recent year for which data is available. In 1977, the actual average regional-development-grant award was 12.3 per cent of eligible investment. Disaggregating this figure according to whether the award was made locally (projects with less than FF 10 million of eligible investment) or centrally (larger projects) reveals that the average local award was 16.8 per cent of eligible investment, whereas the average central award was a more modest 8.8 per cent. The relatively small size of central awards would appear to be primarily a reflection of the greater capital intensity of larger projects, thus causing the job-related ceilings to 'bite harder' for such projects. As regards the actual value of awards in each of the three award zones, the available figures relate only to awards made in Paris. In the Maximum-rate Zone (up to 25 per cent of eligible investment) the average award was 16.8 per cent, while in both the Intermediate-rate and the Minimum-rate Zones (up to 17 per cent and 12 per cent respectively) the average was only 6.3 per cent. This may be because more labour-intensive projects locate in the Maximum-rate Zone, but it may also reflect a greater willingness of Paris to use its powers to exceed the normal job-related ceilings on award values in the case of projects located in the Maximum-rate Zone.

So far, we have talked only about the nominal value of awards, i.e. the value of an award as calculated according to the job- and investment-linked formula described above. In practice, the effective value of an award to a firm will be less than this nominal value because of the influence of a number of different factors. Three factors in particular tend to reduce the nominal value of a regional-development grant: the ineligibility of certain items of expenditure, delays in the payment of awards and taxation. We now consider these in turn.

The eligible items of investment for the regional-development grant are land, all buildings other than those buildings or parts of buildings used for residential or purely social purposes and plant and machinery (but excluding second-hand plant and machinery). Working capital is not eligible, nor are vehicles, except those employed on-site (e.g. for materials handling). Also eligible are site-preparation expenditures (levelling, piling, drainage, etc.), as well as legal and consultancy fees directly related to the Designated Area location. Works other than those of an ornamental nature also qualify (e.g. vats, reservoirs, access roads). There are no specific rules with regard to low-value items, although it is laid down that only office equipment with an economic life of at least one year and held in the balance sheet may qualify. The value of each qualifying item is its cost price exclusive of all taxes but, in the case of imported items, inclusive of customs duties.

The ineligibility of assets is further affected by the manner in which they are financed. Assets acquired by cash purchase, whether by outright payment or by phased payments, are eligible. Assets acquired by hire purchase or by analogous leasing arrangements (i.e. arrangements whereby the asset enters contractually into the ownership of the lessee immediately or at some contractually specified time in the future) qualify insofar as the assets are provided by a recognised company specialising in such forms of asset supply and financing and as long as the full benefit of the award made to the firm supplying the assets (the portion of the award relating to the supplied assets is paid to the supplier) is fully passed on to the user. The other common form of asset financing is, of course, simple renting. Rented assets are not eligible.

Turning now to the timing and phasing of payment, a regional-development grant is almost always paid not as a lump sum but in two or three instalments spread over the three-year period during which the set job and investment targets must be met. To the extent that the investor makes investment expenditures today but only receives the corresponding portion of grant at some time in the future, the effective value of the award is reduced. In practice, the impact of delays in the payment of regional-development grants is small compared to other incentives in France as well as to many incentives in other countries. There are two reasons for this. The first is that because of disbursement of awards in instalments they are, by and large, paid out to the investor in line with need (i.e. the delays between incurred actual expenditure and receipt of grant are kept to a minimum). Second, it is usual practice in France to give the investor an advance on his award equal to one-third of its value. This advance payment is usually disbursed within about three weeks of the award decision. It is not impossible, therefore, for the investor to receive a portion of the grant even in advance of his having incurred actual expenditure. Similarly, advance payment may compensate an investor for the fact that the following instalment payments will be made only after he has incurred actual expenditure.

As far as tax treatment is concerned, a regional-development grant is always viewed by the revenue authorities as an addition to corporate income and hence is subject to corporation (profits) tax. The nominal rate of corporation tax is 50 per cent of taxable profits, but the impact of taxation on the grant is less than this. The principal reason for this, apart from the fact that firms may not make sufficient profits for the grant to be fully subject to tax, is that the incorporation of the grant into taxable income is phased according to the depreciation schedules of the assets on which the grant is paid. Typical depreciation lives for tax purposes are 20 years (straight-line) for industrial buildings and between 5 and 10 years (reducing-balance) for plant and machinery. In the case of non-depreciable aided assets, notably land, the grant is normally brought into income in ten equal annual instalments starting in the year following that in which the grant was received. The effect of this phasing of the incorporation of the grant into income is to postpone the tax burden borne by the grant — for a substantial period in the case of an industrial building, and often to substantial effect when one considers that buildings often make up half of the total fixed-capital expenditure associated with projects. Because of this postponement, the effective rate of tax on the grant is considerably less than the nominal rate of 50 per cent.

Tax treatment, the timing and phasing of payment, and item coverage all go some way towards reducing the effective value of the regional-development grant. But even more important in the French context is the fact that regional-development grants may be 'clawed back' by the authorities whenever the job and/or investment targets agreed between the applicant and the administration are not met within the stipulated three-year project-realisation period. If the shortfall is such that the project fails to achieve even the minimum job and/or investment requirements set for a project of that type in the location in question, then the whole of the award may be recalled by the administration. If the shortfall is less than the agreed targets but not such that the project fails to meet the minimum requirements for a project of that type in that location, then the amount of grant clawed back is proportional to the shortfall. Although several countries have clawback conditions in their incentive schemes, they often make little use of them. In France, by contrast, the regional-development-grant clawback conditions are enforced with relative stringency; and indeed in recent years, the amount clawed back in any one year has been as high as 10 per cent of the total value of grants awarded in the same year – a figure far in excess of that found in any other European Community country.

The Local-business-tax Concession

The local-business-tax concession requires a brief preface on France's local business tax if it is to be properly understood.

The local business tax (*taxe professionnelle*) is an annual tax levied by each *département* and by each *commune* within each *département* on all business establishments operating for profit. The tax is assessed partly on the theoretical rental values of all fixed assets employed by the firm in its day-to-day business and partly on the firm's annual wages and salaries bill. This taxable value is multiplied by a tax rate, set by each *département* and *commune* separately, to obtain a firm's liability to the tax. All *départements* and *communes* within the areas designated for this incentive have the opportunity of offering a concession on the tax. Any concession which they wish to offer is subject to the agreement of the Ministry of the Budget in Paris. The maximum possible concession which they may give is limited to five years, after which time the firm becomes liable to the tax in the ordinary way. The concession may be up to 100 per cent of liability in each of the five years, or a lesser amount. In a given locality, the concession may be available on only the *commune* levy or on both the *commune* and the *département* levy.

As should be clear from the preceding paragraph, France's local-business-tax concession is an incentive which jointly involves sub-national and national government. Sub-national government decides whether it wishes to make the incentive available in its area. National government decides whether to allow the incentive to be awarded in each particular locality (a procedure intended to ensure that sub-national governments do not jeopardise their finances) and sets the condition of award for the scheme. As in the case of the regional-development grant the award decision is taken in the *département* (by the local tax inspector) for projects involving qualifying investment of less than FF 10 million and in Paris (by the Minister of the Budget) for all larger projects (as well as for 'problem' cases).

Eligibility Conditions. In terms of its spatial coverage, the local-business-tax concession is among the least restrictive regional incentives on offer in France. For *industrial* projects, the concession can be offered in all those areas qualifying for the regional-development grant (Zone A in Figure 4.2) as well as in a number of other areas (Zone B), while in certain additional areas (Zone C) projects are eligible if they involve relocation from either the Paris or Lyons regions and if their old premises are closed down. For *service* projects coverage is even wider, virtually the whole country being eligible except for the Paris Basin (as defined for the service-industry schemes) and the Lyons region. Within those areas which are eligible, there is variation in the conditions of award regarding both minimum levels of investment and minimum job-creation/maintenance requirements — especially for industrial projects where, as we shall see, the conditions set are similar to those laid down for the regional-development grant (favouring the Upland and Rural Areas and Corsica over the remaining Designated Areas, and small localities over large).

Moving on to consider activity coverage we again find substantial similarity with the regional-development grant. Thus the concession is available to the manufacturing sector but generally not to the extractive, haulage or construction industries; nor to the agricultural sector, apart from food-processing industries. One point of difference, however, is that the local-business-tax concession is as freely available for tertiary investment as it is for industrial investment (it will be recalled that the regional-development-grant scheme is rarely paid for tertiary-investment projects because of the availability of specific grant schemes for service-sector investment). The eligible tertiary activities are those which qualify for the regional-development grant (and for the two service-grant schemes). These are the headquarters functions of industrial firms (including their data-processing and research and

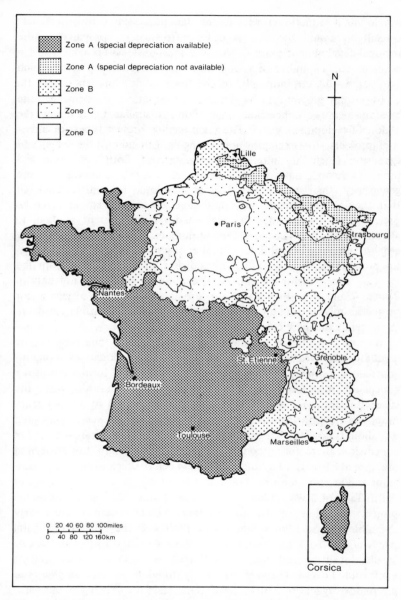

Figure 4.2: Designated Areas in France (Fiscal Concessions to Industry)

development functions) as well as data-processing firms, technical consultancies and the like. Another difference as compared to the regional-development grant is that the local-business-tax concession is available for a number of tourist and hotel investment projects. Such projects would not normally receive regional-development-grant aid.

Regarding project-type eligibility, the situation in respect of the local-business-tax concession once more is similar to that for the regional-development grant. The main eligible project types for industrial projects, for example, are setting-up (including take-overs) and extension (including internal re-organisation). Both take-overs and internal re-organisation are, however, treated somewhat more generously than under the regional-development-grant scheme in that the job requirement is simply that the original labour force be preserved (whereas under the regional-development-grant scheme, as already noted, it is necessary for the number of maintained jobs to be at least as high as the minimum number of jobs to be created by setting-up projects in that location). In addition, decentralisation from the Paris or Lyons regions is eligible – and, as we have seen, not only in Zones A and B in Figure 4.2 but also in Zone C. For service-sector projects, only setting-up projects, extensions and transfers from the Paris region are eligible.

Beyond these broad parameters of spatial, activity and project-type eligibility, and bearing in mind, too, that – like regional-development-grant-aided projects – any project in receipt of a local-business-tax concession must be viable, the main additional condition which the successful applicant must fulfil is that the project satisfy the set minimum job-creation/maintenance requirements. Before describing these, we should however stress that, in respect of the local-business-tax concession, there are no conditions regarding the amount of associated investment. This is a key difference between the regional-development-grant and local-business-tax-concession schemes.

In Table 4.2 we set out the job conditions attached to industrial projects applying for the local-business-tax concession. Quite clearly the table has much in common with Table 4.1: the Upland and Rural Areas and Corsica are favoured over the rest of the Designated Areas; smaller localities are favoured over larger ones; and setting-up projects are favoured over extensions. As already noted, however, take-overs and internal re-organisation 'only' have to maintain the existing labour force – not, as with the regional-development grant, the number of jobs setting-up projects in the same area would have to create.

Service projects also have to meet job conditions. But these

Table 4.2: Local-business-tax Concession: Job Conditions of Award (Industrial Projects)

	General Case		Upland and Rural Areas and Corsica	
Size of locality	< 15,000	15,000+	< 15,000	15,000+
Setting-up Projects:	10	30	6	15
Extensions:	10 & 25% increase	30 & 25% increase	6 & 20% increase	15 & 20% increase
	or	or	or	or
	50 & 10% increase	120	50 & 10% increase	50 & 10% increase
	or		or	or
	120		120	120
Take-over/internal re-organisation	Maintain existing labour force	Maintain existing labour force	Maintain existing labour force	Maintain existing labour force

conditions are not those of Table 4.2 but rather those set out in our description of the specific service-industry schemes in the previous section. Thus, for research and development projects, setting-up requires the creation of at least ten new research-related jobs and extension requires, in addition, that the original labour force be increased by at least 30 per cent. However, extensions which involve a transfer from the Paris region, the extension of an existing establishment by the addition of research and development functions, or a first extension following the setting-up of research and development activities need, *alternatively*, create only 50 new jobs. For service projects other than research and development, the usual requirement for a setting-up project is 30 new jobs, reduced to 20 when the project involves the creation of the firm's registered offices in the Designated Areas. For extension projects there is the additional requirement that the pre-extension labour force be increased by at least 50 per cent, except when the project involves the creation of new functions or the decentralisation of functions from the Paris region; in this case 100 new jobs then suffice to fulfil the job-creation requirements, irrespective of the percentage increase in the labour force which these 100 jobs represent.

The further job conditions of award are similar to those attached to the regional-development grant. Account is taken only of permanent, full-time employment (although part-time jobs may be counted by converting them into full-time equivalents), and apprentices and outworkers as well as temporary and seasonal workers do not normally qualify. The major difference compared to the regional-development grant in terms of job conditions of award is that award of the local-business-tax concession is conditional upon multi-establishment firms not shedding labour in any of their other establishments except in the case of relocation from the Lyons region. There is, however, doubt about whether this condition of award is systematically enforced.

Finally, it should be noted that every project in receipt of a local-business-tax concession must fulfil the job target agreed between the administration and the applicant firm within a maximum period of three years. There is, however, no provision for the granting of a period of grace, as in the case of the regional-development grant. Moreover, the three-year period begins from the date of application for an award, and the application must precede the commencement of the investment for which assistance is being sought. Thus, in contrast to the regional-development grant, there is no provision allowing an earlier start to investment by the submission of a letter of intent to the awarding authorities up to six months in advance of formal application.

Award Levels. It is exceedingly difficult to make general statements about the value of awards under the local-business-tax-concession scheme. As noted earlier, the value of an award is a function of the rate of local business tax as well as of the value of the concession itself. Each *commune* and *département* sets its own rate of taxation and determines whether it will give a full concession of 100 per cent of liability or some lesser amount, as well as whether it will award the concession for the maximum period of five years or for some shorter period.

Rather surprisingly, there are no systematic data available on the rates of concession actually awarded. Impressionistic evidence suggests, however, that the typical concession is the maximum possible concession − a 100 per cent concession over five years on both the *commune* and *département* levies applying in the particular location. But this still gives little indication of the money value of the award, because tax rates can vary substantially between localities. Indeed, the variation in local-business-tax rates is such that a location offering no concession may in the long run be more attractive than one in which a concession is available since, once the concession runs out, the rate of local business tax to be paid may be so much higher. Clearly, it is very difficult to attach a value to the concession. Some indication, however, is provided by a government study, now rather out-dated, which suggested that on the assumption of a maximum concession on the forerunner of the local business tax, the *patente*, the typical concession might be worth some 11 per cent of initial-project fixed-capital investment.[11]

But even this figure, however tentative, must be viewed with caution when trying to assess the effective value of the local-business-tax concession to recipient firms. In particular (and in addition to the points already made about, for example, variations around the average) it takes no account of the fact that the local business tax in France can be offset against corporation (profits) tax. As a consequence, when a local-business-tax concession is received, the firm bears a higher than usual corporation-tax burden since it has no local-business-tax liability with which to diminish its taxable profits. Given that the ordinary rate of corporation tax is 50 per cent of taxable profits, this is a factor which can reduce substantially the effective value of a local-business-tax concession.

Comparative Conclusions

One of the striking features of the French regional-incentive package is the relatively large number of individual incentives on offer — about a dozen. On the other hand, there is not the rich variety of forms of incentive which this figure might lead one to expect; there are, for example, virtually no soft loans, nor are there any 'national' profit-tax concessions. In fact, despite the relatively large number of individual incentives, only two of them may truly be called major, the regional-development grant and the local-business-tax concession.

Although a number of the countries in the European Community operate taxes which are not dissimilar to the French local business tax, none offers a regional incentive in relation to that tax like the one to be found in France — or of its scale. It will be recalled that the French local-business-tax concession accounts for about one-third of annual regional-incentive spending (and the regional-development grant for a further one-half). The local-business-tax concession is also remarkable in that it continues to operate despite the fact that there are probably few who would rally to its support if some other incentive were proposed to replace it. The business community is unlikely to find it attractive because it is so difficult to value. Similarly, the Commission of the European Community is not particularly enthusiastic about it, partly because it is difficult to value and partly because it can be viewed as a virtually ongoing form of assistance. Even the French national government would probably prefer to abolish the concession, for the reason that it has little effective scope to control the rates of taxation set by each *commune* and *département* and to that extent cannot influence the value of awards. Nevertheless, it seems likely that any attempt to do away with the local-business-tax concession will meet with difficulties; it will certainly experience the stubborn resistance of the *communes* and *départements*, which will be most unwilling to yield 'their' most valuable regional incentive.

Another interesting feature of the French package is represented by the four incentive schemes directed at small-scale investment projects. Three of these are specifically intended to encourage small-scale investment in the rural areas of France — a reminder of just how much of France is rural and sparsely populated, and a recognition of the limited ability of incentives geared towards medium- and large-size projects to contribute to resolving the regional problem in an extensive rural 'periphery'.

Also of note within the French package are the two grant schemes specifically intended for tertiary-investment projects. France, to a greater extent than most other European Community countries, has been experimenting with incentives for the tertiary sector for a number of years, in particular since 1972. Between 1972 and 1975 the success of France's tertiary grant was modest; in those three years only twenty tertiary awards were made, whereas almost 1,500 regional-development grants were awarded. It is therefore not surprising that in 1976 a number of important modifications were made to the major tertiary-grant scheme, the service-activities grant. Whereas prior to 1976, for example, award was conditional (even in the most favourable circumstances) upon the creation of a minimum of 50 new jobs, the threshold was reduced to six new jobs after 1976. Similarly, whereas before 1976 there were minimum investment conditions to be met (and not all forms of investment were eligible for aid), after 1976 all restrictive investment conditions were dropped. Again, in 1976 the maximum rate of award was set at FF 25,000 per job created, whereas previously the maximum had been FF 15,000 per job created, limited to 20 per cent of eligible investment. Moreover, since this investment condition would most likely have resulted in actual awards prior to 1976 being less than FF 15,000 per job, the increase in the maximum award is even more significant than it might appear. A final important change in 1976 was that the Designated Areas for the service-activities-grant scheme were much more widely defined; whereas previously the scheme had applied, by and large, only in those areas where the regional-development grant could be obtained, after 1976 assistance was made available throughout the country with the exception of the Paris Basin and the partial exception that only qualitatively significant projects may be assisted in the Lyons region. The impact of these changes is reflected in the award statistics for 1976 and 1977. In the single year 1976 more tertiary awards were made than in the three preceding years (25 awards in 1976 as against only 20 in the period 1973 to 1975). Moreover, 56 awards were made in 1977, as against the 25 in 1976. Although the number of tertiary awards is still much lower than the number of regional-development grants awarded (the number of service grants awarded in 1977 represents slightly more than 6 per cent of the number of regional-development grants in the same year) there would appear to be the start of a trend which will be deserving of considerable interest in the years to come.

Finally, there is the regional-development grant to consider. With a maximum nominal rate of 25 per cent (albeit job-constrained) the regional-development grant is certainly on a par with most other capital grants in the European Community, although some way behind those on offer in Ireland, Italy and Northern Ireland. Tax treatment, the timing and phasing of award and item coverage are all fairly standard compared with other capital grants in the Community (although both the possibility of submitting a letter of intent before a formal application and the availability of advance grant payments soon after the project is approved are certainly worthy of note) so that in effective-value terms, too, the French regional-development grant is in line with most others in the Community (at least as regards award maxima).

There are, however, a number of respects in which the regional-development grant can perhaps be viewed as somewhat restrictive relative to capital grants in other Community countries. First, it is available basically only to setting-up and extension projects and then only if minimum job and investment conditions are met. Elsewhere in the Community, a wider range of project types is normally eligible and, if there are job and investment requirements, then they are usually less explicit than within the French scheme. Secondly, job and investment targets are set for the project to meet within three years. And finally, it is expected that these targets actually be met — all or part of the award being clawed back if there is a shortfall. Nowhere else in the European Community are such specific targets set, and nowhere else is clawback so extensive. As already noted, the amount clawed back in any one year has been as high as 10 per cent of the total value of grants awarded in the same year — well in excess of capital-grant clawback anywhere else in the Community.

Notes

1. Unless otherwise stated, the figures in this paragraph are taken from Institut National de la Statistique et des Etudes Economiques, *Statistiques et Indicateurs des Régions Françaises* (INSEE, Paris, 1977).
2. See M. Astorg, 'Le Développement Régional et l'Aménagement du Territoire' in J.-P. Pagé (ed.), *Profil Economique de la France* (La Documentation Française, Paris, 1975), p. 304.
3. SESAME, *Activités et Régions: Dynamiques d'une Transformation*, Travaux et recherches de prospective, Schéma générale d'aménagement de la France, no. 75 (La Documentation Française, Paris, 1978), p. 39.
4. See R. Froment and S. Lerat, *La France en 1974* (Bréal, Paris, 1974), vol. 1, pp. 199-200; and SESAME, *Activités et Régions*, p. 49.
5. See P. Durand, *Industrie et Régions* (La Documentation Française, Paris, 1974), pp. 20-3.
6. J. Gravier, *Paris et le Désert Française* (Le Portulan, Paris, 1947).
7. See J. Jalon, *Primes et Zones Industrielles* (Berger-Levrault, Paris, 1967), p. 32 ff.

8. See Durand, *Industrie et Régions*, pp. 24-9.

9. See B. Nicol and R. Wettman, 'Background Notes on Restrictive Regional Policy Measures in the European Community', in Kevin Allen (ed.), *Balanced National Growth* (Lexington Books, Mass., 1979).

10. See P. Merlin, *Les Villes Nouvelles Françaises* (La Documentation Française, Paris, 1976).

11. DATAR, *Effet Cumulè des Aides Financières Accordèes Pour une Implantation Industrielle en Province* (DATAR, Paris, 1968).

5 REGIONAL INCENTIVES IN THE FEDERAL REPUBLIC OF GERMANY

This chapter is in five sections. After a brief introductory section concerned with the nature of the regional problem in the Federal Republic, the second section covers the development of regional policy — with particular emphasis on the efforts made to harmonise Federal and *Länder* policies. The next two sections then describe the current incentive package and the main regional incentives in turn, while a final section compares and contrasts German regional-incentive policy with similar policies in other European Community countries.

The Nature of the Problem

In the Federal Republic of Germany regional problems were recognised, and regional policies developed, rather later than elsewhere in Western Europe. In the first decade or so after the war the prime policy preoccupation was, not unnaturally, with recovery and reconstruction while the 1960s saw a period of sustained economic growth spread throughout the German *Länder* (the states of the Federal Republic). Although certain regions benefited more than others from the general advance of the economy (an advance which led to Germany being ranked among the world's major economic powers by the end of the 1960s) dramatic disequilibria were avoided. As a result, the German regional problem is rather different *from* the regional problem found in many other countries in that

> there are neither the major structural disequilibria characteristic of Italy or the United Kingdom, nor the striking contrasts between 'developed' and 'underdeveloped' regions, remote and backward peripheral regions, or regions of marked geographical and physical features which prevent their participation in the general progress of the country.[1]

Rather, the German regional problem is perhaps best described as 'sub-regional', being concentrated in a limited number of sub-regions distributed throughout the country.

A further characteristic of the German case is that the regional problem cannot be defined in terms of a single criterion. Rather, the problem regions are characterised by a variety of features, ranging from deficiencies in infrastructure provision to distance from large population centres, from the effects of adverse industrial change to rural depopulation. Thus, the assisted areas in Germany include both areas with a lop-sided industrial structure and rural agriculture areas which have relatively high unemployment and are seeking new industrial employment opportunities, as well as areas bordering on Eastern Europe which have suffered from the loss of their historic economic hinterlands.

Given the nature of the German problem, and bearing in mind, too, that Germany is a federal country, a very interesting question concerns just how the problem areas have been identified and designated. This is one of a number of questions considered in detail in the next section.

The Development of Policy

Regional policy in Germany can be viewed as having developed in three phases. The first phase covered roughly the first decade after the end of the Second World War. Policy during the period was, by and large, of a 'fire-fighting' character, designed to alleviate local distress resulting from the devastation brought by the war. The main objectives of policy were the reconstruction of areas with severely damaged productive capacity and the alleviation of high local levels of unemployment (often exacerbated by the inflow of evacuees and refugees). Policy measures were largely directed at clearing away war damage and reconstructing plant and infrastructure which had either been damaged in the war or had been dismantled and removed after the war by the occupying powers.

From 1951 onwards 'Emergency Areas' (*Notstandsgebiete*) were delineated annually. These areas were of two types — areas of general economic depression and areas of agricultural destruction. Both were delineated using (different) unemployment indicators. In 1953, after the Iron Curtain had ensured the division of Germany and Europe, a 40-50-km-wide belt of territory along the borders with East Germany and Czechoslovakia and along the Baltic Sea was delineated as the 'Zonal Border Area' (*Zonenrandgebiete*) and assistance was made available to compensate for the loss of its natural economic hinterlands.

The essentially *ad hoc* policy operated in this first period was administered by an interministerial committee set up in 1950 — the Interministerial Committee for Emergency Area Questions (*Interministerieller Auschuss für Notstandsgebietsfragen*, IMNOS). The assistance, mainly in the form of soft loans, was paid from the Federal

Regional Promotion Programme (*Regionales Förderungsprogramm*) to industry and local government in some 10,000 localities. The Zonal Border Land Promotion Programme (*Zonengrenzlandfőrderungsprogramm*) of 1953 introduced more specific incentive measures for firms (e.g. special depreciation allowances) plus the guarantee that the border areas would receive preferential treatment in other regional-development programmes.

The second phase of German regional policy began in the late 1950s. Despite considerable population outflows from agricultural areas brought about by structural change within agriculture, full employment had by then been reached and, indeed, manufacturing industry was facing labour shortages. As a consequence, many firms were willing to decentralise from the major population centres, with the result that the main orientation of policy was on concentrating assistance on localities with economic growth potential — the so-called 'Federal Growth Centres' (*Bundesausbauorte*). These areas, the forerunners of today's Growth Points (*Schwerpunktorte*), were characterised by a large local labour market, a minimum of sanitary, social and educational infrastructure and an existing core of industry. They enjoyed rates of incentive award higher than those for the other assisted areas and, originally fifteen in number, had increased to 81 by 1968.

It was during the second phase of policy that (in line with developments elsewhere in Europe) a new kind of problem region began to emerge: areas, notably in the Ruhr, affected by structural change in the coal-mining and iron and steel industries. In order to allow the accommodation of these areas in the Federal Regional Promotion Programme, the criteria for area delineation were changed in 1963. The new indicators were gross regional product, industrial-activity rates, unemployment rates and net emigration rates, the first being given greatest weight. A further feature of the second phase was a shift in policy emphasis away from incentives and towards the promotion of infrastructure — a result of the official view that, as a consequence of the 1966-7 recession and the associated decline in firms' propensity to invest, more could be gained from infrastructure investment than from further financial aids to firms.

The third phase of policy began in the late 1960s. The key feature of this phase was — and remains — the attempt to achieve a more concerted regional-policy effort by a greater co-ordination of the economic and regional policies pursued independently by both the Federal government and each of the *Länder*. Three factors made greater harmonisation essential: the areas assisted by the Federal government and the *Länder* often overlapped, but not in any systematic way; similarly, there was unsystematic overlap in the assistance given by both the Federal government and the *Länder*; and finally, there was an increasing awareness of the existence of unequal living conditions between different parts of the nation, a state of affairs inconsistent with the constitutional requirement that there be 'uniformity of living standards in the Federal territory'. The issue of harmonisation is so central to the operation of regional policy in the Federal Republic, and indeed to the operation of regional policy in any federally organised society, that it is worthy of more detailed examination.

The Harmonisation of Federal and Länder Regional Policy

In many ways, 1969 was the key year in the development of German regional policy, for it represented the first material step towards harmonisation of the regional policies operated by the Federal government and by the individual *Länder*. Up until 1969, the individual *Länder* had operated their own policies for those areas which they held to be problem areas, while, at the same time, the Federal government operated its policies aimed at what it considered to be problem areas. Although an attempt had been made to achieve some degree of harmonisation via IMNOS it was widely recognised that this was not adequate to ensure meaningful harmonisation. The shortcomings of such harmonisation as had been achieved prior to 1969 are well illustrated by the position in respect of promoted areas. By the late 1960s there were three types of promoted areas: areas in receipt of Federal aids, areas in receipt of *Länder* aids and areas in receipt of both. Since, as we have seen, very few attempts had been made to co-ordinate Federal and *Länder* aids, this gave rise to a situation conducive to competitive outbidding between areas. Moreover, because there were no agreed priority areas (i.e. agreed by both the Federal authorities and the *Länder*), there was no certainty of regional promotion in any nationally meaningful sense. In a society where equality was, in the latter half of the 1960s, as important as growth, and in a society which was increasingly experiencing severe structural change (particularly in the energy industries and in the iron and steel industry), it was recognised that greater co-ordination of Federal and *Länder* policies was necessary. Federal expenditure on regional policy had, anyway, reached such proportions that the *Länder* were feeling that their powers were being usurped, while the Federal government felt frustrated by *Länder* policies which, even if they were not in outright contradiction to

Federal policy, often appeared not to be in the national interest.

The outcome of these various developments was an Act in 1969 concerned with the Programme for the Improvement of Regional Economic Structures (*Gesetz über die Gemeinschaftsaufgabe 'Verbesserung der regionalen Wirtschaftsstruktur'*). This provided the institutional basis for a more harmonised regional policy in the Federal Republic and constitutes the origins of current policy. The importance of this law and the problems encountered in winning its passage through Parliament were considerable since, inevitably, some surrender of power was required by all the parties involved. Indeed, before the Act could be passed, a change of constitution was required to allow a joint Federal/*Länder* initiative in what had previously been a policy area constitutionally reserved for the *Länder*.

The 1969 Act provided for the establishment of a planning committee (*Planungsauschuss*) of Federal and *Länder* representatives. The principal issues with which the committee had to deal, other than finance, long-term planning and the setting of objectives, are two-fold: first, the delineation of the areas to be assisted; and second, the harmonisation of Federal and *Länder* incentives. We deal with each of these in turn.

The 1969 Act did not specifically delineate the areas which would qualify for assistance, other than to designate the Zonal Border Area. It simply provided that assistance could be offered in two kinds of area: areas with a level of economic activity 'substantially below' the average (or where it was expected to fall below the average); and areas suffering or liable to suffer major adverse structural changes arising from strong dependence on dominant but declining industries. Not surprisingly, the actual delineation of specific areas proved a difficult and delicate task and it was not until 1974 that a list of areas was agreed.[2] The task was a difficult one because of the technical and methodological problems of delineating meaningful areas, and it was a delicate one because of the political problems of designating mutually acceptable areas.

Because the Germans have probably devoted more time and effort than anyone else to the development of methodologies for designating assisted areas, we have added an appendix to this chapter in which we briefly describe the delineation methodology. Briefly, the method consisted of identifying actual labour-market areas and then ranking these according to three weighted criteria: a measure of employment-opportunity shortage; income per head; and a measure of infrastructure provision. The areas which were finally designated, after lengthy political discussion, were termed the GA Areas (*Gemeinschaftsauf-gabengebiete*). These areas, which are shown in Figure 5.1, presently cover some 60 per cent of the surface area of the country and hold some 36 per cent of the population.[3] Superimposed on them are Tourist Promotion Areas (*Fremdenverkehrsgebiete*), the Zonal Border Area and a system of Growth Points (*Schwerpunktorte*, SPOs). As we shall see, the regional incentives on offer in Germany (and the GA programme as a whole) discriminate in favour of the Zonal Border Area. They also discriminate in favour of the Growth Points. There are some 331 of these in the GA Areas and they, too, are shown in Figure 5.1.

The second major task facing the planning committee after the passage of the 1969 Act was the working out of a harmonised system of Federal and *Länder* incentives. As part of this system, an investment grant (half-financed by the Federal authorities and half-financed by the *Länder* in the GA Areas) was introduced, and so-called 'maximum preferential rates' were set. These maximum preferential rates represent the maximum value (in grant-equivalent terms) of all public aids (i.e. all Federal aids and all *Länder* aids) which may be paid to firms in the GA Areas. The system of maximum preferential rates is a complicated one, not least because the maximum rates are not uniform, either within the GA Areas as a whole or between project types. There is discrimination between the Zonal Border Area, the Growth Points (and even further discrimination by type of Growth Point) and the remaining GA Areas. Similarly, there is discrimination between setting-up projects, extension projects, rationalisation and re-organisation projects. In brief, what one has is a matrix of maximum preferential rates. We shall return to the matrix when we discuss the investment grant since it is for this incentive that the matrix is of greatest importance.

It should be stressed that the maximum-preferential-rates system represents a policy of 'minimum harmonisation'. In other words, the *Länder* retain considerable freedom of decision-making as long as they keep within the maximum preferential rate set for a particular locality. On the other hand, that freedom is not entirely unconstrained. In order to ensure meaningful harmonisation it was essential to go further and to try and establish common conditions of award for the main incentives on offer, such that projects would face similar conditions of eligibility no matter in which part of the GA Areas they located. These conditions of award are described in detail later.

The areas designated, the maximum preferential rates and the conditions of eligibility for award are not immutable. Each year the

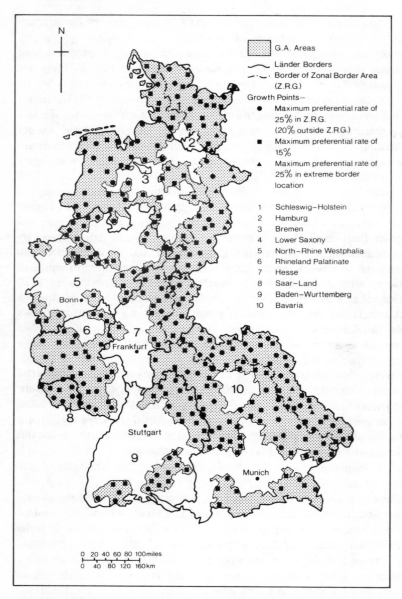

Figure 5.1: Designated Areas in Germany (GA Areas)

planning committee issues an annual Framework Plan (*Rahmenplan*). In this plan, the opportunity is taken to make changes in areas or maximum preferential rates or conditions of award in an attempt to ensure continuing and improved harmonisation of the regional incentives on offer.

We have now set the scene for the following two sections of this chapter, where we describe, at some length, the main regional incentives currently available in Germany. Before doing that, however, we should mention, albeit very briefly, other non-incentive aspects of contemporary German regional policy. In practice, the main non-incentive component of policy involves infrastructure investment. It is not possible here even to begin to give an overview of infrastructure policy in the Federal Republic, since this is a highly complex policy issue involving expenditures and programmes operated independently by the Federal authorities, by the *Länder* authorities and by local authorities − in addition to joint expenditures and programmes. Suffice it to say that, at the Federal level alone, infrastructure spending encompasses a very wide range of policies, including transport policy (motorways and other major highways), urban-renewal policy, agricultural policy and vocational-training policy − many of which are biased in favour of the problem regions. Moreover, it should be noted that the GA programme itself is not limited to incentive assistance but also covers joint Federal/*Länder* infrastructure policy, the major kinds of infrastructure which qualify being the preparation of industrial sites; the improvement of communications networks; the production and supply of energy and water; and infrastructure to promote tourism.

Apart from infrastructure policy, none of the other regional policies commonly found in Europe exist in Germany. There is, for example, no disincentive policy along the lines of the French *agrément* or the British Industrial Development Certificate. Such a policy has so far not seemed essential in Germany, primarily because the existence of a relatively large number of major urban centres, widely distributed over the national territory, has meant that spatial concentration of population and economic activity has been less of a problem than in most other countries. A second type of policy which is operated in some countries (and, above all, in Italy) requires state-owned industry to make its location decisions according to regional-development priorities. Such a policy has little application in Germany for the simple reason that there is very little state-owned industry. We might also add that Germany does not have a marked policy of encouraging the dispersal of government offices from central locations, not least because the scope of this (given the Federal system) is very limited.

The Current Incentive Package

There are four major regional incentives currently on offer in the Federal Republic of Germany:

(1)   the *investment allowance*, which is the cornerstone of the German regional-incentive system, is a fairly automatic project-related capital grant on a fixed 10 per cent of eligible investment in the Zonal Border Area and 8.75 per cent of eligible investment elsewhere in the GA Areas;[4]

(2)   the *investment grant* is a discretionary project-related capital grant with rates of up to 25 per cent of eligible investment, depending on a matrix of location and project-type criteria;

(3)   the *ERP regional soft loan*, which is project-related and largely automatic, can only be awarded to small or medium-sized firms for projects that are not eligible for the investment allowance or investment grant (so-called 'non-primary-effect' projects);

(4)   the *special depreciation allowance*, which is available only in the Zonal Border Area, is an item-related concession involving a high initial depreciation allowance of up to 50 per cent of eligible costs for plant and machinery and up to 40 per cent for buildings.

In addition, there are a number of more minor incentives on offer, including labour-removal assistance, concessions on the purchase of land and preferential public-supply contracts. Further, there is a freight-transport subsidy (the only one of its type in the European Community countries) paid to establishments located in the Zonal Border Area. None of these minor incentives is, however, of any real importance — and certainly not in terms of expenditure. For this reason, we concentrate in the remainder of this chapter on the major regional aids — the investment allowance, the investment grant, the ERP regional soft loan and the special depreciation allowance.

Within the German system, the investment allowance (administered by the Federal authorities) is the basic incentive. Over the period 1972-7 almost 22,600 investment allowances were approved to the value of DM 3,800 million in respect of eligible investment of almost DM 52,600 million. In comparison, the investment grant (administered by the individual *Länder* within the constraints of the Framework Plan) is much more rarely awarded (6,376 cases have been approved between 1972 and 1977 to the value of less than DM 1,500 million and with associated investment of DM 23,800 million) and, indeed, is best viewed as a form of 'topping up' of the investment allowance in 'deserving' cases. While the investment allowance and the investment grant are aimed at the manufacturing sector and similar 'regionally exporting' activities (i.e. activities with a so-called 'primary effect') the ERP regional soft loan is available only to local industries (i.e. industries which have no primary effect). Between 1972 and 1977 over 23,000 such loans were approved, to the value of just under DM 1,800 million, in respect of eligible investment of almost DM 7,300 million. Comparable figures for the special depreciation allowance, which, it will be recalled, is restricted to the Zonal Border Area, are difficult to find — partly because of its fiscal nature and partly because it is item-related. It is, however, estimated that over 64,000 awards were made over the period 1972-7 to the value of some DM 2,700 million in terms of postponed tax.

Having indicated the relative importance of the main regional incentives in the Federal Republic, we turn in the next section to consider each in detail, concentrating in particular on eligibility conditions and award levels.

The Main Incentives

The Investment Allowance

The investment allowance (*Investitionszulage*) was introduced in 1969. As noted above, it is the major component of the German regional-incentive system — the base on top of which investment grants may be awarded. The central position of the investment allowance is well illustrated by the fact that few who get an investment grant do not get an investment allowance, while only 21 per cent (in the period 1972 to 1977) of those who got an investment allowance also got an investment grant. The legal basis of the investment allowance is the Investment Allowance Act (*Investitionszulagengesetz*) of 1969, as subsequently amended (the most recent amendment being in 1978). The investment allowance has its origins in the earlier investment premia of Section 32 of the Coal Act (*Gesetz zur Anpassung und Gesundung des deutschen Steinkohlebergbaus und der deutschen Steinkohlebergbaugebiete — Kohlegesetz*), which were paid in specified coal-mining areas in an attempt to encourage new investment. The 1969 Act not only extended the areas to include non-coal-mining areas in economic distress, but also made further important changes. The investment premium had been awarded as a direct income-tax or corporation-tax reduction, with the result that it had been paid only to applicants who made profits. In that many new projects did not make profits in the first few years this was a major drawback of the scheme. The investment allowance avoids this problem, since it is payable to all who are *liable* to income or corporation tax, with no requirement that such taxes actually be paid. Initially, the areas in which the investment allowance was payable were specifically designated 'Investment Allowance Areas'. Over time, these have been aligned with the GA Areas.

In many ways the investment allowance is a delightfully straightforward incentive. In spite of its name, it is in fact a non-discretionary project-related investment *grant* of a *fixed* 10 per cent of eligible investment in the Zonal Border Area and 8.75 per cent elsewhere in the GA Areas. In terms of administration it is much more of a Federal instrument than is the investment grant. Applications are made at the *Länder* level and are passed on to the Federal authority (principally the Federal Ministry of Economics) for final decision. The award decision takes between one and a half and four months, but projects can start before the submission of an application, and an application can be submitted even after the completion of the project. If the decision of the Ministry of Economics is positive, the subsequent administration is largely the responsibility of the local tax boards, which make the final award — checking, amongst other things, the eligibility of submitted terms of expenditure.

Eligibility Conditions. The investment allowance is by and large restricted to setting-up and extension projects (these accounting for 22 per cent and 68 per cent, respectively, of the total number of awards made between 1972 and 1977) though basic rationalisation and re-organisation projects are eligible in the Zonal Border Area. But not all setting-up projects qualify. Only those locating in Growth Points within the GA Areas are eligible. Extension projects, too, must be located in Growth Points unless the expanding firm established itself in the GA Areas before 1972 (when the Growth Points were first designated).

Turning to activity eligibility, the basic requirements which an applicant firm must fulfil are very broad (being liable for income or corporation tax and operating business premises for profits, plus an almost inoperable rule that the firm must not be too profitable — the 'prosperity clause') but, in addition, there are a number of more stringent conditions attached to the project to be assisted, and encompassed by the term 'especially worthwhile promoting economically' (*volkswirtschaftlich besonders förderungswürdig*). Within this term, the most important condition is that the project must have a 'primary effect'. This condition has its intellectual origins in export-base theory and means, in practice, that the project must belong to an industry where 50 per cent or more of the goods or services produced are of a type which is normally distributed outside the region of production. A list of eligible industries and services has been drawn up with this criterion in mind, but applicants have the right to claim eligibility if they belong to an activity not on the list, as long as they can prove that they can fulfil the condition. In general, however, eligibility is limited to mining, manufacturing, mail-order firms, import/export trades, head offices of banks, credit and insurance groups, producers of computer soft-ware or data-processing equipment and publishing businesses. Excluded (beyond agriculture, forestry and the free professions) are retailing, wholesale businesses, handicraft and local trades and services, as well as most of the construction industry.

The primary-effect condition is without doubt the most important of the investment-allowance eligibility conditions. There is, however, a second significant condition (applicable to extension projects), and this is that the project must increase the original labour force by at least 15 per cent or 50 jobs. There are no quantified job targets for setting-up projects or for rationalisation and re-organisation projects. In addition to these two conditions, there are a number of other project-related conditions which are vague and/or of little importance. These include a maximum-cost-per-job condition (i.e. total investment costs per job) of DM 3.6 million (which would eliminate only the most capital-intensive chemical plants and power stations) and a condition that the project must not exacerbate structure concentration in an area.

The investment allowance cannot be cumulated with other public aids beyond the maximum preferential rate set for the particular area/project/industry (except with the express permission of the GA planning committee). In theory, the maximum-preferential-rate calculation takes account of a great variety of awards (Federal, *Länder*, European Community) irrespective of whether they be grants, allowances, loans, subsidised interest or any other financial advantage. In practice, the main incentive taken into account when assessing whether or not an investment allowance will take the project over the maximum preferential rate is the investment grant; as we shall see, other incentives are either *de jure* excluded or — and this is particularly true of *Länder* aids — are excluded in practice. In fact, it is misleading to imagine that the investment allowance would be cut back if the total award exceeded the maximum preferential rate for an area. Rather, as we have said, the investment allowance is the basic award on top of which the investment grant is paid. It would, therefore, be the investment grant that was adjusted if there was a danger of exceeding the maximum preferential rate.

Award Levels. The nominal value of the investment allowance is, as we have seen, 10 per cent of eligible investment in the Zonal Border Area and 8.75 per cent elsewhere in the GA Areas, but what of its effective value (i.e. its value after taking into account incentive tax treatment, payment delays and eligible items and forms of expenditure)? The nominal value of award is unaffected by tax treatment since the investment allowance is one of the few capital grants in the European Community countries which is tax-free. The other factors do, however, cut back on the nominal value.

Beginning with eligible forms of expenditure, a key requirement of the investment allowance is that the assets on which it is paid must be entered on the asset side of the firm's balance sheet. This means that assets purchased under phased-payment agreements are eligible but that assets bought under hire-purchase or leasing arrangements are not — except where the hire-purchase or leasing arrangement allows the asset to be carried in the balance sheet of the lessee, a rare occurrence. A second factor reducing the effective value of the investment allowance is the list of conditions which determines eligible items of expenditure. In order to be eligible, items must be new, fixed assets, must have a life of more than one year and must be worth more than a set minimum value (in practice DM 800). Excluded items cover, therefore, land; second-hand items (including previously occupied buildings); intangibles like goodwill or patents; and working capital. The third factor influencing the effective value of the investment allowance is that the incentive suffers from considerable delays in payment. Applications for payment can only be made within three months of the end of the calendar year in which the financial year of the firm undertaking the expenditure ended. It takes about half a year to verify claims and one month to pay the money. This means that the average period between the purchase of an asset and receipt of the investment allowance in respect of that asset is of the order of 12 to 15 months. These delays considerably reduce the effective value of the investment allowance. They certainly compare unfavourably with delays under the investment-grant schemes, where payment is normally made about one month after purchase has been made and a claim submitted. It is to the investment grant that we now turn.

The Investment Grant

The investment grant (*Investitionszuschuss*) was introduced in 1969 and represents a major arm of German regional-incentive policy. Although, in terms of sums awarded, the investment grant is the 'poor cousin' of the investment allowance, both the monies which have been expended and the investment associated with assisted projects are, as we have seen, not insubstantial.

Unlike the investment allowance, the investment grant is administered almost wholly by the *Länder* (although the scheme is half-financed by the Federal authorities and half by the *Länder*). It is the *Länder* which, within the regulations of the Framework Plan of the GA programme, decide on the eligibility of applicants and on rates of award, as well as on eligible items of expenditure. The Federal level is not involved in any of these decisions, unless there is a wish to exceed the Framework Plan guidelines, in which case the *Länder* have to secure the permission of the GA planning committee. On average (although there is wide variation) the award decision takes some ten months – a long time for a capital-grant scheme, certainly in comparison to other capital grants in the European Community.

Eligibility Conditions. Investment grants are payable on any project type (setting-up, extension, rationalisation, or re-organisation) located in the GA Areas. Between 1972 and 1975, 65 per cent of assisted projects were extensions, 24 per cent were setting-up projects and the remaining 11 per cent were rationalisations and re-organisations. Projects must fulfil a number of conditions in order to be eligible for an award. Many of these conditions are identical to those already discussed in the context of the investment allowance. First, the project must be from a listed primary-effect industry or, failing that, must be able to demonstrate a primary effect. The industries which are eligible for the investment grant are therefore essentially the same as those which are eligible for the investment allowance – even though the lists of eligible industries for the two incentives are drawn up on a different basis.[5] Thus, the main eligible industries for the investment grant are manufacturing, tourism and specified service-sector activities. Ineligible are the primary sector, construction, public utilities and most of the service sector. Second, extension projects must fulfil specified minimum job-creation targets of at least 15 per cent of the original labour force or 50 jobs. Third, total project-investment costs per job must not exceed DM 3.6 million. All three of these conditions are found, too, within the investment-allowance scheme. Some investment-allowance conditions, however, are not required of applicants for the investment grant (for example, there are no monostructure conditions, nor does the prosperity clause apply — although such conditions can be imposed if the *Länder* so wish), while other conditions are unique to the investment grant. For example, the grant can only be paid on up to DM 250 million of investment costs (in practice, rarely a hurdle for most projects); the project cannot start before application (but it can start before the final award decision); and the project must be in a sufficiently advanced stage of operation that it can be started soon after the award decision has been made.

Award Levels. A point about the investment grant which cannot be overstressed is that it is highly discriminatory in terms of rates of award. In the Framework Plan a matrix of rates is specified above which the investment grant, in combination with other public aids including the investment allowance, cannot go. This matrix (of maximum preferential rates) discriminates both by project type and by area. There are, for example, higher rates for setting-up and extension projects than for rationalisation and re-organisation projects; for locations within the Zonal Border Area than for those elsewhere; and for Growth Points than for non-Growth Points (and indeed for certain types of Growth Point than for other Growth Points). This complex project-type/location matrix is made even more complicated by the fact that higher rates can be awarded when certain additional conditions are met (e.g. when a project has a 'very strong structural effect'). The complete maximum-preferential-rate matrix is shown in Table 5.1.

The main points to arise from Table 5.1 are the following. Within the Zonal Border Area, the maximum 25 per cent award is normally available only to setting-up and extension projects, and then only when located in 'superior' Growth Points or Growth Points in extreme border locations. Setting-up and extension projects located in 'normal' Growth Points face a 15 per cent maximum. Outside the Growth Points, setting-up projects are generally ineligible for assistance, while extensions normally qualify (for a maximum 15 per cent award) only where the expanding establishment located prior to 1 January 1972 (when Growth Points were first designated). In comparison, setting-up and extension projects located outside the Zonal Border Area (but still within the GA Areas) are eligible for a maximum award of 20 per cent in superior Growth Point locations and 15 per cent in normal Growth Points. Outside the Growth Points only extensions are eligible for the maximum award of 10 per cent (15 per cent if the project has a significant structural impact) and then only where the expanding

Table 5.1: Maximum Preferential Rates by Locality and Project Type*

	Setting-up	Extension	Re-organisation or basic rationalisation
		Within Zonal Border Area	
Within the Growth Points:			
'Superior' Growth Points	25	25	10
Growth Points in extreme border locations	25	25 ⎫	(15)c (25)a ⎫
Normal Growth Points	15 (25)a	15 ⎭ (25)a	(15)c (25)a ⎭
Outside the Growth Points:			
Taking-over/setting-up of premises			
after 31 December 1974	15b,c (25)a	15b,c (25)a	10b (15)c (25)a
between 1 January 1972 and 31 December 1974	–	15d,c (25)a	10d (15)c (25)a
before 1 January 1972	–	15 (25)a	10 (15)c (25)a
		Outside Zonal Border Area	
Within the Growth Points:			
'Superior' Growth Points	20	20 ⎫	10
Normal Growth Points	15	15 ⎭	(15)c
Outside the Growth Points:			
Taking-over/setting-up of premises			
after 31 December 1974	10b (15)c	10b	10b (15)c
between 1 January 1972 and 31 December 1974	–	10d	10d (15)c
before 1 January 1972	-	10	10 (15)c

Note:

a In exceptional cases if adjacent to the border.

b If mainly female-employing or if bound to the locality by raw material supply or if difficult to relocate on environmental grounds.

c If project helps to diversify significantly the industrial structure of the area.

d If the establishment was set up or taken over when the location was a Growth Point.

* The information in this table refers to the situation in 1976. In the sixth Framework Plan (1977-80) the conditions for projects located outside Growth Points were changed slightly. Where the establishment was set up or taken over after 31 December 1976 then such projects are eligible only if b or c hold.

establishment located prior to 1 January 1972. For their part, re-organisation and basic rationalisation projects are eligible for a maximum award of 10 per cent throughout the GA Areas, rising to 15 per cent if the project has a significant structural effect.

On the basis of the maximum-preferential-rate matrix illustrated in Table 5.1, it is obvious that the investment-grant scheme is highly discriminatory. But it is also highly discretionary. The conditions of eligibility and range of maximum preferential rates set out above are guidelines only. Within these guidelines the individual *Länder* enjoy considerable freedom (and indeed there is even provision for *Länder* to go beyond the formal guidelines with the consent of the GA planning committee). It is the *Länder* which decide upon the eligibility of projects and of investment costs. And, even more important, it is the *Länder* which decide whether or not to assist a project (even if formally eligible) and what level of award to offer.

But this power of discretion is not only available to the *Länder*; it is actively exercised by them. Although there is no comprehensive information on turndown, the evidence which is available suggests that turndown is not uncommon since, between 1972 and 1977, only 21 per cent of projects awarded an investment allowance also received an investment grant. Sometimes turndown is because of a failure to meet the primary-effect conditions and sometimes it is a result of the fact that the project started before an application for aid was made; but most often it is probably simply because the *Länder* did not feel that an investment grant was justified. Further evidence that the *Länder* utilise the discretionary power available to them comes from the fact that actual awards made are normally substantially below the possible maxima. Over the period 1972-5 the average setting-up/extension award where the investment grant alone was awarded was 6.5 per cent of eligible investment; for re-organisation/rationalisation projects in Growth Points it was 8.5 per cent. For projects which also received an investment allowance, the average investment-grant award was 6.8 per cent and 2.9 per cent, respectively.

Actual awards, then, tend to fall well below the nominal maximum values. There are, in addition, a number of other features of the investment-grant scheme which similarly reduce the effective value of awards to well below their possible maxima. First, the investment grant, unlike the investment allowance, is subject to income/corporation tax as well as to the local tax on business earnings (*Gewerbeertragssteuer*). In practice, firms have a choice in the accounting treatment of the grant: it can either be entered into corporate accounts as income or it may be used to reduce fiscal-depreciation charges (i.e. the assets on which the grant is paid may be depreciated on the basis of their purchase price less the grant received). Either way, the grant is taxed. The tax rate, including the local tax, normally lies between 40 and 50 per cent. Second, like the investment allowance, assets purchased under hire-purchase or leasing arrangements are not generally eligible for an investment grant unless the hire-purchase or leasing scheme allows the assets to be carried in the firm's balance sheet. Only rarely is this possible. The third feature of the investment-grant scheme which can affect the effective value of an award concerns eligible items of expenditure. Although the Framework Plan does not explicitly exclude any particular item, in practice the items deemed to be eligible are generally those which are eligible for the investment allowance — although the *Länder* do have the right to vary the generosity of treatment of eligible items according to the desirability of each individual project. In so far as the *Länder* use the investment-allowance list of eligible items of expenditure, the permitted items are new fixed assets with a life of at least one year and a value of more than DM 800. On the same basis, the excluded items are land, second-hand items (including previously occupied buildings), intangible assets such as goodwill and patents, and working capital.

Tax treatment, eligible forms of expenditure and eligible items of expenditure are the main factors reducing the effective value of the investment grant. In contrast to the investment allowance, the value of the grant is not further reduced by the timing and phasing of award payments. This is because the investment grant is paid in instalments, on the basis of receipted bills which can be submitted by the applicant at any time. The processing delay between the submission of such bills and the disbursement of the corresponding part of an award is insignificant. There is, in addition, the possibility of receiving an advance grant payment, i.e. in advance of actual payments by an applicant to the supplier of an asset.

ERP Regional Soft Loans

The European Recovery Programme (ERP), which was financed by the United States of America, was introduced in 1947 with the general aim of aiding the economic recovery of Germany after the Second World War. The ERP fund was used largely to enable the German economy to import capital and other goods. The fund, which was in dollars, enabled exporters to Germany to be paid in dollars while the German importer paid marks into a special account opened for this purpose by the German government. In 1953 the ERP as originally conceived was terminated and the funds in the special account were used to set up a new programme (though still called ERP) involving a wide range of long-term measures aimed at the 'promotion of the German economy'.

A number of different programmes are currently financed, through soft loans, out of the ERP fund. The most important concern aid for underdeveloped countries, export financing and the economic development of Berlin, as well as schemes of assistance for small and medium-sized firms. The section of the fund relating to small and medium-sized firms (which accounted for some 19 per cent of the total ERP budget of more than DM 2,500 million in 1975) includes a number of specific schemes of assistance. The most important of these (making up nearly 50 per cent of the total loans under the programme for small and medium-sized firms) is the regional programme. It is the soft loans paid under this programme (*ERP Regionaldarlehen*) which are described here. As already noted, over 23,000 loans to the total value of DM 1,793 million were awarded under this scheme between 1972 and 1977.

Although the ERP fund is generally administered by the Ministry of Economics in Bonn, the administration of wards under the regional programme is the responsibility of a public-sector credit institution, the *Kreditanstalt für Wiederaufbau* (KW) in Frankfurt. The Ministry of Economics is involved in the administration of awards only in very special cases and only then on the request of the KW. Applications for a soft loan are not made direct to the KW, but through the applicant's bank, which acts as a guarantor of the ERP loan to the KW, requiring for this purpose mortgage guarantees from the applicant. The bank's main task is to examine the viability of the project and of the applicant firm; it acts as a filter between the applicant and the KW, eliminating ineligible applications. After the initial application has been processed by the bank, it is sent to the KW for further checks, in particular with regard to conditions of eligibility and permitted items of expenditure.

Eligibility Conditions. ERP regional soft loans are payable only on projects located in the GA Areas. All project types (setting-up, extension, rationalisation and re-organisation) are eligible, although the majority of awards tend to be for extension and rationalisation projects. In 1975, extension projects accounted for some 37 per cent of awards made and rationalisation projects for a further 36 per cent. Regarding activity eligibility, the ERP scheme is not available to agriculture, forestry, fishing and the free professions, and there is a long list of conditions which reduces eligibility still further. First, the applicant must be a small or medium-sized firm. Although there is no specific definition of what constitutes 'a small or medium-sized firm', only rarely would an ERP soft loan be awarded to a firm employing more than 500 employees or having a turnover of more than DM 25 million. In fact, the great majority of awards go to firms of a much smaller size than this. More than 90 per cent of ERP regional soft loans are awarded to firms with less than 50 employees and a turnover of less than DM 5 million. Second, extension projects (but not other project types) must increase the original labour force by at least 20 per cent. Third, firms where more than 50 per cent of the capital is owned by a holding company or by some other firm (25 per cent where the capital is owned by a bank) are not eligible. Fourth, the project must not have started before application for a loan although it may be started before a decision on the application is reached. Fifth, the applicant must be able to demonstrate that he is in need of a soft loan and must be able to provide guarantees (*dingliche Sicherheiten*) from a bank or from the *Länder*. Sixth, but a condition little used in practice, the project must be 'worthwhile promoting economically'. Finally, the most important condition — quite the reverse of that applying in investment-grant and investment-allowance schemes — is that the project must *not* have a 'primary effect', i.e. the project must not normally export more than 50 per cent of its output outside the region. This is, without doubt, the main condition of award. Together with the size condition, it means that soft loans are only rarely paid to manufacturing industry. The great majority of loans go to local/regional craft and service activities. In 1975, the retail and wholesale sector accounted for 38 per cent of the loans awarded, craft industries for a further 27 per cent and catering for 11 per cent.

Award Levels. Apart from the eligibility conditions noted above, the ERP regional-soft-loan scheme is fairly straightforward and non-discretionary. There is, moreover, no explicit project-type or activity discrimination in terms of the softness of the loan. Since September 1977 the interest rate on the loan has been a fixed 5.5 per cent (4.5 per cent in the Zonal Border Area). Repayment is six-monthly on a straight-line basis. Principal-repayment holidays are granted virtually automatically — one year for loans of up to six years' duration and between 18 months and two years for loans above this. Most loans run for between ten and fifteen years; their actual duration is linked to the life of the assets being financed by the loan.

The maximum amount which can be loaned under the scheme is DM 200,000 and loans may cover up to two-thirds of eligible investment. In practice, only small projects involving eligible costs of DM 75,000 or less get the maximum. For projects with qualifying expenditure of DM 75,000 to DM 150,000 the loan coverage steadily declines from two-thirds to one-third. When even larger amounts of qualifying expenditure are involved, the coverage of the loan remains at one-third. But, and this is important, whenever the ERP loan covers less than two-thirds of qualifying expenditure the difference is met by additional loans under a special programme also administered by the KW. Indeed, this special programme is specifically intended to top up ERP loans; it has similar conditions of award to the ERP loan conditions, except that the rate of interest is approximately one percentage point higher. However, since the loans paid out under this special programme are available throughout Germany, they are not a regional aid and are not considered further.

Moving now from the nominal value of an ERP regional soft loan to its effective value, it should immediately be noted that, since the loans are drawn down as expenditure is incurred, their value is not affected by the timing and phasing of payment. There are, however, other features of the ERP scheme which do reduce the effective value of any award made. First, in order to be eligible an asset must have a life of five years or more (as against one year in the case of both the investment grant and the investment allowance). Second, working capital is not eligible nor, generally speaking, are vehicles and small-value items of less than DM 800. On the other hand, land is eligible and so, too, is second-hand equipment. Third, assets financed by leasing and hire purchase are not eligible. Fourth, the concessionary element of the loan is taxed, since interest payments on loans are tax-deductible. For the firm, therefore, the post-tax value on the concession is not simply the nominal interest-rate difference between an ERP regional soft loan and an alternative source of finance but, rather, the *taxed* nominal value of this difference. Finally, the effective value of an ERP regional soft loan is further reduced by the fact, noted above, that the ERP scheme is only slightly more generous than the scheme operated by the KW for small and medium-sized firms located anywhere in Germany.

The Special Depreciation Allowance

The special depreciation allowance (*Sonderabschreibungen*) is provided for in the Zonal Border Promotion Act (*Zonenrandförderungsgesetz*) of August 1971. It is a relatively straightforward incentive payable only on investment located in the Zonal Border Area. It takes the form of an initial-depreciation allowance (on top of normal depreciation) of up to 50 per cent for movable fixed assets and up to 40 per cent for buildings. The assisted assets must be depreciated on a straight-line and not a reducing-balance basis. The allowances can be used in the year of acquisition or at any time during the succeeding four years. The firm itself decides, in a technical and quantitative sense, how and when they are used.

Application for a special depreciation allowance (SDA) is made in writing (although there is no standard form of application) to the applicant's local tax board, and the decision whether or not to make the award is normally made by the local tax board within a period of between two and four weeks. In the case of allowances involving DM 2 million or more in one year or DM 6 million or more over a period of three years or longer, applications are passed on by the local tax board to the Minister of Finance of the *Land* in question, who makes a recommendation on the application and passes on both application and recommendation to the Federal Ministry of Finance for a final decision. In only a very small number of cases, however, is the decision not taken by the local tax board — only 216 cases between 1972 and 1975 out of a total of more than 39,000. Applications can be made after the investment on which assistance being sought has started, as long as the tax board's final assessment for the tax year in which the assets were acquired has not yet been sent to the applicant. In practice, tax assessments are normally sent out with a delay of roughly one and a half years. However, there is an advance-payment system of tax. Advance payments are calculated on the profits of recent years as well as on likely future profits and losses. When an SDA is awarded, the recipient may apply for a reduction in his advance tax payments on the basis of the award. In this way, the award can be of almost immediate benefit.

One further feature of the SDA scheme which increases its value to recipients is that firms may apply for permission to set up a tax-free reserve to cover anticipated investment. These reserves (*Steuerfreie Rücklagen*) can be awarded on conditions similar to those applying to the SDAs prior to the year of acquisition of the assets and irrespective of whether or not advance payment on those assets has been made. Between 1972 and 1977 some 64,000 SDAs, having a total value of nearly DM 2,700 million, were used; of this total value, just over two-thirds were for investment in plant and machinery and the remainder for investment in buildings and associated works. In the same period, the total value of tax-free reserves created (involving some 632 cases) was approximately DM 145 million.

Eligibility Conditions. In many ways, the SDAs are less restrictive than either the investment allowance or the investment grant. This is the position, for example, in respect of industrial coverage. A wide range of activities are eligible for the SDAs — much wider than for either the investment allowance or the investment grant. Within the Zonal Border Area virtually any firm which is liable for income or company tax and which operates for profit is eligible to apply, although, in practice, certain technical conditions (in particular, accounting requirements) tend to eliminate much of agriculture and forestry as well as the free professions.

There are, moreover, far fewer conditions of award than for the investment allowance or the investment grant, perhaps primarily because the scheme is item-related and not project-related. In fact, the main conditions which attach to an SDA concern the matter in which it is used by the firm. These conditions involve, in particular, a 'loss clause' whereby an SDA may not be used if it would either cause a loss or increase an existing loss. On the other hand, this clause is applied on a firm basis and not on an establishment basis, with the result that the losses of the factory or outlet where the investment was made can often be offset by profits from other establishments of the same firm — even if these are located outside the Zonal Border Area. Moreover, the importance of the loss clause is further diminished by the fact that allowances can be used at any time over a five-year period following the date of acquisition of the asset. Thus, even firms which incur losses in the short term will have some significant scope for being able to use the SDA — even though its value is obviously reduced the later it is taken.

Award Levels. As already noted, the SDA is in addition to normal (straight-line) depreciation and takes the form of an initial allowance of up to 50 per cent for movable fixed assets and up to 40 per cent for buildings. Although the 'up to' clauses give scope both for discrimination and discretion, in practice the vast majority of applicants get the maximum award.

In terms of eligible items of expenditure, the SDA scheme is similar to the investment grant and investment allowance. Special depreciation allowances are payable on purchased or self-produced new fixed assets (excluding second-hand equipment) with a life of more than one year and located anywhere in the Zonal Border Area. The excluded items, therefore, are land, patents, goodwill, bonds, stocks and other working capital, as well as assets having a life of less than one year or a value below DM 800. With respect to eligible forms of expenditure, the SDA scheme also resembles the investment-allowance and investment-grant schemes in that assets acquired under leasing and hire-purchase arrangements are not eligible for an award (except in the relatively rare event that such arrangements permit the assets to be carried in the balance sheet of the firm).

One final point should be made about the SDA, and this concerns its cumulability with other incentives. Although the SDA is not included in the calculation of maximum preferential rates, it does have an impact on the value of other incentives, and in particular the invest-ment grant. When an SDA is awarded in conjunction with an investment grant, the effective value of the investment grant is reduced since tax payments on the building and plant elements of the grant are brought into income, and hence taxable profits, more quickly under the SDA regime.

Comparative Conclusions

The key aspect of German regional policy, and a point which distin-guishes it from policy in all other European Community countries, is that it operates in the context of a federal system. It is this, for example, that has led to the considerable technical input into the development of area-designation methodologies (the German system must surely be among the most sophisticated in Europe), and which has meant that, at the end of the day, broad political factors (i.e. the reconciliation of different *Länder* interests) have nevertheless played an important area-designation role. It is this which has been at least one of the causes of the emphasis on infrastructure and incentive policy, and of the disinterest in and/or irrelevance of other policy instruments, especially disincentive and office-dispersal policy. And, most important, it is this which has made the co-ordination of incentive policy a necessity, and yet has produced a system whereby co-ordination has been combined with considerable flexibility. In no other European Community country is a similar emphasis placed on incentive co-ordination.

The need for co-ordination has itself had an important influence on the German incentive package. In particular, it has resulted in a concentration on the most transparent of incentives, capital grants, to the exclusion not only of tax concessions and labour subsidies, but also of soft loans[6] – at least as far as regionally exporting projects are concerned. Prior to the 'Joint Task' approach in 1969 soft loans had always been an important part of the German regional-incentive scene, and indeed soft loans were the major incentive instrument at that time. The question may, of course, be posed that, if co-ordination is so crucial, then why is the special depreciation allowance not included within the maximum-preferential-rate limits? The simple answer is that there is in practice no need to take it into account for co-ordination purposes. Since it is available on set conditions at a fixed rate, and is restricted to the Zonal Border Area, it cannot anyway be utilised by *Länder* for competitive outbidding purposes.

But the German federal system has not only resulted in a co-ordination solution which keeps the competitive instincts of the *Länder* *vis-à-vis* mobile investment in check, it has also meant, as noted above, that the *Länder* have been given considerable operational flexibility within the co-ordination limits. Indeed the element of flexibility is such that, as we have seen, the preferential-rate maxima can even be broken on occasion, given the consent of the GA planning committee. In many ways the system represents a minimum of co-ordination consistent with the avoidance of competitive outbidding.

A clear indication of the desire to maximise *Länder* flexibility lies in the fact that the investment allowance (the fixed Federal element of the system) has a low value while the investment grant – by and large *Länder*-determined – has at least the scope to reach high levels. The combination of a fixed base plus a discretionary upper tier is not uncommon in the European Community countries. For example, the United Kingdom combination of regional-development grant and selective financial assistance and, at least for large projects, the investment premium in the Netherlands also incorporate this feature. In so doing they try to avoid either being 'too automatic' (with a consequent 'waste' of public money) or being 'too discretionary' (with the danger that they are then ignored during the investment/location decision). However, nowhere in the European Community is the base as low as that provided by the investment allowance and nowhere is the upper tier quite as discretionary as the investment grant.

As a result, the average value of the German regional-incentive package lies very much below its maximum value, particularly outside the Zonal Border Area. In effective-value terms, the German package maximum, while well below the Northern Irish, Irish and Italian maxima, is nevertheless towards the top of the range of the packages provided by the remaining Community schemes. However, the average investment grant was (in 1976) less than 9 per cent of eligible investment (compared with a possible maximum at that time[7] of 17.5 per cent when awarded with an investment allowance) and was obtained by only one-fifth of eligible cases. As a result, the 'standard' package in the Zonal Border Area (i.e. investment allowance plus special depreciation allowance) was, in 1976, worth just over half the possible maximum in effective-value terms. Only with the addition of an average investment grant was the value of the German package raised sufficiently to bring it within the middle range of effective package values found in the Community countries. Outside the Zonal Border Area, the German incentive package is of course very much less valuable, since no special depreciation allowance is available. Awarded on its own, the investment allowance is worth very much less than other capital grants in the Community and, even with the addition of an average investment grant, the German package outside the Zonal Border Area remains low by European Community standards in effective-value terms.

Turning to the individual elements of the package, the investment allowance, as already noted, represents the base. As we have seen, however, it is a low base and indeed, as just noted, is the least valuable grant in the European Community in terms of both nominal and effective values. Moreover, and this is most unusual for the base element of a package, it is characterised by a very high rate of turndown — averaging well over 30 per cent between 1972 and 1975. Since the investment allowance is operated in a non-discretionary manner this can only be attributed to stringent (not to say, unclear) award conditions. They are certainly tighter and more numerous than in most comparable grant schemes. Most important, eligible projects must have a primary effect and, for extension projects, must increase the labour force by at least 15 per cent or 50 jobs. A further interesting feature of the investment allowance is that it has fiscal roots, and indeed can be taken in the form either of a grant or of a tax allowance. As a result it is not subject to taxation, one of only two capital grants in the Community countries in this position (the other is the regional-development grant in the United Kingdom). Finally, we should note the role that project type and location play in the conditions of award. In probably no other country in the European Community is so much emphasis placed on project type and location as in Germany.

But if project type and location are important within the investment-allowance scheme, they are crucial to the investment grant. As we have seen, the entire maximum-preferential-rate matrix is dependent on both type of locality (with distinctions being drawn not only between locations in and outside the Zonal Border Area but also between Growth Points and non-Growth Points and even between different types of Growth Points) and type of investment project (setting-up, extension and rationalisation or basic re-organisation). Further features of the investment grant are that it is highly conditional (many of the conditions reflecting those of the investment-allowance scheme) and, as already noted, highly discretionary. This discretion is, of course, simply a reflection of the freedom given to the *Länder* within the co-ordination system. There are, however, less flattering reflections of *Länder* flexibility. For example, the processing period required in respect of investment-grant applications is among the longest in Europe. Moreover, despite the fact that a central task of the GA planning committee is to harmonise Federal and *Länder* aids, there remain significant differences between the investment grant and the investment allowance — not only in respect of tax treatment and the timing and phasing of applications but also in terms of award conditions and eligible items of expenditure. Quite clearly there is still much which could be done at a technical level to bring about greater harmonisation.

The two remaining regional incentives in Germany are of less import-ance — the special depreciation allowance because it is available only in the Zonal Border Area, and the ERP regional soft loan because it is restricted basically to small local services. Nevertheless, both schemes do contain a number of interesting comparative features. The special depreciation allowance, for example, is far and away the most valuable regional accelerated-depreciation allowance in the European Com-munity in effective-value terms, and this primarily because it is available on both building and plant and machinery costs. It is also interesting to note that, quite unlike SDAs in other countries, the German special depreciation allowance can be used to reduce advance tax payments. For its part, the ERP regional soft loan is probably of most interest because it is limited to small 'non-primary-effect' industries, i.e. local services — making it one of the few schemes in the European Com-munity restricted to this sector. However, in contrast to those schemes in the Community countries aimed specifically at the service sector, no attempt is made to tailor the incentive to the needs of the service sector (leasing, for example, is an ineligible item of expenditure). Moreover, the regional impact of the scheme is very much reduced by the availability of similar, if somewhat less generous, soft loans on a national basis.

Throughout most of this concluding section we have emphasised the influence which the federal system has had on the German incentive package, and indeed on German regional policy in general. Since there are no other federal systems in the European Community it may be felt that the German experience is therefore of little relevance elsewhere in the Community. Such a feeling would be mistaken. The German case has important lessons, particularly in respect of co-ordination, not only for those Community countries faced by devolutionary pressures in the regional-policy sphere but also for the European Commission itself in its attempts at Community-wide co-ordination.

Appendix: The Delineation of the Assisted Areas[8]

As described in the body of the text, the co-ordination of the regional policies previously pursued independently by the Federal authorities and the individual *Länder* included the attempt systematically to define those areas which would qualify for assistance under the GA programme. It should be self-evident that mutually agreed affiliation of assisted areas is of crucial importance for any meaningful attempt to co-ordinate regional policies pursued by different levels of government within a single nation. Setting this aspect to one side, however, the manner in which Germany sought to create its assisted areas is of particular interest both at a technical level and because of the serious political difficulties which had to be overcome. The purpose of describing these difficulties is to emphasise that the criteria ultimately employed in the designation procedure reflect the necessity of securing the agreement both of the Federal authorities and of the individual *Länder* to the final definition of the assisted areas. As we shall see, in many instances it proved necessary to redefine criteria during the course of delineation in order to accommodate particular regional interests.

The basic objective of the delineation exercise was to operationalise the criteria contained in the 1969 Act which introduced joint regional policy by the Federal and *Länder* governments. This law had simply provided that the areas in which assistance would be made available would be areas with economic activity which had fallen, or threatened to fall, significantly below the national average, as well as areas with dominant sectors experiencing structural change such that adverse consequences had been experienced or were to be feared for the affected areas. Thus, the objective of the delineation exercise was to operationalise these generally formulated criteria in a quantified manner and on the basis of available official statistics.

At the outset, the Federal authorities intended that areas would be delineated according to the single criterion of a 'labour-reserve quotient', i.e. a measure of projected labour surplus. To them, this was an attractive criterion because it would enable inclusion in the newly defined GA Areas of the existing 'Emergency Areas', as well as the problem areas characterised by lop-sided industrial structure which had emerged in the wake of the 1966-7 recession. However, various *Länder* suggested other criteria for delineating the assisted areas, because they feared that use of the labour-reserve-quotient criteria would lead to a reduction in the number of their areas qualifying for assistance. Thus, for example, Baden-Württemburg, fearing that use of the labour-reserve quotient would mean that the majority of its previously assisted areas would no longer qualify for aid, argued the case for including a measure of regional income differences in addition to the labour-surplus measure. Similarly, those *Länder* with the classic problem regions – in particular Bavaria – argued that a third criterion should be included, namely a measure of infrastructure provision. These demands led North Rhine Westphalia, which had most to gain from the use of the labour-surplus measure, to insist that any infrastructure definition must be generously framed so as to include recreational infrastructure, i.e. should be framed in such a way that the infrastructure criterion would only minimally influence the delineation of the areas to be assisted relative to the labour-reserve measure.

Given these conflicting views as to how the areas to be assisted should be defined, the Federal authorities were faced with a two-way choice. They could either attempt to devise a totally objective and scientifically grounded delineation methodology which none of the *Länder* would be able reasonably to challenge, or they could accept the fact of specific regional interests and manipulate the criteria used in delineation in order to facilitate a political solution. In practice, the chances of being able to establish an unchallengeable objective delineation methodology meant that the second option had to be chosen.

Thus, the Federal government initially retained two of the three criteria mentioned above – the labour-surplus measure and the regional-income measure – and prepared 16 alternative delineations (using different threshold values for the two variables) of the areas to be assisted. Even at this time, political considerations were playing an important role, in that the whole of the Zonal Border Area was included in the areas assisted *a priori*. At the same time, however, a side condition was imposed, in the sense that the total size in terms of population of the assisted areas should be smaller than hitherto, i.e. the new assisted areas should embrace less than the 33.9 per cent of the total population which the areas previously qualifying for assistance had contained.

In line with expectations, the 'winner' of this exercise was North Rhine Westphalia, while Schleswig-Holstein, Lower Saxony, the Saarland and Bavaria were all 'losers': all these *Länder* lost previously assisted areas. Despite the large number of losers there seemed, at the time, every chance that some such solution could be adopted because *Länder*, governed by the same political parties as were in office in Bonn, were prepared to join forces with political colleagues at the Federal level to force through such an area of delineation. However, this coalition proved fragile as parliamentary elections in one of the affected *Länder* (Lower Saxony) drew closer; regional political interests came to the fore, and in the election campaign any loss of previously assisted areas in that *Land* was rejected.

The Federal authorities had no option but to revise the delineation model in a bid to find a solution which was agreeable to all the *Länder*. Thus, at this juncture, the measure of infrastructural provision was added to the other two criteria and, at the same time, the previous side condition that the total size of the assisted areas should be less than previously was relaxed. The objective now was simply to ensure that the assisted areas were no greater in population terms than hitherto. Ultimately, the three criteria were assigned weights of $1:1:0.5$ (labour-reserve quotient:income:infrastructural provision) and index measures were then calculated for labour-market areas covering the whole country. These areas were then ordered such that those with the lowest score came at the top of the list, and a cut-off line was drawn through the list such that the areas above the line, the new assisted areas, represented 33.9 per cent of the national population.

Although agreement was reached to retain this solution, other political considerations had had to be taken into account. Thus, not only was the whole of the Zonal Border Area retained *a priori* as an assisted area, but so too was the whole of Saarland. Similarly, in order to ensure that the city-state of Bremen was also included in the assisted areas, the two labour-market areas into which it had previously been divided were merged, so that Bremen then achieved a sufficiently high placing in the ranking. Even the weights assigned to the three variables represented political compromise in the sense that assigning equal weights would have defeated the objective of biasing the new delineation of assisted areas in favour of the newly emerged problem areas with lop-sided economic structures. The Federal authorities argued that, in view of the deficient statistical basis for measuring infrastructural provision, and because of unsolved methodological problems in its measurement, it would be unreasonable to assign a weight to this variable equal to that assigned to each of the others. The result of the area-delineation exercise was that 38 local-government areas which previously had not qualified for assistance were now included in the designated areas, whereas 37 other local-authority areas which had previously been assisted no longer qualified. Of particular interest, however, is the comparison of changes in the proportions of territory which would qualify for assistance in each of the *Länder*. In fact, the changes at the level of the *Länder* were minimal. By and large, each of the *Länder* was able to preserve its existing proportion of assisted areas.

Notes

1. OECD, *Regional Problems and Policies in OECD Countries* (OECD, Paris, 1976), vol. 2, p. 152.
2. Between 1972 (the date of the first Framework Plan) and 1974 the 'agreed' designated areas were those which had been delineated prior to 1972 – by the *Länder* or by the Federal government (or by both).
3. Area designation is reviewed periodically. The next redelineation is planned for 1980. Originally the GA Areas held some 34 per cent of the national population.
4. Until the end of 1977 the investment allowance was a fixed 7.5 per cent of eligible investment throughout the GA Areas.
5. The list of eligible industries under the investment-allowance scheme is based on a product classification, while that under the investment-grant scheme is based on an industrial classification.
6. Soft loans are, however, still available in some *Länder* schemes.
7. Up until the end of 1977, as already noted, the investment allowance was a fixed 7.5 per cent of eligible investment. Given a maximum preferential rate of 25 per cent, the maximum investment grant was therefore 17.5 per cent. Currently the maximum investment grant is 15 per cent, since the investment allowance is now 10 per cent in the Zonal Border Area.
8. The appendix draws heavily on F.W. Scharpf, B. Reissert and F. Schnabel, *Politikverflechtung: Theorie und Empirie des Kooperativen Föderalismus in der Bundesrepublik* (Scriptor, Kronberg, 1976); and H. Mehrländer, 'Die Weiterentwicklung der Gemeinschaftsaufgabe "Verbesserung der regionalen Wirtschaftsstruktur" ' in *Innere Kolonisation*, vol. 4, no. 3 (1975), pp. 106-10.

6 REGIONAL INCENTIVES IN THE REPUBLIC OF IRELAND

The Nature of the Problem

Although there is certainly a regional problem in the Republic of Ireland, the basic economic difficulties facing the country are national rather than regional in character. At the national level, income per head is less than half the European Community average; this is at least in part a consequence of the fact that almost one-quarter of the working population (in a total population of almost 3.2 million) is employed within the agricultural sector. In the European Community as a whole less than 10 per cent of the labour force is employed in agriculture. In terms of unemployment, too, the Republic shows up badly, unemployment rates being almost double the Community average in the mid-1970s. As might be expected, emigration has also been high — averaging 1.4 per cent per annum over the period 1951-61 and 0.5 per cent annually between 1961 and 1971 — but in recent years the position has much improved, and there is now little or no net out-migration. This, however, may be more a reflection of economic conditions in recipient countries than of the economic performance of Ireland itself.

Given national economic problems on this scale, it is not surprising that the thrust of the Irish development effort has been towards raising the level of activity in the economy as a whole rather than on concentrating assistance on particular problem regions and thus trying to balance development within the country. Nor, given these problems, is it surprising that Ireland as a whole qualifies as a less-developed 'region' for European Regional Development Fund aid. With a Gross Domestic Product well below the Community average, a heavy dependence on agricultural activities and both high unemployment and migration rates it does, after all, easily meet the criteria laid down for European Regional Development Fund assistance.

But this emphasis on national rather than regional problems is not to say that the latter do not exist or that they are ignored. The western part of the country has long been overdependent on agriculture and on tourism, and has long suffered from high levels of unemployment, underemployment and out-migration, and from low levels of income per head. In 1969 *per capita* personal income levels in the west,

113

north-west, Donegal and Midlands regions (i.e. the north-west corner of the country) were just over three-quarters the national average, while in the east region (which includes Dublin) they were more than 20 per cent above average.[1] Percentage differentials have perhaps narrowed since then, but in 1973 *per capita* personal income in Donegal was still less than two-thirds the east-region level. The east region, too, was the only region experiencing a net migratory inflow in the decade 1961-71. In the same decade the west, north-west, Donegal and Midlands regions all suffered average annual net migration outflows of well over 10 per 1,000 inhabitants.

Clearly, therefore, there are problem regions within the Republic – a point which is reflected in its regional policy. Although the basic incentive package applies to the nation as a whole, various aspects of it favour particular areas, the so-called 'Designated Areas' (see Figure 6.1 below). For example, the maximum rate of award of capital grants offered by the main grant-giving body in Ireland, the Industrial Development Authority (IDA), is higher in the Designated Areas than elsewhere in the country. Moreover, the investment allowance, a 20 per cent depreciation allowance on top of the national free-depreciation system for plant and machinery, is available only in the Designated Areas.

Nevertheless, the main concentration, as already noted, is on improving the performance of the economy as a whole, and the main incentives are therefore national incentives. Given this, and bearing in mind, as we have said, that the whole of Ireland is viewed as a problem region for European Regional Development Fund purposes, any study of regional incentives in Ireland cannot limit itself solely to the regional level but must consider also those national-incentive instruments on offer. We begin our study of the Irish incentive package (national as well as regional) by tracing out the development of incentive policy. In the two sections which then follow we first give a brief overview of those incentives currently on offer, before turning to consider the main incentives in more detail. In a final section, we compare and contrast the Irish incentives with those available elsewhere in the European Community.

The Development of Policy

A prime objective of development policy in Ireland has been to secure a structural transformation of the economy through the expansion of the manufacturing sector. Since the foundation of the state in 1921, policy has moved through three broad phases: an initial decade in which open-market free-trade policies prevailed; a second phase (lasting from about 1932 until the mid-1950s) during which the attempt was made to induce the development of domestic industry through tariff protection and the regulation of foreign investment under the Control of Manufactures Act; and a third, current, phase which saw a swing away from protectionism.

The move against protectionist policies began with the Industrial Development Authority Act of 1950 and was a direct response to rising levels of unemployment and emigration after 1945. This Act established the IDA and charged it with the promotion and development of Irish industry. While the Authority was not required to promote industrial development in specific locations, it was hoped that particular regard would be paid to the needs of areas outside the main population centres.

More explicitly regional was the Underdeveloped Areas Act of 1952 which set up a statutory body, *An Foras Tionscail*, to administer a system of non-repayable grants towards the costs of establishing industries in certain Designated Areas. The areas designated in 1952 were located mainly on the western seaboard and included the counties of Donegal, Sligo, Leitrim, Roscommon, Mayo, Galway and Kerry, together with Clare and West Cork. Taken together, these areas comprised the major proportion of what were formerly known as the 'Congested Areas' — a curious term in current times but one used by the Congested Districts Board towards the end of the nineteenth century when referring to an area which, by reason of its poor resource endowment (including quality of soil and land configuration, together with average size of agricultural holding), was incapable of providing a reasonable living for its residents. Designation recognised that these areas had been bypassed in terms of industrialisation, had an unbalanced demographic structure because of high emigration and suffered high unemployment or underemployment and poor incomes. In 1956 the counties of Monaghan, Longford and Cavan were designated. These areas and the 1952 areas are still the main Designated Areas in the Republic (see Figure 6.1), covering over 55 per cent of the national land mass, and holding just under one-third of the population. But, in addition, Designated Area status can be given for a limited period to areas which have suffered a serious industrial loss. At present the Ballingary colliery area is so designated (until September 1979).

While the Underdeveloped Areas Act and subsequent regionally differentiated measures were to result in the improved flow of new industries to the Designated Areas, the economy of the nation as a whole

Figure 6.1: Designated Areas in the Republic of Ireland

continued to decline. This led to the dropping of the previous protectionist policy in favour of a policy based on efforts to encourage national
economic growth and in particular the growth of exports. As part of
this new policy, the Industrial Grants Act of 1956 gave the IDA powers
to offer capital-grant assistance to firms locating outside the Designated
Areas where these firms were in a position to make a significant contribution to both employment and export growth. The IDA was, moreover,
directed to encourage the dispersal of industry throughout the country.
The Designated Areas were, however, still accorded some priority
through a grant differential ranging from 10 to 15 percentage points.

At the same time as these new national financial measures were
being introduced, the Finance Act of 1956 brought in a five-year
50 per cent tax-relief scheme for company profits deriving from new
export sales or from an increase in the export sales of Irish manufactured goods. Accelerated-depreciation allowances for plant and
machinery were also introduced, while foreign investment was given
a stimulus by lifting the restrictions on foreign ownership imposed by
the Control of Manufactures Act.

Together, these grants and reliefs, extended and adjusted over the
years, constitute the essence of the current incentive package, and as
such form the main subject-matter of the remainder of this chapter.
But before turning to discuss these measures in detail, we should first
mention a number of other related developments in the last twenty
years or so.

In 1958 *Gaeltarra Eireann* was founded with the aim of encouraging
the economic development of the *Gaeltacht* areas of Ireland, areas
located mainly on the western seaboard where Irish is the commonly
spoken language. *Gaeltarra Eireann* operates independently of, but in
co-operation with, the IDA and aims to stabilise the *Gaeltacht* population and thus preserve the Irish language. It tends to offer slightly
higher incentives than those available elsewhere and operates two main
grant schemes: the major-industries scheme, aimed at attracting
established industry either from overseas or from other parts of Ireland;
and the minor-industries scheme, aimed primarily at the residents of the
Gaeltacht. In addition, it is empowered to take share capital in
companies and, indeed, presently has holdings in a wide range of firms.
Although obviously of major importance to the *Gaeltacht*, *Gaeltarra
Eireann* is less significant nationally since the *Gaeltacht* areas hold less
than three per cent of the national population.

In the following year, 1959, the Shannon Free Airport Development
Company was established, with responsibility for the promotion of

Shannon Airport (the future of which had been threatened by the introduction of long-range aircraft on the North Atlantic routes) and for the development and management of an industrial estate and new town at Shannon. A Custom-free Zone was set up at Shannon and, for a time, the Development Company also acted as an agent of the IDA in the mid-west region. However, the financial incentives on offer at Shannon were not, and are not, materially different from those available elsewhere in the Republic, apart from a slightly more favourable treatment of the service sector.

Also in 1959, an important change took place on the incentive front with the passing of a new Industrial Grants Act. This Act withdrew the grant-giving powers awarded to the IDA only three years earlier and transferred them, instead, to *An Foras Tionscail*, which then became the national grants-payment agency. At the same time the differential between Designated and Non-designated Areas in terms of incentive values was further diminished.

During the 1960s there was in Ireland, as elsewhere in Europe, pressure to introduce a growth-area policy, a policy aimed at spatially concentrating investment and development. In the case of Ireland, the initial success of the Shannon experiment was one factor contributing to such pressures, but there was also a general feeling that more 'value for money' could be achieved by such a policy. Particularly influential in this period was a report by Colin Buchanan and Partners in association with Economic Consultants Limited,[2] which not only put forward persuasive arguments in favour of a concentration strategy but, more important (since the growth-area idea was not new in Irish policy-making circles[3]), identified a hierarchy of towns to be favoured. However, in common with the difficulties experienced elsewhere in Europe with attempts at concentration, the main problem was the political one of *having to be seen* to discriminate in favour of particular towns. The problem was made all the more severe in the case of Ireland by the size of the country. 'As a result the government, although it appeared to welcome the report, found difficulty in facing up to its more unpleasant implications and in due course a somewhat more equivocal position has become established in governmental attitudes.'[4]

In the Industrial Development Act of 1969 a number of major changes were made with respect to incentive policy. Most important amongst these, the Industrial Development Authority was reconstituted as an autonomous state-sponsored organisation outside the civil service, and given almost exclusive responsibility for grant awards and the promotion of industrial development. Under the previous (post-1959) system, decisions on the administration of grants and the development of industrial estates had rested with *An Foras Tionscail*, while the IDA had been charged simply with the promotion of industry and the provision of advisory services. In addition to the rationalisation of the organisational system, the Act sought to update, integrate and clarify the incentives available to manufacturing, and in so doing aimed to make Ireland as attractive to investment as other countries, to induce worthwhile investment that might not otherwise take place and to nurture industrial linkages.[5]

Within this new framework it is interesting to note that there was no move towards the explicit concentration strategy proposed by Buchanan. Rather, the areas to be assisted were 'broad-banded', the Designated Areas as a whole being eligible for higher maximum grant awards than the Non-designated Areas. In addition, outside the Designated Areas a distinction was drawn between Dublin and the rest of the country — the Dublin area qualifying for the lowest grant rates and, until the recent economic recession, setting-up projects not being encouraged within Dublin.

In this chronology so far, we have tended to concentrate on incentive policy, and to make only passing references to other methods of stimulating industrial development. In this context we should first mention the important role played by physical planning in Ireland. No doubt because of the size of the country, physical planning and economic planning are more integrated in Ireland than in perhaps any other European Community country. Thus, for example, the physical-planning objective of limiting the growth of Dublin to the natural increase of its population led to the already-noted situation whereby, until the recent high levels of unemployment in the metropolitan area, new manufacturing development was not encouraged through the award of grants in Dublin. Infrastructure development and economic planning are also very much inter-related, not only because of the close contacts which the IDA has with local authorities, but also because particular aspects of infrastructure policy, such as the provision of government factories, is in fact the responsibility of the IDA. One arm of regional policy not found in Ireland is a control policy along the lines of the British Industrial Development Certificate (although developments in excess of £5 million do have to submit an environmental-impact statement to the planning authorities). Rather, the government has chosen to 'rely on inducements to encourage balanced development',[6] basically because of the desire not to discourage foreign investment. Nor have any significant attempts been made as yet to encourage office dispersal (public or private) — except insofar as office employment is included within a manufacturing project. The government has, however, recently become strongly committed to encouraging service-type employment as an instrument of regional policy. As a first step, it is proposed to disperse some 2,000 civil-service jobs to medium-sized urban areas over the next few years.[7]

Having traced out the development of policy generally we now want in the remainder of this chapter to consider the incentive package in more detail, beginning with a brief overview of the incentives on offer.

The Current Incentive Package

As we have seen, one of the important features of the Industrial Development Act of 1969 was that it placed almost complete responsibility for the *financial* incentives on offer in Ireland in the hands of the IDA. Only the spatially limited measures offered by *Gaeltarra Eireann* fall outside direct IDA control, but even here the level of co-operation with the IDA is high. The current section therefore concentrates on IDA assistance. It ends, however, with a brief description of the fiscal incentives available in the Republic — the unique export-profits tax-relief scheme and a variety of capital-allowance aids, including the regionally specific investment allowance.

IDA grant assistance is divided into a number of programmes. Between April 1973 and December 1977, expenditure approved under these programmes amounted to some £360 million, an annual average of just over £77 million. Almost three-quarters of this total — more than £55 million annually — was devoted to the new-industry and major-expansion programme, while a further fifth (just over £15 million annually) was in respect of the re-equipment and modernisation programme. These schemes clearly account for the lion's share of IDA grant aid, and are thus considered in detail in the next section, where we concentrate on the main incentives on offer in Ireland. For the present, we need simply note that under the former scheme the maximum rates of award, for administrative purposes, are 50 per cent in the Designated Areas and 35 per cent in the Non-designated Areas, including Dublin (although prior to the recent recession the Dublin maximum was 25 per cent), while re-equipment and modernisation projects qualify for award maxima of 35 per cent in the Designated Areas and 25 per cent elsewhere in the country. For such projects there is, moreover, an absolute upper limit of £850,000, although this may be exceeded with government approval.

The remaining IDA grant programmes are of much less importance and indeed, in terms of grant expenditure approved in the period April 1973 to December 1977, accounted for less than 9 per cent of the IDA grant total. Just over half of this (on average some £3.6 million worth of approved expenditure per annum) was devoted to the small-industry programme, designed to assist small manufacturing industry employing up to 50 persons and with fixed assets not exceeding £300,000. Under this programme, grants of up to 60 per cent of fixed-asset costs in the Designated Areas and of up to 45 per cent of fixed-asset costs in the Non-designated Areas are available, except in the Dublin area where the 45 per cent maximum applies only to building expenditure. Plant and equipment in Dublin qualify for a maximum award of only 35 per cent under the small-industry scheme.

Other programmes, minor in terms of expenditure even though significant in the context of the development process, include the joint-venture, the service-industries and the product- and process-development schemes. The primary objective of the joint-venture programme is to encourage the establishment of new manufacturing capacity through the promotion of partnerships between foreign and domestic entrepreneurs. The service-industries programmes (which, like the joint-venture scheme, offers grants at the new-industry/major-expansion-programme maximum rates) is aimed at both domestic and overseas firms in certain areas of the service sector such as engineering consultancy and computer technology, with a view to developing export services. The product and process scheme, together with grants towards the provision of research facilities, has the objective of improving both the competitiveness and growth potential of Irish manufacturers through innovation and the development of industrial processes. Under this scheme, the maximum rates of grant award are the same as those under the re-equipment/modernisation programme.

A recent (January 1978) addition to the list of IDA schemes is the enterprise-development programme, aimed at encouraging the establishment of new industrial projects by first-time entrepreneurs. A particularly interesting feature of the scheme is that, in addition to the normal grant finance available to new projects, loan guarantees are on offer to help in the raising of working capital, together with interest grants to reduce the interest payable on any working-capital loans raised. The programme also provides for equity participation and, if necessary, for direct IDA assistance at the project-planning stage.

But this is simply to emphasise that the IDA incentive package extends well beyond simple capital grants. Under the Industrial Development Act, the Authority can offer interest rebates and loan guarantees and, moreover, can take equity in firms. It can also award training grants; it can help companies both to identify new manufacturing opportunities and to take advantage of these opportunities by supplying appropriate technical, financial and managerial resources; and it is empowered to arrange the provision of housing for industrial employees (through buying, leasing or selling land and through subsidising rents). Such non-grant measures, however, either have been little used in the recent past (and some, like equity participation, are explicitly reserved for special circumstances) or involve only minor expenditure. As already stressed, far and away the most important financial incentives in the IDA armoury are the two main capital-grant schemes — the subject-matter of more detailed study shortly.

Turning from financial to fiscal incentives, the most important is the export-profits tax-relief scheme — generally considered to be of key significance in attracting foreign investment to Ireland. Under this scheme, up to 100 per cent relief from income and corporation tax is given until April 1990 in respect of the percentage of sales attributable to the export of Irish manufactured goods. In recent years, export-profits tax relief is estimated to have 'cost' the exchequer £25 million in revenue foregone. Both because it has an important role to play within the Irish incentive package, and because it is, of its type, unique in the European Community, this incentive is also considered further in the next section, even though it is wholly national in character.

Also national in character are most of the Irish capital allowances. This is true, for example, of the allowances on new plant and machinery, which take the form of a 100 per cent initial allowance or of free depreciation, and of the industrial building allowances which involve an initial 50 per cent allowance plus a straight-line writing-down allowance of 4 per cent per annum.[8] Indeed, only the so-called 'investment allowance' is truly regional. This allowance of 20 per cent of capital expenditure on new plant and machinery in the Designated Areas is available on top of the already-noted capital allowances, thus permitting a total of 120 per cent of the cost of new plant and machinery to be set against tax in these areas.

It may be wondered just what the value of capital allowances can be within an incentive system which has profits tax relief. The first point to make here is that not all profits (although certainly most manufacturing profits) are eligible for export-profits tax relief since it applies only to export profits. But secondly, and more importantly, the existence of the leasing sector means that many firms for which capital allowances would be nominally worthless can lease rather than buy their assets, and thus obtain the benefits of the available capital allowances through reduced leasing charges (since the companies doing the leasing will themselves be in receipt of capital allowances).

The various capital allowances available in Ireland are administered by the Revenue Commissioners and 'cost' the exchequer some £10 million annually, most of this being paid under the national schemes. Given the low *regional* expenditure on these schemes, and bearing in mind that capital allowances are widely found at the national level in Europe (indeed the Irish scheme is almost identical to that on offer in the United Kingdom), we do not consider these allowances in any further detail. Rather, the next section is devoted to a discussion of the two main IDA capital-grant schemes — the new-industry/major-expansion and re-equipment/modernisation programmes — and of the very powerful export-profits tax-relief scheme.

The Main Incentives

IDA Capital Grants

By way of introduction we should first say something about the administration of the various capital-grant schemes. Grant administration is the responsibility of the IDA for all of the Republic except the *Gaeltacht* areas, for which *Gaeltarra Eireann* is responsible and where, as already noted, rates of award are somewhat higher than elsewhere in the Designated Areas. In general, and in common with the position in the other small European Community countries, the IDA's grant programmes are administered in a highly centralised manner (from Dublin), although certain functions — including the monitoring of grant entitlement — are regionally devolved. Indeed, centralisation, and in particular the fact that industrialists have a single 'contact point' as far as financial incentives are concerned, is a key selling point of the IDA. Centralisation also allows a large element of discretion whether or not to make an award and the level of award made. As a final administrative feature, it should be noted that the IDA is an autonomous state-sponsored organisation outside the civil service but falling within the parliamentary responsibility of the Minister of Industry and Commerce. The Department of Industry and Commerce also supplies the funds for the IDA from its voted capital.

Of the many different IDA capital-grant programmes only two, for reasons explained earlier, are considered in detail here — the new-industry/major-expansion scheme and the re-equipment/modernisation scheme. Together, these programmes accounted for well over 90 per cent of approved grant expenditure between April 1973 and the end of 1977. In this period, 201 new-industry/major-expansion projects were approved in the Designated Areas and a further 397 outside these areas, to the value of £93.6 million and £164.1 million respectively, giving an average award of around £450,000 in both Designated and Non-designated regions. Over the same period 1,170 re-equipment/modernisation projects were approved, to the value of £70.5 million,[9] giving an average award of only £60,000 — very much lower than that under the new-industry/major-expansion programme.

Having made these introductory remarks, we can now turn to a more detailed discussion of these two grant programmes, beginning with those eligibility conditions which determine whether or not an award will be made, and going on to consider those factors which have a bearing on the level of award made and the value of that award to recipient firms.

Eligibility Conditions. In most countries, project location is a key feature determining eligibility for incentive award. In Ireland it is far less important, since the capital grants on offer are normally available on a national basis. True, new-industry/major-expansion grants were not generally encouraged in the Dublin area in the early 1970s (in line with the government's stated objective of holding down population growth in the capital city to the level of its natural increase) but, with the present depressed economic conditions, awards are now made throughout the country. Location is therefore not a significant factor in the determination of award eligibility, although it does play an important role, as we shall see, in the setting of award levels.

In addition to the obvious condition that any project assisted must be viable, there are three basic conditions to the award of a new-industry/major-expansion grant: the investment must be of a reasonably permanent nature; the project must be in need of assistance; and, above all, employment must either be created or maintained. Indeed, until recently, most projects (i.e. those undertaking investment of less than £1 million or of less than £15,000 per job created) faced explicit aid-per-job limits — of £7,500 in the Designated Areas, £5,000 in the Non-designated Areas outside Dublin and £4,000 in Dublin. Under present conditions, with the economy in recession, specified limits have been dropped. While this gives the authorities greater flexibility, it should not be interpreted to mean that job creation/maintenance is now of less importance. On the contrary, the political emphasis on job maintenance and creation is even greater than in the recent past.

As well as these basic conditions of permanence, need and employment impact, there are a number of other conditions laid down as part of the new-industry/major-expansion scheme. These relate to the significance and character of the employment created (skilled male jobs being favoured); the degree of local linkage; the growth potential of the undertaking; and its technological and scientific content. As set out in the Industrial Development Act, the main purpose of these supplementary conditions is to determine whether or not the basic grant award should be 'topped up' by an extra, discretionary, amount (and we return to this point shortly) but, in practice, they also tend to play a role in deciding whether or not any award should be made. The IDA has developed sectoral priorities on the basis of the above criteria under which aid tends to be concentrated on the manufacturing sector, and indeed on particular product areas[10] — even though no economic activity or sector is explicitly excluded in law.

Although re-equipment and modernisation projects have never faced the explicit aid-per-job limits noted earlier, they are expected, at a minimum, to preserve existing employment. In 1977 the IDA-grant commitment to modernisation resulted in a new-jobs potential of 830 at a cost per new job of £21,200 compared with £4,400 for each job provided by new industry. Actual job costs would of course be very much lower if jobs preserved were also taken into account. As well as preserving existing jobs, re-equipment and modernisation projects must be part of a fully integrated and realisable development plan. Within this plan, the objective must be to achieve reasonable economies of scale and/or to improve competitiveness by increasing productivity and reducing costs. The plan must not, however, result in industrial overcapacity, and must be in line with future market trends and with the IDA's sectoral priorities. On average, as many as 40 per cent of re-equipment/modernisation applications are turned down, largely for reasons of overcapacity in the product area, project non-viability, lack of growth potential and financial inadequacy. No comparable figure is on hand for new industries and major extensions. Any such figure would, in any event, be meaningless, since projects which would fail the IDA criteria are normally discouraged at an early stage from making formal application.

Award Levels. We mentioned earlier, almost in passing, that as initially envisaged in the legislation the IDA-grant structure was to be two-tier.

On top of a relatively rigid first or basic level was to be a more discretionary second tier, the aim being to ensure both certainty for the developer and flexibility for the awarding authorities. If the basic-level criteria (as set out in the previous sub-section) were met, then a grant not exceeding 40 per cent of eligible fixed investment was to be offered in the Designated Areas and one not exceeding 25 per cent of eligible fixed investment elsewhere in the country. On top of this basic grant, a further award of up to 20 per cent was to be awarded if the supplementary criteria noted above were met. The legal maximum-award levels were therefore 60 per cent in the Designated Areas and 45 per cent elsewhere.

In practice, the position has been far more complex than this. In the first place, there appears to have been no basic/discretionary split in the grant-award system; rather, negotiation has taken place within the relevant maxima on the basis of job content, skills, location linkages, etc. Second, administrative (operational) maxima have been established which are lower than those set out in the law. As we have seen, maximum awards under the new-industry/major-expansion scheme are 50 per cent in the Designated Areas and 35 per cent in the Non-designated Areas, while for re-equipment projects and modernisations the administrative maxima are 35 per cent in the Designated Areas and 25 per cent in all other parts of the country. An additional constraint (although in practice not an important one since the average re-equipment award, as we have seen, is only £60,000) is that re-equipment grants may not exceed £850,000 except with government approval.

Moving away from maxima, both legal and administrative, to actual awards, an interesting picture arises. Over the period April 1973 to December 1977, awards under the new-industry/major-expansion scheme averaged some 23 per cent of eligible investment costs, compared with 24 per cent under the re-equipment/modernisation scheme — and this despite the higher award maxima under the former scheme. There is, however, considerable variation around these averages at the individual-project level. One single project, for example, reduced the average award for incoming projects under the new-industry scheme in 1977 from 29.4 per cent of eligible investment to only 15.9 per cent (the comparable figure for domestic projects was 33.2 per cent). As a result, such averages must be viewed with some caution. On the other hand, they do show that the discretion available to the authorities in the setting of award levels *is* used, with at least some projects receiving very much less than the advertised award maxima.

Discretion within the system is one factor which means that the value of grant awards tends to be below the nominal/advertised rate maxima. But other factors which can have a bearing on the effective value of incentives to recipient firms are incentive tax treatment, the timing and phasing of incentive award and the eligibility or otherwise of particular items and forms of expenditure. These factors, however, often have less impact in respect of IDA capital grants than with regard to similar incentives in other countries.

Beginning with tax treatment, only the building element of the capital grant is taxed (as long as taxable profits are made, of course) and then only indirectly, since grant-aided buildings can only be depreciated for tax purposes net of any grant received. The plant and machinery element of the grant is, in contrast, tax-free since the available capital allowances apply to the total cost (i.e. ignoring grants) of aided plant and machinery. But even in respect of the building element of grant, the amount of tax which is likely to fall due will be small, and this for two main reasons. In the first place, the capital allowances on offer in Ireland greatly reduce the level of taxable profits, especially in the early years of a project (years which, anyway, may not be very profitable). And second, manufacturing projects in the export field qualify for export-profits tax relief and will therefore be paying no tax. Taken together, these measures mean that little or no tax will be paid in respect of IDA capital grants.

The timing and phasing of grant payment also does little to reduce the effective value of the grants on offer. Claims for payment are submitted as bills are paid, and the claim-verification period is only about one month. Until recently claim verification was carried out from Dublin, but now it has been devolved to the IDA's regional offices. As well as bringing the regional staff into closer contact with existing and newly established industry in the regions, this administrative devolution will, if anything, further speed up the verification process.

As far as eligible items and forms of expenditure are concerned, the position in respect of IDA capital grants is similar to that of most other project-related grants on offer in the European Community countries. Almost all the fixed-capital costs of a project — including site purchase and development, infrastructure works and installations (e.g. electrical services, water, telephones) — are eligible, as long as they are 'reasonable', are directly relevant to the production process (this would include offices and canteens on the premises) and are not incurred as part of the leasing contract. Working capital, off-site vehicles, second-hand items, plant and machinery of less than £1,000, tools and implements and office decorations are all ineligible, as is office equipment of less than £2,000.

A final point to note in respect of the IDA grants is that they can be combined unconditionally with the fiscal incentives on offer. They can, moreover, be added to other, more minor, IDA assistance, but only up to the administrative maxima already noted.

Export-profits Tax Relief

As mentioned earlier, this concession had its origins in the depression conditions of the 1950s. Increasing unemployment and high emigration emphasised the need for economic growth. The realisation that, given the size of the Irish domestic market, any expansion of industrial production would have to rely on export growth led to the introduction of a limited measure of export tax relief in 1956.

The basic scheme, which was amended and adapted over the years, involved a 50 per cent tax relief on specified export profits (those derived from new export sales or the increase in export sales over such sales in a standard year). The relief was extended to 100 per cent in 1957, and in the following year the period over which it could be claimed was increased to ten years. Since 1969, all export profits (not simply, as before, the increase in export profits) derived from eligible activities (basically manufacturing) have been eligible for 100 per cent relief for a period of 15 years and partial relief for an additional period of five years. Partial relief begins at 80 per cent in the first year, reducing to 65, 50, 35 and 15 per cent respectively, in the second, third, fourth and final years.

Although export-profits tax relief has generally been viewed as a very important part of the Irish incentive package, it has been 'frowned upon' by the Competition Directorate in Brussels. From 1981 it is envisaged that the scheme will be replaced by a special rate of corporation tax for all manufacturing companies in Ireland, covering the period up until the turn of the century. Even so, the export-profit tax-relief scheme remains of considerable interest, not least because it will remain available up until 1990 to qualifying companies already in receipt of it.

The scheme, liberal in concept and simple in operation, is administered uniformly throughout the country as part of the general taxation system. Decisions on borderline cases (where it is not clear that the product to which the concession attaches falls within the definition of a manufactured good) lie with the Revenue Commissioners, who are the authority charged with the administration of tax legislation and tax collection. Because, as we shall see, the interpretation of what constitutes a manufactured good can be extremely broad, manufacturers normally seek the advice of the revenue authorities before starting production. Thereafter, the standard practice is that certified business accounts are submitted to the Inspector of Taxes, together with a claim for export-profits tax relief showing the proportion of goods manufactured going to export sales. The Inspector then assesses the tax due.

Eligibility Conditions. There are three basic conditions to be satisfied before export-profits tax relief is granted. These relate to the claimant, to the product or activity and to the geographic origin of profits.

Export-profits tax relief is restricted to companies, no matter where incorporated and whether or not managed or controlled in the Republic. Only those profits which originate from export sales are eligible, and then only where they are attributable to the sale of goods *manufactured* in Ireland or to certain other specified activities. These activities include certain planning, design and other consultancy services for projects executed abroad, repairs to non-resident-owned ships and (somewhat strangely) both fish farming and mushroom cultivation. Manufacturing processes carried out on goods brought into the country for that purpose and subsequently taken out without a change of foreign ownership also qualify.

In general, the main ineligible sectors are the primary sector, construction, tourism and services other than those consultancy services mentioned above. At Shannon Airport, however, all activities certified by the Minister of Finance as exempt activities are eligible for 'Shannon Relief'. Unlike standard export-profits tax relief, Shannon relief can be claimed in full, without any scaling down, for all qualifying profits made before April 1990.

Award Levels. The export-profits tax-relief scheme is a very straightforward incentive, being awarded automatically and at a uniform rate to all qualifying projects. As we have seen, the basic award involves full relief of profits derived from export sales in manufacturing over a fifteen-year period (or until 1990, whichever is the earlier) and there is, in addition, partial relief for a further five years (again with 1990 as the terminal date). In those cases where output is sold both abroad and domestically, 'export' profits are calculated by determining the percentage of output sold abroad and applying this percentage to the total profits figure. The resultant estimate of 'export' profits is then exempt

from tax. If, for example, total trading profits for the year amount to
£20,000 and 90 per cent of the product is sold abroad, then, given the
full relief, £18,000 would be exempt from tax.

On average, export-profits tax relief (outside of the Shannon area)
cost the Exchequer — in terms of revenue foregone — £15.6 million
annually in the period 1970-4, rising to £23.8 million in 1974/5 and
£24.6 million in 1975/6. On top of this, Shannon relief is estimated to
have cost the Exchequer about £5 million a year.

From a national point of view the immediate benefit of the export-
profits tax-relief scheme (and the other incentives received by industrialists) lies in the employment generated by export industries. Other
benefits are not as clearcut. Although foreign enterprises may price-
down imported intermediate goods (with a resultant positive balance-
of-payments effect), this must be set against an increasing proportion of
tax-free, easily repatriated, profits and the high import content of
industrial production (both of which have a negative impact on the
balance of payments). Moreover, commentators have noted that the
scheme has done little to encourage 'across-the-fence' trading, with the
result that industrial-linkage and technology-transfer effects have
tended to be weak.

Functionally, the object of the incentive is to attract new exporting
industries. Generally it is agreed that in this regard the scheme has been
efficient. The Survey of Grant Aided Industry in 1966 reported as a
prima facie conclusion that export-profits tax relief has proved particularly attractive in inducing foreign industrialists to establish relatively
large-scale projects in Ireland, whether these be judged in terms of
employment, output or exports. But this is understandable, given that
the relief is available more or less automatically to eligible applicants,
will continue for a specified period and is subject only to the export
capacity and profit-making capabilities of recipient firms.

Comparative Conclusions

As noted at the outset, the problems facing Ireland, whether measured
in terms of unemployment rates, levels of industrial employment or
standards of living, are among the most severe in the European Community. Indeed, as we have seen, the country as a whole is viewed as
a problem 'region' by the Community for the purpose of the Regional
Development Fund. Not surprisingly, the severity of the problem in
Ireland has had a number of very important influences on policy.

It has, for example, led to a very strong emphasis on capital grants
within the Irish incentive package. Grants are the most visible incentive

type and can, moreover, be pushed up to very high values. The Irish grants have particularly high nominal values, the legal maximum being 60 per cent of eligible investment (a percentage which is not matched by any other regional-grant scheme in the European Community), while the administrative maximum is 50 per cent. Only the grants on offer in Italy and Northern Ireland can compete with this administrative maximum. In most other Community countries, the nominal or advertised rate is between 20 and 25 per cent. In effective-value terms, too, the Irish grants compare very favourably with others in Europe — being worth more than double the Community 'norm'. This, however, is only to be expected since, as we saw earlier, taxation is insignificant, claim-processing delays are minor and item coverage is in line with most other capital grants (in that working capital is the main ineligible item).

The severity of the problem in Ireland also does much to explain the existence of the export-profits tax-relief scheme. No other country in the European Community has such an extensive profits-tax concession (the various Italian schemes are of just ten years' duration and cover less than 100 per cent of taxable profits, while the Luxembourg concession is only for eight years and is in respect of only 25 per cent of tax liabilities). The form of the concession has, however, caused problems in Brussels since it cannot be incorporated *ex ante* into the European Commission's co-ordination methodology (see Chapter 11). As already noted, a replacement scheme will be introduced in 1981, involving a special rate of corporation tax for *all* manufacturing companies in Ireland. It will be interesting to see whether this new measure proves to be as valuable and attractive to incoming industry as export-profits tax relief would seem to have been.

But, of course, in respect of fiscal aids, Ireland not only has export-profits tax relief; it also has very wide-ranging and generous capital allowances on offer, allowances well in advance of those available in most other Community countries (at either the regional or the national level). Certainly no other country can match the 120 per cent allowance on plant available in the Republic's Designated Areas.

A further feature of the Irish incentive package is the large number of minor incentive schemes aimed at specific problems and/or points of potential. As we have seen, there are, for example, aids to encourage new entrepreneurs (including two which are rare in Europe — working-capital loan guarantees and interest grants), aids to promote partnerships between foreign and domestic entrepreneurs, aids aimed at small firms and aids to help maintain the Irish culture and language. There is also a specific programme for the service sector — though this is restricted to a very limited part of that sector, namely export services (and, in particular, engineering consultancy and computer technology). It is, in fact, in the area of service-sector assistance that, if anything, the Irish lag behind a number of other countries, and perhaps especially the United Kingdom and France.

We mentioned earlier that a key feature of the Irish incentive package was the extent to which capital grants were emphasised. In respect of these grants it is interesting to note that at the policy-formulation stage the aim was to introduce a two-tier approach, consisting of a basic award to go more or less automatically to applicant projects plus a discretionary second tier. The hope was that such a system would combine certainty of award to potential applicants with administrative flexibility. In the event, however, the grant system has been operated in a wholly discretionary manner and the idea of a basic, automatic grant award has been dropped. To some extent it could be argued that this is unfortunate, since it tends to reduce the visibility of the grants on offer and certainly makes firms wary of incorporating them at an early stage of their investment/location decision-making procedures. On the other hand, the Irish obviously consider themselves sufficiently small to be able to overcome the problems posed by discretion (and in this regard it is worth mentioning that discretion is also of major importance in Denmark, Belgium and Luxembourg) and, in particular, feel that they can indeed tailor the incentives on offer to the needs of applicant firms. Certainly, high maximum rates of award are likely to produce plenty of applications – a situation well suited to the IDA, one of the most streamlined and persuasive industrial-promotion agencies in Europe.

If one has to try to sum up the Irish incentive system one would seek out words such as 'discretionary', 'comprehensive' and 'valuable'. But in a country up against the problems facing Ireland these features are the least one can expect from the incentives on offer.

Notes

1. Calculated from OECD, *Regional Problems and Policies in OECD Countries* (OECD, Paris, 1976), vol. 1, Table 5, p. 72.
2. C. Buchanan and Partners, *Regional Development in Ireland* (An Foras Forbartha, Dublin, 1969).
3. A growth-area policy was first advocated in official circles in Ireland in 1958. See Department of Finance, *Economic Development* (Stationery Office, Dublin, 1958), PR 4803, p. 160.
4. J.H. Johnson, 'Republic of Ireland' in H.D. Clout (ed.), *Regional*

Development in Western Europe (John Wiley and Sons, London, 1975), p. 228.

5. The aims emerge clearly from National Industrial Economic Council, *Report on Industrial Adaptation and Development*, Report No. 23 (Stationery Office, Dublin, 1968).

6. OECD, *Regional Problems and Policies*, p. 67.

7. For the background to this move, see National Economic and Social Council, *Service-type Employment and Regional Development*, Report No. 28 (Stationery Office, Dublin, 1977).

8. Making a 54 per cent allowance in the year in which the expenditure is made and 4 per cent annually thereafter.

9. There is at present no breakdown of these projects into Designated Area and Non-designated Area projects. Between April 1973 and the end of 1975, however, 151 re-equipment/modernisation projects were approved in the Designated Areas, to the value of £7.0 million, while 608 such projects were approved elsewhere in the country, to the value of £31.8 million.

10. The favoured product areas are: electronics and computers; mechanical engineering, including industrial machinery, valve compressors, engines, vehicles; selected areas of the textile industry; consumer products including sports and leisure equipment, photographic equipment, health-care products; intermediate and related chemical products; industrial support industries, iron and steel foundries, contact forging. See *IDA Industrial Plan 1977-80* (IDA, Dublin, 1978), p. 22.

7 REGIONAL INCENTIVES IN ITALY

The Nature of the Problem

The main problem area in Italy, the *Mezzogiorno* (roughly mainland Italy south of Rome plus Sicily, Sardinia and a number of smaller islands) covers about two-fifths of the national territory, and currently holds some 35 per cent of the national population. In physical terms, it is larger than many Western European countries (over 47,000 square miles) and, with a population of almost 20 million, it has more inhabitants than most. Despite the fact that Italy is among the ten most highly industrialised Western countries, the *Mezzogiorno* exhibits features more characteristic of many underdeveloped countries: extremely high rates of rural-urban migration, high regional out-migration, low income-per-head levels and low activity rates, lack of public and urban services and poor social infrastructure. In Table 7.1 we present some of the key socio-economic indicators of the scale of the problem currently facing the Italian south.

Table 7.1 shows a clear north-south gap in the socio-economic development of the country. Between 1951 and 1976 the *Mezzogiorno* suffered an overall net migratory loss of over 4 million, while the centre-north experienced a net migratory gain of over 2.5 million. Despite the massive net outflow from south to north, and despite the fact that most southern migration has been at the expense of its rural areas, agricultural employment remains of major importance in the *Mezzogiorno*. Over one-quarter of southern employment was in agriculture in 1977, compared with just over 10 per cent of employment in the north. Partly as a result, but also as a reflection of high levels of unemployment and underemployment, average income per head in the *Mezzogiorno* is less than two-thirds the average centre-north figure. Finally, it is evident from Table 7.1 that in terms of 'non-economic' indicators, too, the south fares badly *vis-à-vis* the north. Illiteracy, for example, is four times more common, while infant mortality is over a quarter higher.

But the Italian regional problem is not as straightforward as the simple north-south dichotomy shown up by Table 7.1.[1] At least two other spatial disequilibria which affect *all* regions in Italy should be mentioned. Although both are highly inter-related with the north-south problem, they also have aspects and causes of their own. First,

Table 7.1: Some Indicators of the North-South Gap in Italy

		Centre-North	Mezzogiorno	Italy
Population (millions)	1951	29.7	17.5	47.2
	1977	36.6	19.9	56.4
Net migration (millions)	1951-76	+ 2.5	− 4.1	− 1.6
Active population (per cent)	1977	41.2	34.5	38.8
Unemployment rate (per cent)	1977	5.8	10.1	7.1
Agricultural employment (per cent)	1977	10.5	27.6	15.7
Industrial employment (per cent)	1977	43.2	26.6	38.2
GDP per head (mill. lire)	1977	3.6	2.2	3.1
Illiteracy (per cent)	1971	2.6	10.9	5.2
Infant mortality (per cent)	1971	22.7	28.8	27.0

Sources: ISTAT publications and *Relazione Generale sulla Situazione Economica del Paese (1977)* (Rome, 1978).

there are marked rural-urban differences. On the one side, high congestion and deteriorating living conditions can be found in the large metropolitan areas (like Milan, Rome, Turin, Genoa, Naples), while, on the other side, vast zones of abandoned and eroding agricultural land lie in decay. And, second, there is the contrast between the inner mountainous areas (the Appenines, the Alps and the mountainous hearts of Sardinia and Sicily) and the few large fertile plains in northern, central and south-eastern Italy. Any economic development in Italy, be it in agriculture, industry or the tourist sector, seems to concentrate in the urban and non-mountainous areas along the coast.[2] Although this chapter concentrates on the *Mezzogiorno* it must be obvious, in view of its mountainous character, that the centre-north also has serious regional problems of its own.

In addition to the spatial differences mentioned above, there are other, more structural, disequilibria in Italy, many of which are strongly related to the basic regional problem. Most important, the size structure of Italian industry is highly dualistic — with very large (and often multi-national) firms on the one hand and very small firms, often of prevalently handicraft (or 'artisan') character, on the other. Where very large firms dominate the regional economy (like car manufacturing in Turin, shipbuilding in Genoa, steel and chemical plants in certain areas of the *Mezzogiorno*), there are the usual problems of over-reliance on single industries. Moreover — and this is a problem found particularly in the south — many large plants are only poorly related to other local economic activities, and have virtually no 'ancillary' relationships to small local producers and local or regional markets; rather, they relate to markets outside the region, both for supplies and sales. For good reason, therefore, such plants are known in Italy as 'cathedrals in the desert'. Despite the fact that small and medium-sized firms have long been among the targets of industrial-development policy in Italy (and regional-incentive policy in particular), the gap between small and large industry has proven an especially difficult one to bridge.

One consequence of the perseverance of dualistic features in Italy, and above all of the north-south gap, is that regional policy has probably been more wide-ranging, and has been subjected to more changes, than in most other European Community countries. It is the purpose of the next section to indicate the breadth of regional policy in Italy, and to note the policy changes which have taken place since the war. The two sections which then follow concentrate in turn on the current incentive package and the main incentives, while a final section compares and contrasts Italian regional-incentive policy with incentive policies found elsewhere in Europe.

The Development of Policy

Regional policy in Italy is long-standing. Even in the immediate post-war period, with its desperate economic conditions, financial aid was provided for small and medium-sized firms through a soft-loans policy with marked regional features. As we shall see, soft loans have since developed into one of the major incentive instruments in Italy. The main policy thrust in the regional sphere in the early post-war years, however, was not in respect of incentives, but rather was towards the development of infrastructure. In 1950 a special development agency, the *Cassa per il Mezzogiorno* (hereafter referred to as the *Cassa*), was set up to encourage southern development. The basic idea behind the *Cassa* was that it should complement the normal infrastructure activities of the state (i.e. the central, regional, provincial and local authorities) by undertaking co-ordinated 'extraordinary interventions' wherever the standard state apparatus was shown to be inadequate or inappropriate. In practice, however, these additive aspirations have been frustrated, and the *Cassa* has tended to substitute for the state in the infrastructure sphere.

In its initial phase the *Cassa* concentrated its resources on agricultural infrastructure and on more general infrastructure programmes (the provision of roads, harbours, airports, schools and hospitals). During this period, land reform was underway in the south (large land holdings being distributed amongst some 90,000 new peasant farmers) and, although not directly involving the *Cassa*, much 'extraordinary intervention' by the *Cassa* went towards supporting this land-reform policy. Indeed, during its first ten-year plan, the *Cassa* devoted about three-quarters of its financial resources to agriculture. Through land reform it was hoped that a change in the socio-economic conditions of the *Mezzogiorno* would be brought about such as to lead to some endogenous industrialisation. Basically, then, land reform and related activities were seen as pre-industrialisation measures. When it became clear that spontaneous industrialisation would not happen, or at least not with sufficient speed, a more direct strategy for industrialisation emerged.[3]

As part of this move, the *Cassa* was given a number of new functions in 1957. In the field of infrastructure provision, for example, it became responsible for initiation, direction and financing of infrastructure for industry — including, amongst other things, the preparation of industrial land and the connection of industrial sites to energy sources, water supply and sewage. In addition, whenever specific infrastructure was needed in connection with the location of particular new projects, the *Cassa* either provided it directly through its special agencies and contractors or, if the firm preferred, made at least a partial financial contribution towards it. The *Cassa* therefore became responsible for supplying direct infrastructure to industry, whereas previously it had been concerned only with more general infrastructure projects.

A second important new role for the *Cassa* in 1957 concerned the administration of a southern financial-incentive policy. This was a major step forward since, prior to this time, there had been no purely regional incentive schemes of any significance on offer in Italy. The 1957 incentive package had three main ingredients: soft loans, capital grants and tax concessions; it also contained a variety of small miscellaneous benefits including rebates on energy and transport tariffs. Although 1957 is rightly viewed as the 'date of birth' of the *Mezzogiorno* incentive package, the sums available for the payment of industrial incentives were in fact fairly limited, and indeed it was only with the *Mezzogiorno* Law of 1965 that the incentives on offer became more substantial. The package was further strengthened in 1968 with the introduction of very valuable social-security concessions, such that it is currently one of the most generous incentive packages in the European Community. We return to consider the incentives on offer in detail in the sections which follow.

So far, we have mentioned those two strands of the industrialisation policies developed for the south in 1957 which involved the *Cassa* – the provision of industrial infrastructure and the award of industrial incentives. Away from the *Cassa*, a third important element of policy, and one which has remained of major importance, is the use of state industry as an arm of regional policy. The state-holding companies in Italy are an inheritance from the inter-war period. They are organised into holding groups (of which IRI and ENI are the two most important) and are active in almost every sector of the Italian economy, and in particular in steel, heavy engineering, shipbuilding, telephones, banking and petrochemicals. Alitalia, Alfa Romeo, Ducati, RAI, Cinecittà, AGIP and the Bank of Rome are just some of the major names falling within the state-holding net. In total, the 350 or so state-holding firms currently employ about 700,000 people.

From 1957 onwards, the state-holding sector was obliged to place at least 40 per cent of its total investment in the south, and to allocate at least 60 per cent of its new investment to the south. In 1971 these proportions were increased to 60 per cent and 80 per cent respectively. Even though these percentages have in practice been applied only to potentially mobile investment, they have had a significant impact; southern employment in the state-holding sector has more than doubled since their introduction. In 1978 over 27 per cent of state-holding-sector employment was located in the *Mezzogiorno*, compared with 18 per cent in 1965 and 13 per cent in 1958.

The final strand of the 1957 industrialisation measures involved the start of a growth-centre strategy. By 1959 so-called 'areas of industrial development' and 'nuclei of industrialisation' had been designated in locations thought to have marked development potential. Perhaps the climax of this growth-centre policy was the plan to create an inter-related-industry complex at Bari-Taranto.[4] In the event, this ingenious and imaginative attempt to locate simultaneously a complex of industries, inter-related in as far as they made demands on each other, failed at the practical level; and the growth-centre approach itself soon came up against considerable political and practical problems. Indeed, by the late 1960s such a large number of growth areas and nuclei had been designated in the *Mezzogiorno* that the distribution of aid could no longer be described as 'concentrated' (the essence of the growth-centre idea) but rather involved, at best, 'dispersed concentration'. In

1971 the picture became even more complex, special attention being given, within the incentive package, to those areas and nuclei doing less well, while economic activities were to be encouraged to settle along so-called 'lines of territorial penetration' drawn into the inner parts of the country. The resultant situation was certainly one of diffusion (and some would say confusion) and was obviously a long way away from the growth-centre concept. In fact, over the post-war period, area-designation policy in the south has turned full circle — from diffusion (aid being given to the *Mezzogiorno* as a whole) to growth centres, and then back again to diffusion.

During the 1960s, the problems to be tackled by regional policy developed beyond the simple north-south dichotomy. In particular, serious internal problems appeared within the *Mezzogiorno*, in the form of acute depopulation of large inner areas. The problem is best explained in terms of migration patterns: first, there was international emigration with migrants coming prevalently from the poorest areas of the south; second, there was internal migration in Italy from the south to the north (and, of course, the places of most massive out-migration were again the worst-off parts of the south); and third, there was also internal migration within the south from rural hinterland to urban agglomerations like Naples, Bari, Taranto and Reggio Calabria. Thus, beyond the basic north-south differences, the problem in the *Mezzogiorno* consisted of two other elements — on the one hand, population erosion in the rural areas and, on the other, congested and overcrowded urban living conditions.

But congestion was not only a problem in southern cities. In the centre-north, massive migratory inflows led to a saturation of both industrial sites and housing areas in the main cities, as well as creating considerable pollution problems. In response to this, attempts were made in the late 1960s to introduce a location-control system which included the possibility of financial penalties against large investment in already-congested areas. However, it was not until the 1971 *Mezzogiorno* Law that a requirement that quoted companies with equity capital of more than 5 milliard lire inform the Ministry for the Budget and Economic Planning of their investment plans was introduced. In addition, any expansion by companies, whether quoted or not, in excess of 7 milliard lire had to be communicated to the Ministry. Under the law, a decision on an application had to be taken by the authorities within three months of submission, otherwise the investment plans were deemed acceptable. Any investment carried out in the face of a negative decision was liable to a fine of 25 per cent of the investment.

Although the negative side of sanctions had a role to play, the positive side of location control was considered far more important. The information on investment plans obtained was viewed as a vital element of economic planning, one which would give the authorities the scope for initiating from their side the process of 'planned bargaining' — a procedure whereby the state and individual firms established in a bargaining process the infrastructure and incentives to be provided by the state in exchange for a state-preferred location of industrial plants.

However, this bargaining procedure (and indeed the disincentive system in general) has never developed into a major instrument of Italian regional policy. Both the hopes and disillusion relating to the whole location-control system have been large. But its lack of impact is perhaps not surprising in the event, since neither the explicit delineation of areas where location was prohibited nor the establishment of sector priorities was undertaken nor were clear procedures defined for the administrative process of information, authorisation and planned bargaining.[5] In recent years some slight changes to the system have been introduced by new laws and amendments, but on the implementation side there is still much embarrassment and confusion about this regional-policy instrument.

In addition to the introduction of a disincentive policy, 1971 also saw important changes in the incentives on offer. Perhaps not surprisingly in view of the wide range of problems to be tackled, the *Mezzogiorno* legislation for the 1971-6 quinquennium is probably one of the best Italian examples of an 'overloaded' policy, with individual incentives being designed in such a way as to allow highly discriminatory use to be made of them. This approach, however, soon ran into problems, not least because of its inherent complexity. As early as 1972 there was a general disenchantment with highly sophisticated and complicated incentives, and first proposals aimed at simplification were put forward.

Simplification was anyway necessary on other grounds. On top of the complex mixture of incentives available as part of the southern package, various national soft-loan schemes (and, in particular, the *Mediocredito* and Law 623 soft-loan schemes for small and medium-sized firms, to which we return) were also available in the south, creating a situation known in Italy as 'the incentive jungle', wherein knowledgeable entrepreneurs were able to get subsidised credit virtually everywhere in the country and, in the *Mezzogiorno*, could draw on assistance from a variety of sources such as to cover most, if not all, of their project costs. Adding further to the complexities, the five autonomous regions of Italy (Aosto Valley, Trentino-Alto Adige, Friuli-Venezia Giulia, Sicily and Sardinia) developed their own supplementary incentive schemes. Clearly the time was ripe for a serious attempt to harmonise and co-ordinate the various incentives on offer. The result was that the 1976 *Mezzogiorno* Law — due to run until 1980 — introduced a very much simpler incentive system than its predecessor. In particular, the various soft-loan schemes which had previously been available were merged into a single national soft-loan scheme. But there was another important feature about the 1976 Law: it was 'twinned' with a national law aimed at tackling the general structural problem of industry. Clearly this new approach was occasioned by the changed economic circumstances of the 1970s. However, despite declarations that southern problems will continue to have top priority, it carries with it the obvious danger that the relative advantage to be gained from investing in the south will be reduced — to the serious detriment of the south.

In the two sections which follow, we describe the incentives on offer under the 1976 *Mezzogiorno* Law in more detail. But before that, we should briefly mention one further change which took place in the regional-policy sphere in 1971. In that year the *Cassa* was given yet another new task, one which in the meantime has developed into a very major activity — the supervision of the financing (and sometimes also physical implementation) of so-called 'special projects'. Such projects can be put forward by groups of regions or other public or semi-public entities, and must have a number of specific characteristics: they must be inter-regional as well as inter-sectoral; they need to have a clear and 'organic' relationship to existing environmental, social, urban and other structures; and they must lead to the better use of natural and human resources. The projects currently under way can be grouped into five main fields of intervention: the development and distribution of water resources; agricultural-development projects; specific infrastructure for industrial development; inter-regional road systems; and environmental reclamation and the restoration and improvement of areas with special tourist characteristics. In the period 1971-5 special projects accounted for over 10 per cent of *Cassa* expenditure on regional policy.

The Current Incentive Package

As we have seen, there are four main incentive types presently on offer in the Italian problem regions — soft loans, capital grants, tax concessions and concessions on social-security contributions. However, all four incentive types are obtainable only in the *Mezzogiorno*. In the designated areas of the centre-north the package consists of just two incentives — the national soft loan (but at rates of award lower than in the south) and a ten-year concession on the ILOR profits tax (one of three southern tax concessions). Neither the two remaining tax concessions, nor the INPS social-security concession, nor the *Cassa* grant — the other southern incentives — are available outside the *Mezzogiorno*. We now turn to look in more detail at the various incentive measures currently available in the south, beginning with the national soft loan.

Loans on favourable conditions and at generous rates of interest are offered through so-called 'Special Credit Institutes' (SCIs), banks specialising in the medium- and long-term credit field. There are about thirty such institutes in Italy, many of them having a public or at least semi-public status. The system of Special Credit Institutes developed rapidly in the post-war period, the main aim being to allow easier access to business finance for small and medium-sized companies. With the growing importance of regional policy in the *Mezzogiorno*, a number of SCIs were set up to fulfil a specific task in the soft-loan system: that is, to award and control, together with the *Cassa*, soft loans available to southern projects. Loans issued by these '*Cassa*-related' SCIs (ISVEIMER, IRFIS and CIS) are aided somewhat indirectly through subsidising the issuing of bonds by the SCIs. In contrast, 'non-*Cassa*-related' SCI loans are directly subsidised by the *Cassa*. Apart from this administrative difference, however, both types of SCI operate in the same manner. Moreover, the 'softness' of loan awards is determined by law and is the same for comparable applicants, irrespective of SCI. Currently, and as already noted, soft loans for projects locating in the *Mezzogiorno* are awarded according to regulations issued in 1976. These regulations co-ordinated existing soft-loan systems and brought them together in one national scheme, with marked regional discrimination. The scheme distinguishes between four areas: the *Mezzogiorno*; the insufficiently developed zones of Central Italy; the insufficiently developed zones of Northern Italy; and the rest of the country (see Figure 7.1).

Depending on area, the loans cover between 40 and 60 per cent of eligible fixed investment plus 'technically necessary' stocks. Maximum loan duration is 10 years, except for southern setting-up projects where it is 15 years. Repayment holidays, related to the time taken to draw down the loan, are available for up to 3 years on 10-year loans and up to 5 years on 15-year loans. Loan repayment is half-yearly and is made up of equal (interest plus principal-repayment) instalments spread over the period of the loan. The concession on the interest to be paid on the

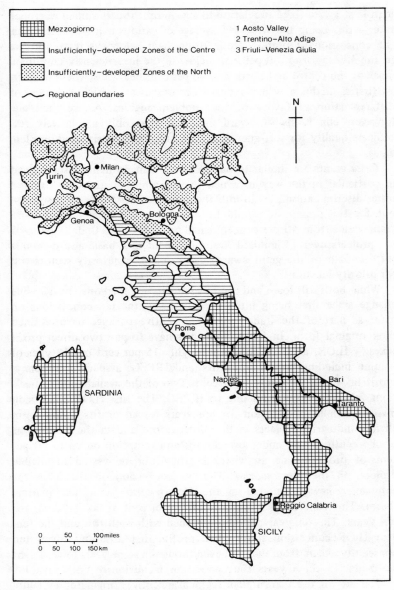

Figure 7.1: Designated Areas in Italy

loan is at a rate fixed in relation to a government-determined reference rate — this being the weighted average of various market rates. Thus, the concessionary interest rate is 70 per cent below the reference rate in the *Mezzogiorno*, 60 per cent below in the insufficiently developed areas of the centre and north and 40 per cent below elsewhere in Italy. At first sight this may not appear to represent a significant element of differentiation in favour of the problem regions. As we shall see, however, conditions of award are such that only a relatively few projects qualify for soft-loan assistance outside the designated problem areas.

Cassa grants are similar to national soft loans in many respects, and in particular in the way in which they combine spatial with size and other discrimination. We go into the details of this in the next section, but for the present it should be noted that the *basic* rate of *Cassa* grant varies from 40 per cent for small projects to less than 26 per cent for projects over 15 milliard lire. On top of this, basic award premia (of one-fifth of the grant award) are available in priority sectors and for priority locations.

While both soft loans and capital grants have undergone considerable change since first being introduced in 1957, the tax concessions on offer as part of the Italian regional-incentive package have retained their original form. In Italy, companies have to pay two direct profit taxes — ILOR, a tax of currently roughly 15 per cent on all types of income including company profits, and IRPEG, a specific company-profit tax of, at present, 25 per cent. Two of the available tax concessions relate to ILOR, and one to IRPEG. The first ILOR concession involves full tax exemption for ten years for all profits arising from eligible industrial projects in the *Mezzogiorno* and in the aided areas of the centre-north; and the second is an exemption on up to 70 per cent of profits made anywhere in Italy but reinvested in eligible projects in the *Mezzogiorno*. The tax concession on IRPEG is for companies newly founded in the *Mezzogiorno* (with headquarters there). This concession is a rebate of 50 per cent of tax liabilities for ten years. The ten-year period mentioned with both this and the ten-year ILOR concession starts when profits first arise and covers ten consecutive years from then on, even though in some years losses might be made. In these years the concession is obviously not 'payable'.

The last of the main Italian regional incentives originated in 1968, is limited to the *Mezzogiorno* and takes the form of a rebate on the social-security contributions payable to INPS, the most important Italian social-security institution. On average, INPS liabilities amount to about 27 per cent of an employer's wage costs, including overtime. Initially, the rebate was 10 per cent of the wage bill (excluding overtime), split between the employer (8.5 per cent) and the employee (1.5 per cent). This distribution, however, proved difficult to operate in practice. Through a series of additions and amendments the social-security concession developed into a complicated set of different percentage rebates on wage costs excluding overtime (8.5 per cent, 18.5 per cent and 28.5 per cent), relating to different 'categories' of employees according to their hiring dates. Thus, by 1972, a firm in the south could have been in receipt of a 28.5 per cent concession for labour hired after January 1971 and increasing the work force (not pure turnover), an 18.5 per cent concession on workers hired after October 1968 and increasing the work force, an 18.5 per cent concession on labour hired before October 1968 and still under contract, and an 8.5 per cent concession for the remaining workers, that is, all those hired in the meantime but not representing an addition to previous employment levels (i.e. turnover cases). In 1976 a new concession was added to the above rebates: this concession was for labour hired after 1 July 1976 over and above the employment level at that date, and amounted to the total employer's contribution to INPS, which, as we have seen, is currently about 27 per cent of the wages bill including overtime. This new concession relates only to jobs created until 31 December 1980 and is payable only until the end of 1986. The pre-1976 INPS concessions, in contrast, are payable only until the end of 1980.

Beyond these four main incentives, there are a number of smaller 'national' regional aids, as well as some incentives awarded by the autonomous regions. Among the minor national incentives is the already-mentioned *Mediocredito* scheme for soft loans. This is a project-related loan scheme for small and medium-sixed firms with concessionary elements being available in the *Mezzogiorno* and the problem areas of the centre and north. A feature of the *Mediocredito* scheme is that it combines size discrimination with spatial discrimination. The maximum size of loan which can be awarded is 1.25 milliard lire in the *Mezzogiorno* and 1.0 and 0.75 milliard lire in the centre and north, respectively. Because, however, of the presence of more generous loan systems in the *Mezzogiorno*, virtually no *Mediocredito* loans have been taken up there. They primarily go to the centre and north, and even there they are taken up only if there is no prospect of obtaining an award under the national soft-loan scheme.

Other minor 'national' regional incentives include soft loans available as reconstruction aids after catastrophes such as floods, earthquakes, epidemics, or because of especially acute political situations (e.g. in some areas around Trieste). In addition, and limited to the *Mezzogiorno*, there are three other minor incentives: a 25 per cent reduction in electricity tariffs for firms with electrical-power requirements below 30 kW (important only to the smallest of firms); a (similarly unimportant) 50 per cent reduction of the indirect tax on the consumption of electricity for all firms, irrespective of size; and a total exemption from the taxes on oil and natural gas for firms located in the — very few — provinces where these are extracted.

As noted earlier, besides these nationally administered incentives the autonomous regions also run their own schemes. The importance of these incentives is, however, very limited in terms of expenditure involved, especially when compared with the main state schemes. Among the autonomous-region schemes is a combined grant and soft-loan scheme in Sardinia, for industrial projects within the scope of the second 'Sardinia Rebirth Plan'. The aids under this plan are largely in favour of areas of 'regional interest', small projects and problem sectors (like mining) related to local resources. In Sicily there is a soft-loan scheme for industrial projects, covering fixed investment and stocks. A soft-loan scheme is also run for small and medium-sized firms involved in large orders which require several months of production time and give rise to problems of liquidity. Among the autonomous regions in the north, the Aosto Valley region gives grants and soft loans to industrial projects located in specified areas. In addition, 'extraordinary' grants are available for the purchase of industrial land. In the autonomous province of Trento interest subsidies on loans are available for small and medium-sized firms located in specified areas, as well as grants and interest subsidies (not tied to the size of firms) for the purchase of industrial land. The autonomous province of Bolzano also offers interest subsidies for industrial projects of small and medium-sized firms as well as soft loans for the purchase of industrial land, again irrespective of the size of firm. The autonomous region of Friuli-Venezia Giulia runs two soft-loan schemes for industrial projects, and gives grants of up to 20 per cent of investment in new plants and up to 12 per cent in extensions.

Clearly the Italian regional-incentive package is very extensive. But it is also, by European Community standards, very expensive. For example, over 1,000 milliard lire was foregone by INPS in respect of the social-security concession in 1977. *Cassa*-grant expenditure has also been high, reaching a peak of 376 milliard lire in 1974, but then dropping to just 268 milliard lire in 1977 as a result, above all, of a fall in the general level of investment. For soft loans, expenditure figures are more difficult to come by, the national soft-loan scheme having only recently been brought into operation. However, it is estimated that, in 1977, interest subsidies in the south amounted to just over 200 milliard lire. As far as the ILOR and IRPEG concessions are concerned, no information is available on exchequer revenue foregone. Nevertheless, it can be hazarded that spending for the incentive package *as a whole* is in excess of 1,500 milliard lire in the south — a high level in comparison with other European Community countries.

The Main Incentives

Building on the basic information so far provided, we wish in this section to describe the main regional incentives in Italy in detail, concentrating in particular on eligibility conditions and award levels. It is, however, interesting to note at the outset some more general administrative features. We have already mentioned that the SCIs and the *Cassa* have an important role to play in the administration of the soft-loan scheme. Within this scheme, the main function of the SCIs is to lend funds to applicant firms either from their own resources or through state-provided 'endowment funds' or 'rotation funds'. Since the SCIs operate according to commercial criteria, much of their effort is devoted to checking the financial viability of project submissions and the general business standing of applicants. Only with the agreement of an SCI to offer a loan can application then be made to the *Cassa* and to the Minister for the South for a subsidy on that loan (outside the south, applications are submitted through the SCI to the Ministry of Industry). The role of the *Cassa* in the system is to decide whether or not to award interest subsidies in respect of SCI loans. In checking applications, the *Cassa* concentrates on the technical-economic viability and eligibility of projects, and on their further needs in terms of assistance, infrastructure and other incentives. For his part, the Minister for the South (and in special cases the CIPI — the 'Interministerial Committee on Industrial Policy') checks the regional impact of projects to be aided and, above all, their *conformity* with national, regional and other economic and territorial planning.

This three-fold examination of applications is found also as part of the *Cassa* capital-grant scheme, which is not surprising since capital-grant and soft-loan applications are often considered jointly. The SCI decides on the financial viability of the project and the economic situation and reputation of the applicant; the *Cassa* determines the value of the award in addition to checking the technical and economic feasibility of the project; and the Minister for the South (or, in the case of large projects, the CIPI) checks conformity with national and other plans. Not unexpectedly, this three-fold checking of applications and setting of award conditions has, in the past, had the drawback of causing delays and administrative duplication. In 1976, however, steps were taken to improve the procedure administratively and to speed up the processing of applications.

The administration of both the various tax concessions and the INPS social-security concession is far simpler, and avoids the risks of unnecessary delay present in the capital-grant/soft-loan schemes. To obtain a tax concession the applicant simply submits a written statement to the tax authorities, claiming that he is eligible for the incentives. The tax officials then have to check whether the eligibility conditions are indeed met and, if their examination proves positive, the award follows automatically through the tax system. The award of a social-security concession is also largely automatic. On the basis of a questionnaire (supplied by INPS) on the composition of their labour force, employers can readily calculate their net INPS liabilities and are then allowed to withhold the concession when making their social-security payments.

Eligibility Conditions

One reason for the simplicity of the administrative procedures surrounding the social security and tax concessions is that these incentives are available more or less automatically to applicants who meet the conditions of award laid down and, in addition, involve straightforward flat-rate payments (i.e. there is no administrative discretion in the setting of rates of award). Moreover, with one exception, the conditions of award set do not discriminate on other than spatial lines. As far as the INPS social-security concession is concerned, for example, the only notable condition of award, apart from the fact that the jobs created must be located in the *Mezzogiorno*, is that they must be permanent jobs. The tax concessions, too, are limited to *Mezzogiorno* projects, apart from the ten-year ILOR concession which is also available in the centre-north. And indeed it is in respect of the centre-north element of this concession that the single element of non-spatial discrimination within the tax- and social-security-concession schemes arises, the concession being restricted to very small firms having current assets of less than two milliard lire.

In contrast, and despite the fact that they are much more straightforward than their predecessors, the *Cassa* grant and the national-soft-loan scheme exhibit a relatively high degree of discrimination by European standards — and not only along spatial and size lines, but also in terms of sector and project type. Beginning with spatial and size discrimination, soft loans are available in the *Mezzogiorno* only on projects of less than 15 milliard lire (including, in the case of extensions, existing plant), while being restricted in the insufficiently developed zones of the centre-north to firms with current assets of less than seven milliard lire and elsewhere in the centre-north to firms with current assets of less than four milliard lire. As if these restrictions were not enough, assisted projects must involve less than five milliard lire of 'global' investment (i.e. fixed investment plus 'technically necessary stocks' covering up to 40 per cent of total investment) in the insufficiently developed zones of central Italy, less than three milliard lire in the insufficiently developed zones of northern Italy and less than two milliard lire in the remainder of the centre-north. Intraregional differences are also present in respect of the concessionary interest rates offered — these being, as noted earlier, 70 per cent below the reference rate in the *Mezzogiorno*, 60 per cent below in the insufficiently developed areas of the centre and north and 40 per cent below in the rest of the country. Finally, loan coverage can be up to 60 per cent of global investment in the problem areas of the centre-north, up to 50 per cent of global investment elsewhere in the centre-north (where, it must be emphasised, the concession is available only to modernisation projects) and up to 40 per cent of global investment in the *Mezzogiorno*.

It can be seen that the national-soft-loan scheme consistently favours small over large projects and the *Mezzogiorno* over the rest of Italy, except in respect of loan coverage, where, as just noted, a higher proportion of global investment is eligible for soft-loan assistance in the centre-north than in the south. There is, however, good reason for this apparent anomaly. In the *Mezzogiorno*, but not in the centre-north, capital grants are also available within the regional-incentive package. Since all southern projects which obtain a soft loan are almost certain to be in receipt of a basic *Cassa* grant, since, as will become clear below, the basic grant for a soft-loan-assisted project (i.e. a project of less than 15 milliard lire) is at least 26 per cent of eligible investment and since, together, the basic *Cassa* grant and the soft loan cannot cover more than 70 per cent of project investment (it being a condition of award that the remaining 30 per cent take the form of 'own finance'), then the maximum possible coverage of the national soft loan in the *Mezzogiorno* is, in any event, close to 40 per cent of project costs.

Although project size is of considerable importance within the soft-loan scheme, it is perhaps even more important as far as the *Cassa* grant is concerned. Indeed it determines the basic rate of grant award. Projects of up to 2 milliard lire get 40 per cent of fixed investment as a grant, projects of between 2 and 7 milliard lire receive between 40 and 33 per cent, those of between 7 and 15 milliard lire obtain grants of between 33 and 26 per cent and those of over 15 milliard lire receive grant awards of less than 26 per cent. The precise percentage award is determined by a quota system whereby the first 2 milliard lire of eligible investment is aided at 40 per cent, the next 5 milliard lire at 30 per cent, the following 8 milliard lire at 20 per cent and all further eligible project investment at 15 per cent. The basic grant is increased by one-fifth if the project belongs to a designated priority sector, or is located in a priority area. When both conditions are met, these increases are cumulated, so that a priority-sector project located in a priority area receives an award two-fifths above the basic grant level.

The fact that the *Cassa* grant favours particular priority sectors is the sole example of sectoral discrimination in terms of rates of award within the Italian package. In terms of award conditions, all incentives are reserved basically for 'industrial' projects. Non-industrial economic activities like agriculture, transport, construction, banking, insurance, public administration, commerce and tourism are normally ineligible — at least under the main incentive schemes — unless they use modern technology (e.g. food processing and computer centres).

As for project-type eligibility/discrimination, it is especially interesting to note that, within the soft-loan scheme, setting-up projects are treated favourably in the *Mezzogiorno* but discriminated against in the centre-north. On the one hand, loan duration for setting-up projects in the *Mezzogiorno* is a maximum of 15 years with a 5-year repayment holiday (as against 10 and 3 years respectively for all other project types), while, on the other, setting-up projects (and expansions) are totally ineligible for national soft-loan assistance in the centre-north outside of the insufficiently developed zones while modernisation *is* aided.

Award Levels

In the Italian context, it makes sense in any discussion of eligibility conditions to include, also, information on nominal/advertised rates of award since, as we have just seen, there is in fact considerable rate discrimination by area, size, sector and project type. This information on nominal rates of award is not repeated in this section; rather, we concentrate on a group of factors which have the effect of reducing the nominal value of any given award and which thus determine the effective value of that award — eligible items and forms of expenditure; incentive tax treatment; and the timing and phasing of award.

For national soft loans the term 'eligible items of expenditure' covers land purchase, land preparation, buildings, plant and equipment, mains connections and on-site vehicles (and indeed off-site vehicles if they are part of the production process, e.g. mixer lorries). It also includes 'technically necessary stocks' up to the point where these represent 40 per cent of total investment. The very same items of expenditure are relevant for the ILOR concession on reinvested profits. For *Cassa* grants, however, the list is somewhat curtailed with both stocks and land purchase (and land preparation) being ineligible for assistance. While it is quite normal for stocks not to be assisted as part of capital-grant schemes in the European Community, the ineligibility of land purchase and site preparation is unusual. As for the social-security concession, it is, of course, not related to eligible items of capital expenditure as such, but is instead couched in terms of the wages bill. In this regard, it should be noted that between 1968 and 1976 the concession was calculated with reference to wages as used in the calculation of contributions to the INPS compulsory-unemployment scheme and explicitly excluded overtime. The new 'total' concession introduced in 1976 is, in contrast, based on wages as determined for the old-age-pension scheme, with the result that overtime payments are included.

Another factor affecting the effective value of asset-related incentive awards (i.e. grants and loans) is whether certain forms of asset finance are eligible for aid. Of particular importance is the treatment of leasing and hire purchase. Up until 1976, and in common with the position in most other European Community countries, leasing was an ineligible form of expenditure under both the *Cassa* grant and the national-soft-loan schemes. Since virtually every industrial project in the *Mezzogiorno* since the early 1960s has been an aided project, the result has been that the leasing sector has remained largely underdeveloped there — at least in comparison with the centre-north. To remedy this situation, regulations were issued in 1976 to allow for leasing to be aided under the *Cassa*-grant/national-soft-loan schemes by assisting the lessor and then requiring that the subsidy be passed on through lower leasing instalments. For technical reasons, however, hire purchase remains an ineligible form of finance.

Turning now to the tax treatment of incentives, all the Italian incentives (with the exception of the ILOR and IRPEG concessions) are taxed in as far as they give rise to higher taxable profits. The social-security concession increases taxable profits by reducing labour costs, while the loan concession has the same effect by lowering interest payments and hence tax-offsettable debt-servicing charges. For *Cassa* grants the position is more complex. Although, strictly speaking, grants are an item of company income (and hence would normally pass directly into income and therefore taxable profits) it is possible to allocate them to a tax-free reserve. If they are then released from this reserve when losses are being made they will not, in practice, be taxed. But even though the social-security concession, *Cassa* grants and the concessionary element of national soft loans are (in theory at least) taxed, since they all give rise to higher taxable profits, the impact of taxation on the effective value of these incentives is not necessarily major. In the first place, there are significant delays in the payment of tax in Italy (although these are currently being reduced) and second, and much more important, the ILOR and IRPEG concessions mean that the tax burden borne by assisted projects is often not great.

The final factor affecting the effective value of the Italian incentives is the timing and phasing of their award. Tax concessions start in the year when profits are first made and run for ten consecutive years thereafter. Tax declarations are made one year after the relevant financial year, and tax demands are sent out a further year later. As a result, the concession is 'paid' after a delay of at least two years. However, advance tax-payment systems, which will of course reduce this delay, are gradually being introduced. The social-security concession does not involve any 'payment' as such, since it takes the form of a withholding of social-security contributions. Timing and phasing does not therefore have an impact on its effective value.

Both processing and payment delays are more serious in the case of loans and grants. As we have seen, the application-processing procedure for both is broadly the same. The SCI and the *Cassa* need, together, up to six months to carry out their various investigations (for small projects, three months) and a further month is required before the *parere il conformita* (the official statement of the Minister for the South certifying conformity of the project with national economic and other planning) is issued. Loans, once awarded, can be drawn down according to need and, if the award is delayed, bridge finance at subsidised interest rates is available for a period of up to two years. As for grants, claims for payment can only be made when individual parts of the project are completed; 80 per cent of the respective part of the grant is paid some two months later. The residual 20 per cent can only be claimed after completion of the whole project and after verification by the authorities, with a delay of roughly four months between claim and payment.

As a result of these various factors — incentive tax treatment, eligible items and forms of expenditure, and the timing and phasing of incentive award — the effective value of the main regional incentives in Italy is obviously significantly lower than their nominal value. Nevertheless, as we shall see in the next section, the Italian regional-incentive package is, in effective-value terms (as it is in terms of nominal rates of award), among the most valuable in the European Community.

Comparative Conclusions

From the above description of the Italian regional-incentive package there are quite clearly many respects in which it compares favourably with others on offer in the European Community. It includes, for example, a very wide range of incentive types and indeed only an accelerated-depreciation allowance is missing from the line-up of major incentives. But such an allowance would, in any event, probably be superfluous in the Italian regional-incentive context, given the large variety of tax concessions available to firms. Within the European Community, perhaps only in Northern Ireland is a comparable range of main incentive types on offer.

Another measure of the relative generosity of the Italian regional-incentive scheme is the level of incentive expenditure. In the south alone, over 1,000 milliard lire per year is spent on social-security concessions together with over 250 milliard lire on *Cassa* grants and more than 200 milliard lire on interest subsidies. No information is available on the amount paid out in the form of tax concessions, but the regional-incentive package as a whole must surely be worth well over 1,500 milliard lire annually — at current exchange rates considerably in excess of expenditure elsewhere in the European Community.

The Italian system is also generous in that there are few constraints on the cumulation of the four main incentive types — capital grants, soft loans, social-security concessions and tax concessions. We noted in the previous section that projects in receipt of *Cassa* grants and/or national soft loans must be at least 30 per cent 'own-financed'. However, for the purposes of this limit only the basic grant is taken into account, so that a small priority-sector project located in a priority area (and therefore eligible for a 56 per cent grant instead of the basic 40 per cent grant) could have as much as 96 per cent of project costs covered by a grant and loan in combination, and yet still be 30 per cent 'own-financed'. This, plus the fact that neither the social-security concession nor the ILOR and IRPEG concessions are constrained by cumulation rules, means that Italian regional incentives *as a package* can reach very high values for aided projects.

In effective-value terms, too, the Italian regional aids show up well compared to others in the European Community, the *Cassa* grant and national soft loan in combination being worth more than twice the value of all other regional-incentive packages except those in Ireland and Northern Ireland. For larger projects, the incentive element is of course less (both because of a lower rate of *Cassa* grant and because national soft loans are limited to projects of less than 15-milliard-lire eligible investment) but once the social-security concession and the various tax concessions are taken into account, then, even for the largest of projects, the Italian regional-incentive package is among the best in the European Community in effective-value terms.

The relatively high value of the Italian package is reflected, too, at the level of its component incentives. The *Cassa* grant, for example, has a maximum nominal value (56 per cent of eligible investment) on a par with the maximum capital-grant awards in both Ireland (60 per cent) and Northern Ireland (50 per cent), and well in excess of grant awards elsewhere in the European Community, all such awards being 25 per cent or less of eligible investment. In effective-value terms, too, the Italian capital grant has a high maximum value when viewed from a European perspective not only because of the high nominal rate of award but also because the grant is not in practice taxed, suffers comparatively short claim-processing delays (as we have seen, 80 per cent of any claim is met almost immediately) and has a relatively broad coverage (and this despite the fact that the ineligibility of 'land costs' for assistance is rare in the Community among project-related grants).

Apart possibly from its high value, perhaps the most interesting comparative feature of the *Cassa* grant is the extent to which it is size-related. Nowhere else in the European Community does project size play such an important role in a capital-grant scheme. On the other hand, there are no further conditions of award attached to the *Cassa* grant, except that assisted projects must be viable. The absence of major conditions of award (and in particular the condition that jobs must be created) is perhaps another feature which distinguishes the *Cassa*-grant scheme from most other project-related grants in Europe.

Turning now to the second element of the Italian regional-incentive package, the national soft loan, this too is generous by European Community standards, particularly in terms of the available interest subsidy. In the *Mezzogiorno* the concessionary rate of interest, as we have seen, is set 70 per cent below the reference rate such that the southern interest subsidy is of the order of 10 percentage points, compared with between 5 and 7 percentage points in Belgium and about 3 percentage points in Denmark, Germany and the United Kingdom (the other European Community countries offering regional soft-loan assistance). Since, in terms of loan coverage, loan duration and principal-repayment holidays, the Italian loan is either in line with or more favourable than loans on offer elsewhere in Europe, it is not surprising that it has the highest loan-effective value in the European Community – and, indeed, is worth as much as many of the capital grants on offer in the Community countries in net-grant-equivalent terms.

Another element of Italian soft-loan generosity is that working capital is eligible for assistance where it takes the form of 'technically necessary stocks' (covering up to 40 per cent of fixed-capital investment). Of all the other grants and loans on offer throughout the European Community only the selective-financial-assistance loans and interest-relief grants available in the United Kingdom similarly subsidise working capital. As with the *Cassa*-grant scheme, the national soft loan favours small projects; for example, aid is being limited in the south to projects of less than 15 milliard lire. It also, as we have seen, differentiates by project type and, although available nationally, discriminates strongly in favour of the *Mezzogiorno*. By European standards, it therefore exhibits a relatively high degree of discrimination (along spatial, size and project-type lines). It does this, however, with comparatively little recourse to administrative discretion.

Few incentive packages in the European Community have one or other of the two remaining main incentive types on offer in the Italian problem regions, and none has both. The social-security concession is, as such, unique in Europe (although regional labour subsidies of a different form are found in the United Kingdom and, on a very small scale, in Belgium), while, outside Italy, profits-tax concessions are available only in Luxembourg and Ireland. Given this, there is not a great deal which can be said about these incentives from an internationally comparative point of view. We should perhaps simply emphasise that, like the other major Italian incentives, they are administered in a basically non-discretionary fashion, being awarded more or less automatically to applicants who fulfil the set (and easy-to-meet) conditions of award.

The general (but obviously not complete) absence of discretion in incentive award is in fact one of the features which typifies the current Italian approach to incentive policy. A further typical feature, as we have seen, is the emphasis on the promotion of small firms and projects. Finally, and to return to an earlier theme, Italian regional-incentive policy compares favourably with others in Europe — in respect of incentive coverage, incentive expenditure and incentive values. Indeed, the entire Italian approach to regional policy is a generous one. In addition to a wide-ranging and valuable incentive policy, state industry probably plays a more structured and active role to encourage the problem regions than in any other European Community country, and Italy is also one of the few countries which operates a disincentive policy, albeit with little obvious success. But the generosity and intensity of policy in Italy is surely only to be expected given the scale and intensity of the Italian regional problem. For many observers, the problems of the *Mezzogiorno* are the most critical problems facing the Italy of today.

Notes

1. There is a vast literature on the problems of southern Italy, collected in a number of anthologies. See, for example, Rosario Villari (ed.), *Il Sud nella Storia d'Italia:Antologia della Questione Meridionale*, 5th edn. (2 vols., Laterza, Bari, 1974). Among the English-language literature, see Kevin Allen and M.C. MacLennan, *Regional Problems and Policies in Italy and France* (Allen and Unwin, London, 1970); K.J. Allen and A.A. Stevenson, *An Introduction to the Italian Economy* (Martin Robertson, London, 1975); Vera Cao-Pinna, 'Regional Policy in Italy' in N.M. Hansen (ed.), *Public Policy and Regional Economic Development* (Ballinger, Cambridge, Mass., 1974), pp. 137-79; and J.L. Sundquist, *Dispersing Population:What America Can Learn from Europe* (Brookings, Washington DC, 1975), Ch. 4.

2. Another rather peculiar, but typically Italian, point might be noted in the context of Italian land use and urban planning. The whole of Italy is endowed with historical sites and monuments of great international, scientific and touristic value. Any modern development encounters not only the standard ecological and environmental problems, but serious value conflicts about how much of the historical inheritance can be sacrificed to economic development.

3. For the theoretical underpinning to the new policy, see P. Saraceno, *Lo Sviluppo Economico dei Paesi Sovrapopolati* (Editrice Studium, Rome, 1962).

4. For more details, see Allen and MacLennan, *Regional Problems and Policies*, pp. 318-27.

5. A description of 'planned bargaining' in English is given in L. Guantario, 'Planned Bargaining in Italy' in *Review of the Economic Conditions in Italy*, no. 2 (1975), pp. 132-41. For a more extensive analysis, see S. Petriccione, *Politica Industriale e Mezzogiorno* (Laterza, Bari, 1976), pp. 43-84.

8 REGIONAL INCENTIVES IN LUXEMBOURG

With a surface area of just 1,000 square miles and a population of only 350,000, the Grand Duchy of Luxembourg is far and away the smallest member of the European Community. The size of the country, and perhaps more especially its strong dependence on the neighbouring countries of Belgium (to which Luxembourg has been joined by an economic union since 1921), Germany (the main purchaser of Luxembourg's products) and France (after Germany and Belgium Luxembourg's third most important trading partner) mean that the Luxembourg policy-maker must take a broad European perspective when considering national problems and developing policies to tackle these problems. Certainly, in the case of incentive policy, developments in neighbouring states have had an important bearing on the Luxembourg policy. Some observers would even go as far as to argue that incentive policy in Luxembourg is basically a defensive reaction to the proliferation of incentives elsewhere in Europe.

It is of course not easy to identify a 'regional problem' in the normally accepted sense of the term in a country of Luxembourg's size, and indeed there are no officially designated problem areas — although the country is divided into four regions for planning purposes. In the north and east regions the prime problem is the continuing and considerable decline of the agriculture sector. Accounting for over one-fifth of the national labour force in 1960, agriculture employment had fallen to just over 9 per cent of the labour force by the mid-1970s. In the industrialised south and west regions, in contrast, the basic problem is that of over-concentration on the steel industry. Throughout the 1950s almost one-half of the industrial labour force was employed in iron and steel making and, even in recent years, as much as one-third of the industrial labour force has been so employed.

As part of the planning programme adopted in 1971, the Luxembourg authorities took on the objective of assuring reasonable long-term equilibrium between the different planning regions and, more specifically, of holding residential population in each of the regions at current levels. In line with this objective, policy measures, including incentive policy, have aimed at avoiding a rundown of the north and east with an associated loss of private and public capital, while also trying to diversify the industrial base in the south and west.

157

Given the general European and regional background outlined above, the Luxembourg government has undertaken a variety of measures to stimulate economic growth, strengthen the general industrial structure and rectify regional disequilibria. Incentives were first introduced in the General Frame Law of 1962 and the package has been further developed by amending legislation in 1967 and 1973. Although this legislation is strongly oriented towards sectoral imbalances in the economy, and in particular the excessive concentration on a limited number of industries, the regional-equilibrium aspect is certainly not ignored. It is, for example, stipulated in the law (Article 1, Paragraph 2) that aided projects must both comply with the requirements of general country planning and be conducive to the expansion and improvement of the economic structure of the Grand Duchy or to the better territorial distribution of economic activities.

In the next section the main incentive types on offer under the most recent General Frame Law (that of 1973) are described briefly, before concentrating, in the section thereafter, on the two most important measures — a capital grant and a tax concession. The chapter ends with a section which draws out a number of comparative conclusions.

The Current Incentive Package

The main incentives on offer under the General Frame Law of 1973 are interest subsidies, loan guarantees, grants to cover organisational studies and related activities, capital grants and tax concessions. Although only the last two have been used to any significant extent, it is nevertheless worth describing the other incentives at least briefly here since, given the current problems of the steel industry, they may well play a more prominent role in the future.

Beginning with the interest subsidy, this is very similar to that on offer in neighbouring Belgium, the maximum subsidy being three percentage points per annum for a maximum of five years in respect of 75 per cent of the eligible project costs of medium-term loans. Eligible costs for the purposes of the subsidy are fairly wide-ranging — covering organisation and market studies, research and development expenditure on new products and production methods, training and retraining costs and also expenditure on anti-pollution plant and equipment, in addition to items more normally covered by financial incentives like land, building and plant costs. For many years interest subsidies were of considerable importance within the Luxembourg incentive package. Recently, however, the tendency has been to offer capital grants instead (the two incentive types are mutually exclusive), and indeed in 1976 no interest subsidy was awarded.

In addition to the interest subsidy, the government can offer guarantees on up to 40 per cent of a loan. However, these guarantees are restricted to enterprises which finance a substantial proportion of project costs from their own funds and which are themselves financially sound. They are moreover reserved for special cases and have not been used up until now. Two further measures under the 1973 law have similarly not yet been used — government powers to acquire land or buildings for subsequent letting or sale to industrial enterprises, and grants to aid a whole miscellany of activities including organisation, management and promotion studies; mergers; and capital-good sales outside the European Community. Rather, as already noted, the main emphasis has been on the capital grant and the tax concession.

The capital grant is the basic Luxembourg incentive. It is a discretionary project-related grant on up to 15 per cent of eligible investment costs although, as we shall see, actual awards tend to be very much lower than this. Over the period 1974-6 some 44 grants were approved to the total value of FLx 219 million — less than £4 million. In the same period, eight tax concessions were awarded. The tax concession is a fixed 25 per cent relief from taxable profits created by a new enterprise or production line for the first eight years of its existence. Normally, tax concessions are awarded only in combination with capital grants, and indeed they can be viewed as a form of 'topping up' the grant. Although there is no formal limit to any tax-concession award, all aided projects in receipt of Luxembourg government assistance amounting, in total, to more than 15 per cent of eligible investment costs or FLx 120 million must be submitted to the European Commission for approval. Only three projects have so far been submitted for such approval (all because of the FLx 120 million maximum) and in no case was approval withheld. In the next section the tax concession and the capital grant are considered in further detail.

The Main Incentives

In common with the administration of the other incentives on offer in Luxembourg, the administration of the capital grant and the tax concession is the responsibility of a special commission drawn from the 'interested' government departments — Economics (two members), Finance (two members) and Labour (one member). Although this commission is, in law, only a consultative body, the Minister of Economics (who, together with the Minister of Finance, has the final decision) almost always accepts its recommendations. Perhaps the key point to make about the work of this commission is that it is probably less narrowly constrained than in other countries by the law (since award conditions are only very broadly specified) or by precedents (since so very few cases are processed). Far more so than in other countries, each case can be considered 'on its merits' both as regards eligibility conditions and award levels.

Eligibility Conditions

Under the General Frame Law of 1973, as already noted, award conditions are broadly drawn. There is, for example, no spatial restriction to the award of a capital grant (the whole country being eligible) nor are particular activities explicitly excluded. Only in terms of project type are there some limitations — with setting-up projects, conversions and the re-orientation and rationalisation of enterprises being the sole types of project explicitly eligible for capital-grant aid. However, since most investment could undoubtedly be classified under one or other of the above project types, even these restrictions are not in practice very significant.

Despite the relative degree of legislative freedom as regards project eligibility there are, of course, practical restrictions on eligibility (even if it is not always easy to identify general policy because of the limited number of awards). In terms of activity aided, the main factors which appear to be taken into account by the special commission, in addition to the viability of the project, are the extent to which it fits into the local economy (an obviously essential condition in such a small country), the degree to which it helps to diversify the economy (also vital, bearing in mind the overdependence on steel) and its capital intensity (a direct consequence of the fact that Luxembourg's active population is only 150,000 and that unemployment rates have tended to be very low). As a result, aid is, in practice, restricted more or less to the manufacturing sector, although certain services and research and development companies may qualify if strongly linked to industry. In respect of spatial coverage, there is also evidence of some discrimination in practice, even although the grant is available country-wide. During the 1950s and 1960s new firms tended to locate (and be aided) in the agricultural north and east, and in so doing helped to absorb the reserves of manpower liberated from the agricultural sector. Recently, with the down-turn in steel, the interest has swung to the remainder of the country as doubts have grown about the ability of the steel industry to provide secure future employment. Finally we should repeat that, although there is no specific size limitation, aided projects of over FLx 120 million (or 15 per cent of eligible investment) must be notified to the European Commission for approval.

The conditions of award for the tax concession are very similar to those for the capital grant – which is not surprising since, as already noted, the two incentives are commonly administered. The one additional condition, and it is key, is that a new enterprise or production line must be created (since the concession relates to profits generated by new enterprises/production lines). As a result, the tax concession is restricted solely to the manufacturing sector; and moreover to setting-up projects and genuine extensions within manufacturing. That less than one-fifth of capital-grant-aided projects in the period 1974-6 were also in receipt of a tax concession is, however, less due to this condition than to the fact that the tax concession (in contrast to just about every other fiscal aid on offer within the European Community) is administered in a discretionary manner, being reserved solely for projects of particular benefit to the Luxembourg economy.

Award Levels

We have already seen that the maximum capital grant which can be offered amounts to 15 per cent of eligible investment. Within this limit the special administrative commission has complete freedom in the setting of award levels (except, as noted above, in those few cases where the European Commission must be notified). In practice, actual awards have tended to be very much lower than the maximum, and indeed the maximum award has never actually been made. In fact, the average award was only 5 per cent of eligible investment in 1974, 6 per cent in 1975 and 8 per cent in 1976 – very low levels by European standards, and this despite the fact that the competitiveness of the award *vis-à-vis* the incentives on offer in neighbouring countries is, as mentioned above, apparently one of the factors taken into account in making the award decision. Of course, the tax concession can be used to raise the level of award. However, less than one-fifth of aided projects in the period 1974-6 were in receipt of such a concession, and in no case did the tax concession and capital grant in combination exceed 15 per cent of eligible investment costs.

The average value of the Luxembourg capital grant is, as we have seen, markedly less than its maximum value. Its value to applicants is further reduced by a number of other factors. First, the grant is indirectly taxed wherever taxable profits are made, since aided investment can only be depreciated for tax purposes net of any grant received. Only where taxable profits were not being made would the grant not be taxed, although receipt of a tax concession would obviously considerably reduce tax liabilities. Second, the grant is normally not paid until completion of the project, although advance payments may be available where delays are especially severe. Finally, certain items of expenditure – in particular, working capital – do not qualify for assistance. Eligible items include land, buildings and equipment (including leased buildings and equipment) together with more intangible investment like market studies, the development of new products and labour training. Although not out of line with other capital grants in the Community countries in terms of tax treatment, timing and phasing and item coverage, these factors – combined with the low nominal rates of award noted above – mean that the Luxembourg capital grant (and, as a result, the Luxembourg incentive package as a whole) has a very low effective value by European Community standards.

Comparative Conclusions

Many of the points which distinguish incentive policy in Luxembourg from incentive policy in the other countries of the European Community are a consequence, purely and simply, of the size of the country. It is country size, for example, which makes the designation of problem areas virtually superfluous. It is country size (and the associated low number of applications for assistance) which allows the operation of a highly centralised, highly co-ordinated and highly discretionary incentive system. Indeed, in few other Community countries is there so much administrative discretion, be it in the decision whether or not to make an award or in the level of that award. And it is country size which permits close and informal contacts with applicants, speedy decision-making and a tailoring of awards, wherever possible, to meet applicant needs.

But there are, of course, other interesting features of the Luxembourg incentive package, not related to the size of the country. There is, for example, no requirement to apply for assistance before the start of project construction, and this despite the highly discretionary nature of the Luxembourg aid. Indeed, in the case of the tax concession, application need not be made until the end of the first working year of the new enterprise/production line. The danger of such retrospective awards is that they do not have much influence on the investment and/ or location decisions of applicant firms, and will often represent little more than a windfall gain to these firms. The fact that relatively few incentives are on offer is also of note, particularly since a number of the available schemes have never been used. In addition, it is of interest that the recent preference for the capital-grant scheme over the interest-subsidy scheme (the two, it will be recalled, are mutually exclusive) stems apparently from the relative administrative ease of operating the former. Finally, the late start of the Luxembourg incentive scheme (1962) is worthy of comment. An earlier start to incentive policy was made in almost every other European Community country and, in some, policy dates from the pre-war period.

But perhaps the key feature of the Luxembourg incentives at the present time is their low value. The capital grant, for example, as we have seen, not only has a low maximum nominal value of 15 per cent (elsewhere in the Community, grants are normally up to a maximum of 25 per cent, and in three instances grants of 50 per cent or more can be awarded) but average awards are less than half this maximum. For its part, the tax concession does, of course, raise the value of the package in those (relatively few) instances where it is awarded. But it has never taken the combined capital-grant/tax-concession nominal value to beyond 15 per cent of initial investment costs since, as yet, no case has been referred to the European Commission for breaking this limit. As a result, the Luxembourg incentive package is, in both nominal and effective-value terms, by some margin the weakest in the Community countries.

Despite the relatively low value of the tax concession, there are a number of features associated with it which are of considerable comparative interest. Of particular note is the fact that it is administered in a highly discretionary manner. This contrasts with both Ireland and Italy, the other Community countries to offer profits-tax concessions, where awards are made virtually automatically if the conditions of award are met. Also of interest, it has apparently proven possible in Luxembourg to incorporate the concession within an *ex ante* net-grant-equivalent limit (if only for the purpose of submitting cases to the European Commission for approval). In neither Ireland nor Italy − nor indeed within the European Commission's own co-ordination solution − has such incorporation taken place. Indeed, it is unusual for fiscal concessions of any description to be taken into account in the setting of upper limits to incentive awards.

The overall impression one has of the Luxembourg package is that it reflects a lack of enthusiasm for incentive policy and that incentives are offered primarily because they are available in neighbouring countries. But that Luxembourg should have contented itself with a 'reactive' policy of relatively low value is perhaps only to be expected, given the low levels of unemployment it has experienced over the years and the fairly even spread of economic activity. How long this approach will hold, however, is an open question in the light of the serious problems currently facing the steel industry and the need to secure alternative employment opportunities for the labour which is likely to be shed. Luxembourg has, as we have seen, a sizeable arsenal of incentive weapons, most of which have been little used up until now. It would not be surprising if a more active approach to the operation of incentive policy was to be taken in the future.

9   REGIONAL INCENTIVES IN THE NETHERLANDS

As with most other country chapters in this book, this chapter divides into five sections. The first is concerned with the nature of the Dutch regional problem, and the second with the development of policy in the post-war period. The third section then briefly outlines the current regional incentives on offer, while the fourth describes in detail the main regional aid, the investment premium. A final section draws out a number of comparative conclusions.

The Nature of the Problem

The character of the regional problem in the Netherlands has changed over time. In the immediate post-war period the basic problem was that of structural unemployment in particular pockets of the country. In one of the worst-affected areas, South-East Drenthe, for example, the unemployment rate in 1950 was 15.5 per cent, compared to an average rate for the Netherlands as a whole of less than one-sixth that level.

In the mid-1950s and into the 1960s this problem of structural unemployment in particular areas of the country continued, largely as a consequence of agricultural rundown. Between 1950 and 1970 over 250,000 jobs were lost within agriculture. This basic structural problem was, however, complemented by an increasing recognition of the problems facing the congested areas in the west of the Netherlands, and in particular in the *Randstad* (a horseshoe-shaped agglomeration including Amsterdam and Utrecht on its northern wing and The Hague and Rotterdam in the south). In 1956 an influential report[1] painted a bleak picture of future developments in the congested west and concluded that 'sound decentralisation' was desirable. By 1959 the government had come to the view that regional policy should 'henceforth . . . aim not only at combating regional structural unemployment, but also at the dispersion of industry and economic activities'.[2]

In subsequent years the population-distribution aspects of the regional problem remained very much to the fore and, if anything, increased in importance. One measure of this is that, whereas, as we shall see, incentives were available in the 1950s to encourage migration from the depressed east to the prosperous west, by the mid-1960s unemployed workers were aided only to migrate to so-called development nuclei within the problem areas, while employed workers in the *Randstad* were subsidised to move with their firms to the problem regions. Moreover, the importance attached to the attainment of a suitable distribution of population has meant that, perhaps more so than in any other Western European country, regional policy in the Netherlands has been very closely related to physical planning.[3] We return later to this point.

One final facet of the Dutch regional problem which should be mentioned is the rundown of certain basic industries key to particular localities, and especially the coal industry. Coal mining was concentrated in the area of South Limburg so that, when the decision was taken to rely on other energy sources (and, above all, on natural gas), the potential impact on that region, with its few alternative employment opportunities, was severe. Accordingly, the area was designated a problem area in 1966 and attempts were made to attract industry into it.

There have, therefore, been three prime components to the regional problem in the Netherlands over the years: the problem of under-industrialised rural areas (especially in the north of the country, but also in Zeeland in the south-west); the problem of industrial areas in need of rejuvenation (the prime example here being South Limburg); and the problem of congestion in the west (and obviously especially in the *Randstad*). As already noted, the importance attached to each of these problems has varied over time. In response to these changing perceptions of the problem as a whole, policy has also varied, and this in three main ways — in terms of spatial coverage; in terms of the mix of policy measures (basically infrastructure provision, incentives and disincentives); and, within this broad policy mix, in terms of the incentives themselves. In the next section we examine the development of policy in respect of these three aspects of change.

The Development of Policy

Spatial Coverage

Since the inception of regional policy in the Netherlands in the early 1950s, there has always been a two-tier approach to problem-area designation — first, broadly defined problem areas have been identified and then, within these areas, development nuclei have been selected on which to concentrate the available aid.

In terms of the broadly defined problem areas we have seen that the initial focus of policy was on areas facing high rates of structural unemployment. Where the problem could not be solved by out-migration and where there seemed to be at least potential for cost-effective industrial development, then such areas were designated as Development Areas. By 1951 nine Development Areas had been classified[4] and these remained in force until 1959. In that year, population loss joined structural unemployment among the designation criteria. With the provinces of Groningen, Friesland, Drenthe and Zeeland all suffering net out-migration of over 6 per cent per annum the result was that the coverage of the problem areas increased substantially, more than doubling to include almost half the surface area of the country. Further minor extensions to the designated problem areas were made in the mid-1960s, at which time, too, they were renamed 'Stimulation Areas'. More important than these changes, however, the whole of South Limburg was deemed a 'Reconversion Area' in 1966 after the decision was taken to close down the mines there, and the Tilburg area, heavily reliant on a struggling textiles industry, was also designated as a Reconversion Area in 1968. Thus, by the late 1960s, large areas of the country were either Stimulation Areas or Reconversion Areas, and as such were in receipt of regional assistance.

The trend towards widening problem-area coverage, which was apparent throughout the 1960s and especially in the latter half of the decade, came to an abrupt end in 1971. In that year, as a reflection of the view held by many that designated-area coverage had become too extensive, the designated problem regions were cut back dramatically, to include only the Northern Development Area (i.e. the provinces of Groningen, Friesland, Drenthe and a small part of Overijssel) and the Reconversion Area of South Limburg. Together, these areas account for some 30 per cent of the Dutch land mass and hold about 17 per cent of the population. At the present time they are still the main designated problem areas in the Netherlands, at least as far as the most important regional incentive, the investment premium, is concerned. Recently, however, a new national incentive has been introduced with a marked regional dimension – the WIR (*Wet Investeringsrekening* – 'investment account'). This aid will be discussed in more detail at a later stage but, for the present, it should be noted that, as part of the scheme, a special regional allowance is available in certain areas on top of a basic national premium. These areas are limited only to parts of the Northern Development Area and South Limburg, as Figure 9.1 shows, and in fact cover little over 10 per cent of the country as a whole. As far as broad area designation is concerned, therefore, the trend in the 1970s has been towards a more concentrated coverage –

quite the reverse of the trend a decade earlier.

We noted above that the Dutch have always adopted a two-tier approach to area designation, aid being concentrated on selected development nuclei within the broadly defined problem regions. The nine Development Areas of the initial policy phase, for example, contained 36 such nuclei; and the total number of nuclei rose from 40 to 44 with the changes made in 1959. For many observers, this represented too many nuclei.[5] In an attempt to reduce their number (and yet avoid the inherent political difficulties of such a move) the Minister of Economic Affairs introduced a distinction between primary and secondary nuclei. The former, 19 in number, were 'those towns which had already shown important industrial development . . . and where . . . conditions justified the expectation of a reasonably successful policy'.[6] Although aid was concentrated on these primary centres, the secondary nuclei remained in existence until the major area-designation changes of 1971. As a result of these changes, it will be recalled, the problem areas were cut back to cover only South Limburg and the Northern Development Area. In South Limburg no development nuclei were identified, aid being available throughout the region. In the Northern Development Area, however, 28 nuclei were designated (basically what had previously been the primary and secondary nuclei in that area). In addition, a number of municipalities outside the designated problem areas were also declared eligible for the investment premium. In May 1975 the geographical coverage of the investment premium was extended to a further ten municipalities, albeit under slightly more stringent conditions of award and in what was stated to be a temporary move brought about by the down-turn in the economy. But in the latest version of the investment premium (dating from June 1977) not only the 28 nuclei in the Northern Development Area plus the whole of South Limburg are eligible for assistance but also 18 nuclei outside these areas (although − and we return to the details of this below − it has to be said that firms in half of these nuclei receive a lower level of award). Clearly, there have been very real difficulties in the Netherlands both of limiting the number of development nuclei (a not uncommon problem in countries which have tried to implement growth-area policies) and of restricting their coverage to the designated problem regions.

Policy Mix

As in many other countries, the first regional-policy measures undertaken in the Netherlands were very much infrastructure-based. In addition to the provision of industrial sites and buildings in the problem regions, they involved road improvements (and improvements to transport infrastructure in general) and the development of public utilities. Such infrastructure policies have remained of considerable importance within the Dutch package (with, in the period 1959-76, over Fl 1,300 million being paid out to municipal and provincial authorities in the development areas in infrastructure subsidies). Over the years, however, they have been joined and complemented by other policy instruments.

Perhaps the most important of these have been financial incentives to firms locating in development nuclei within the designated problem regions. Such incentives were first introduced in 1953 and, despite a number of changes in subsequent years (to be detailed below), have always remained a major part of the package. Far less important have been incentives to individuals to encourage them to migrate. As already mentioned, such incentives initially attempted to encourage unemployed workers to move from the depressed east to centres where jobs were available in the more prosperous west (including the *Randstad*). They were not, however, very successful in this role, fewer than 3,500 unemployed moving as a result of the scheme in the period 1952-8. Later, as the problems of congestion in the west of the country became more apparent, the focus of attention switched to movement *to* the problem regions. Migration aids were used to help unemployed workers move to development nuclei in these regions and employed workers move with their firms to these regions.

For many years it was felt that financial incentives and infrastructure measures together were sufficient to deal with the Netherland's spatial problems. On more than one occasion a disincentive or control policy for the pressured west was rejected by government spokesmen due to 'the infringement it would mean on the present freedom of the entrepreneur to choose his own location and to bear the full responsibility for, and the full risks of, his choice'.[7] However, by the early 1970s, the drawbacks of increasing concentration of both population and economic activity in the west were becoming increasingly apparent. Accordingly, an attempt was made in 1972 to introduce a disincentive policy for the west (basically the provinces of North and South Holland and Utrecht) based on levies, permits and a system of building notification. But it was not until October 1975 that a disincentive-policy instrument, the selective-investment regulation (SIR, *Selectieve Investerings Regeling*) actually came into force.

Growing opposition from the western part of the country (and especially from the business and industrial community there, as well as from the affected municipalities), together with a significant worsening of the economic climate in the Netherlands (as elsewhere in the world), not only delayed the introduction of the measure but also changed its essential character. Instead of being based on a system of levies, the emphasis came to be placed on the need to seek government approval for industrial building and the construction of 'open-air installations' through permit application (indeed the limited levies remaining in the law, as it was brought into force, were suspended in mid-1976). Moreover, both the investment and spatial coverage of the measure were narrower than originally conceived. Permits, for example, were necessary only in the Rijnmond area, centred on Rotterdam. In the remainder of the control zone, notification of building plans was all that was required. Although such advance warning is not without value for the regional authorities, the scheme as eventually introduced was obviously nowhere near the major policy departure that had originally been proposed.

In June 1978 the SIR levies were reintroduced at higher rates and with a wider coverage, taking in not only the Rijnmond area but also most of the remainder of the provinces of North and South Holland and Utrecht, as well as part of Gelderland. However, and this is an important point, their purpose was not the original one of 'taxing congestion'. Rather they were brought in to increase the regional differential present in the WIR scheme (introduced in the previous month) in a way compatible with the rules of the European Commission's Competition Directorate. We discuss these levies and their relationship to the WIR later.

At the same time as the SIR was initially suggested, systematic attempts were made for the first time to disperse government jobs from The Hague on a large scale. True, dispersion had also taken place in the 1960s, but then it had tended to be *ad hoc* and did not involve major transfers of staff. The new attempts, however, met with considerable resistance, not least from the civil servants who would have to move. Although some jobs have been dispersed, and there are plans to transfer more, the prime emphasis now is on situating *new* government jobs wherever possible in the problem regions, rather than on transferring existing jobs. This change of emphasis has not only been the result of the resistance of public servants but can also be attributed to a deteriorating labour-market situation in The Hague.

A further new development with possible regional implications has been the creation of Regional Development Companies (with majority government shareholding), with powers both to take shares in existing companies and to set up new companies. These Development Companies have, however, moved beyond their initial concentration on the Northern Development Area and South Limburg. One has been established in Overijssel and others have been proposed for Gelderland and North-Brabant. Whether these companies can be viewed as true regional-policy weapons is therefore questionable.

One final point to make in this brief description of the various regional-policy instruments available in the Netherlands is that, increasingly, they have become intertwined with spatial-planning measures. The latest example of this, as we shall see, is the favouring of particular growth centres (inside the *Randstad*) and so-called growth cities (outside the *Randstad*) as part of the WIR scheme. Moreover, overall structure plans (*Integraal Structuurplan*) have recently been developed both for the North and for South Limburg, giving a more comprehensive and long-term approach to regional policy in these areas. As already noted, physical planning has probably played a greater role in regional policy in the Netherlands than in any other Western European country.

Regional Incentives

As we have seen, incentives were first introduced into the Dutch regional-policy package in 1953. Under an Act of that year to promote industrial settlement in the development nuclei (*Bevordering Industrievestigung Kerngemeenten*) grants of 25 per cent of the construction costs of industrial buildings were awarded, but only up to a maximum of Fl 25 per m^2 of floorspace — a very serious constraint. Further limiting conditions of award were that ten new jobs had to be created, and that at least one unemployed worker had to be employed for every 50 m^2 of floorspace. Moreover, eligibility was restricted to firms locating in development nuclei in the designated problem regions.

Levels of award were even more strongly linked to floorspace by changes made in 1959. Under a new Act (*Bevordering Industrialisatie Ontwikkelingskernen*) a grant of Fl 35 per m^2 of floorspace was introduced for both extension projects and small setting-up projects (of less than 1,000 m^2) while larger setting-up projects qualified for awards of up to Fl 75 per m^2. As before, there was a requirement to create jobs and to employ the unemployed — one unemployed worker for every 100 m^2 of floorspace for setting-up projects and one for every 50 m^2 for extensions — and, again, eligibility was limited to development nuclei. In contrast, however, to the previous Act, land purchase was for the first time aided, there being a 50 per cent subsidy on municipal-industrial-site purchase on condition that one-fifth of the purchased land was immediately brought into use.

The 1965 measures to stimulate industrial settlement in the development nuclei (*Stimulering Industrievestiging Ontwikkelingskernen*) were also based primarily on floorspace criteria. There were, however, two important differences over the 1959 scheme (in addition to slightly lower rates of award). First, as already noted, a distinction was drawn between primary and secondary development nuclei, rates of award being higher in the former. Second, although jobs still had to be created, there was no requirement to employ the unemployed. Similar, if marginally more generous, measures were introduced in South Limburg following its designation as a Reconversion Area in 1966. But, here, there was an important additional condition — that former miners had to be employed.

Up to this point, incentive policy in the Netherlands had been restricted, in terms of eligible items of expenditure, to buildings and land. It had, moreover, been linked to both floorspace and employment; and for most of the period there had been a requirement to employ the unemployed. In 1967 a new type of incentive was introduced into the incentive system aiming 'particularly to increase its appeal to the technologically advanced, capital-intensive industries that appeared to the Dutch [authorities] . . . to have the power to attract ancillary enterprise to a lagging region'.[8] The new measure, the investment premium (*Investerungs Premie Regeling*) was available on plant and machinery as well as on buildings and land, was totally unrelated to floorspace and carried with it no requirement to create jobs. Initially seen as an alternative to the incentives then in operation (described above), by 1970 it had completely replaced them.

When first introduced, the investment premium was restricted to industrial setting-up projects, but it was extended to industrial extensions and to service setting-up projects (for services of a regionally exporting character) in 1969. In 1975, regionally exporting service extension projects were also brought within the scheme. These changes, plus changes in rates of award, are set out chronologically in Table 9.1.

Before discussing Table 9.1 we should mention that the rates of award shown are fixed rates for projects up to a given size level (of Fl 12 million up until September 1975, of Fl 14 million between September 1975 and June 1977 and currently of Fl 16 million). Larger projects may receive, at the discretion of the authorities, extra awards of *up to* the shown rates in respect of investment beyond the above investment quotas. Thus, an eligible industrial setting-up project will currently receive an automatic fixed 25 per cent award of Fl 4 million towards the first Fl 16 million of project costs and, in addition, *may*

Table 9.1: Rates of Investment-premium Award since Inception

Rate applicable from	Industry		Services	
	Setting-up projects	Extension projects	Setting-up projects	Extension projects
January 1967	25%	—	—	—
January 1969		15%	25%	—
January 1970		10%		—
October 1972		15%		—
May 1975		25%		25%

receive an extra award of *up to* 25 per cent of project costs beyond Fl 16 million. As we shall see, however, the discretionary extra award made to large projects averages well below the possible maximum.

Turning now to the details of Table 9.1, it can be seen that industrial setting-up projects have qualified for a 25 per cent award in respect of the initial investment quota since the start of the investment-premium scheme, and that both service setting-up projects and service extensions have also been eligible for 25 per cent awards in respect of the initial investment quota since being brought within the scheme. Rates of awards for industrial extensions have, in contrast, varied considerably over the years — from 15 to 10 per cent, back to 15 per cent and finally in May 1975 to 25 per cent. At that time, all four eligible project types qualified for 25 per cent awards in respect of the initial investment quota in all the assisted areas. This is also the position at present, except that in June 1977 (and not shown in the table) an element of geographical differentiation was introduced in the form of a 15 per cent award in certain municipalities outside the main problem regions. Like the 25 per cent award, this 15 per cent award is in respect of an initial investment quota currently of Fl 16 million. In addition, a discretionary award of *up to* 15 per cent *may* be available for project costs of beyond Fl 16 million.

The Current Incentive Package

At the present time the investment premium is still by far the most important regional incentive in the Netherlands, and the next section is devoted solely to it. Within the current section we wish to concentrate on other, more minor, elements of the Dutch package.

We begin with the Lelystad employment premium (*Premieregeling Stimulering Ontwikkeling Lelystad*). This premium is available to industrial projects and to service projects of a regionally exporting character

174 *Netherlands*

which set up in Lelystad, a 'new' city in the reclaimed agricultural Ijsselmeerpolder 'Oostelijk Flevoland'. The premium, originally introduced in 1968, takes the form of a grant of Fl 10,000 for every employee employed permanently by an eligible project as long as the employee has moved to Lelystad to take the job and has settled there, with his family. The aim is therefore not only to attract industry (and industry of a reasonable size, since at least 10 employees have to meet the conditions of award for the premium to be paid) but also to bring people to the city.

Despite the fact that it is an employment premium, directly related to the creation of jobs, the Lelystad premium, as we shall see, has much in common with the investment premium. The total award, for example, cannot exceed 25 per cent of fixed investment costs; and is generally limited in absolute terms to Fl 3,500,000 (although the Minister of Economic Affairs does have the discretion to allow awards beyond this limit). In addition, projects must involve eligible fixed investment of more than Fl 400,000, must be at least 35 per cent financed by 'own capital' and must not involve a transfer from other 'assisted areas'. Even in terms of tax treatment the Lelystad premium mirrors the investment premium. Although an *employment* premium, it has to be deducted from the associated *investment* costs for the purposes of calculating tax-allowable depreciation. But, despite these similarities, the Lelystad premium remains, in national terms, relatively insignificant – not least, since it is restricted to Lelystad (a city, incidentally, not encompassed by the investment-premium regulations). Up to July 1977, only 24 awards had been made in respect of 1,086 jobs created (and associated fixed investment of Fl 60.3 million). Moreover, the premium is due to remain in force only until 1980.

A second minor regional incentive in the Netherlands is a concession on the cost of preparing new industrial sites. This aid is available to municipalities in the investment-premium areas, and in the so-called growth nuclei in the west of the country where the cost price of the site (and hence the selling price to industry) would otherwise have been too high, viewed in relation to site prices in surrounding municipalities. But so far only six municipalities have made use of this subsidy – three in the Northern Development Area and three in the northern part of North Holland – even though it has been available since 1975.

In addition to these two minor incentives and the very important investment premium, which we discuss in the next section, there is one further measure which must be mentioned – the recently introduced WIR scheme. Although basically national, the WIR contains some regional differentiation in terms of rates of award and is therefore worth describing in detail here.

The WIR covers almost all types of fixed investment and is taken in the form of reduced tax payments when profits are made and negative tax payments when there are losses. The basic rate of award is 23 per cent for new buildings, 15 per cent for extensions and modifications to existing buildings and for sea-going ships, 13 per cent for 'open-air installations' (e.g. oil refineries), 12 per cent for commercial aircraft and 7 per cent for other eligible fixed investment (and, above all, plant and machinery). *On top of* this basic award, extra allowances are available for small-scale investment, for large projects, for firms which change their location in accordance with Dutch physical planning priorities and for firms located in particular problem regions. But only the last two have a distinct regional component and we therefore concentrate on them. It should, however, be noted in passing that the small-scale allowance is available to entrepreneurs who undertake fixed investment of less than Fl 800,000 in any one year and has a maximum value of 6 per cent of the investment carried out, the actual award varying inversely with the size of the investment, while the large-project allowance is available at the rate of Fl 25,000 per job in respect of those jobs which can be attributed to that part of project investment in excess of Fl 30 million — up to a maximum of 4 per cent of the total investment.

Turning to the extra allowances with regional implications, the physical-planning allowance can be dealt with quickly since its regional component is not major. To be eligible for this extra allowance (of 15 per cent of building costs and 7.5 per cent of open-air installation costs) an entrepreneur must move the whole or part of his activities from those parts of the SIR area not designated as growth nuclei for physical-planning purposes (and there are twelve such nuclei) to the SIR-area growth nuclei or to one of the five 'growth cities' outside the SIR area.[9] However, only two of these cities (Groningen and Leeuwarden) lie within the investment-premium areas, and in the latter only half the standard allowance is available. The physical-planning allowance is therefore of no great material benefit to the problem regions; indeed, by offering firms an extra incentive to locate in non-problem-area locations (which is what the majority of the physical-planning priority nuclei are) it in fact reduces the incentive advantage of the problem regions.

The special regional allowance, the final extra allowance on top of the basic WIR, is available towards investment in buildings (new as well as existing) at a rate of 20 per cent, and towards investment in 'open-air installations' (as long as such investment does not involve a replacement of productive capacity) at a rate of 10 per cent. It is not available towards any other type of investment (and does not, therefore, cover plant and machinery). The areas where the extra regional allowance can be obtained are indicated in Figure 9.1. It can be seen that they are located in the Northern Development Area and in South Limburg, and cover somewhat less than one-half of these, the designated Dutch problem areas.

With a basic allowance plus four extra allowances it might appear as if entrepreneurs in the Netherlands have been given the opportunity to cover a very large proportion of fixed-investment costs through the WIR scheme. There are, however, a number of restrictions to the combination of the available allowances. For example, the small-scale allowance can obviously not be added to the large-project allowance, while none of the physical-planning priority nuclei lie within the special-regional-allowance areas. Moreover, there is an upper limit to WIR awards — 50 per cent of investment in eligible buildings and 25 per cent of investment in eligible fixed installations. But even more restrictive than this from a regional-policy point of view is the ceiling on aid going to any given project imposed as part of the European Commission's regional-policy-co-ordination solution.[10] In the Netherlands this ceiling is such that the differential in favour of the designated problem regions must not exceed 20 per cent of project fixed-investment costs *after tax*. Obviously, with an investment premium of up to 25 per cent of eligible investment costs *before tax* and a WIR special regional allowance of 20 per cent of building costs and 10 per cent of fixed installation costs, this limit is likely to bite (unless of course tax rates were very high and/or building costs were a very small proportion of total investment costs and/or less than the maximum investment premium was awarded). Where it does bite, the investment premium is reduced so as to bring total project assistance within the co-ordination-solution ceiling.

From this, it is clear that the co-ordination-solution ceiling has the effect of reducing the intended differential in favour of the designated problem areas. To re-establish the relative position of these areas, at least to some extent, the SIR levy was reintroduced, as already noted, in June 1978. The levy on new buildings (with construction costs of more than Fl 250,000) is at the rate of 15 per cent of those construction costs in excess of Fl 250,000. Since the levy is viewed as an investment cost for WIR purposes, this is equivalent to reducing the WIR on new buildings in the SIR area to just over 11 per cent of investment

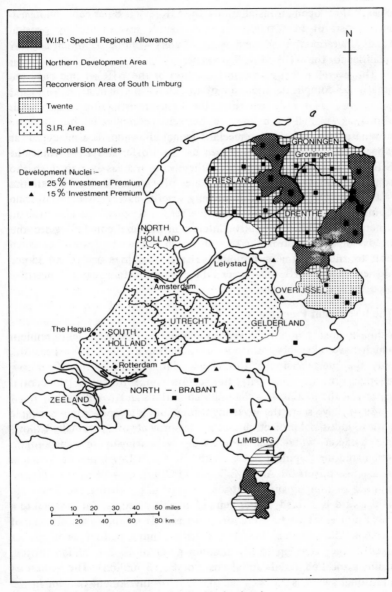

Figure 9.1: Designated Areas in the Netherlands

costs.[11] For 'open-air installations' the SIR levy is 8 per cent (on investment costs of Fl 500,000) and on eligible investments by pension funds, investment funds and savings banks — none of which anyway qualifies for the WIR — it is 5 per cent.

The overall effect of the introduction of the WIR scheme has been greatly to complicate the map of the Dutch problem areas, as Figure 9.1 shows. Not only are there the basic investment-premium areas which, as we shall see below, are themselves complicated, but there are now also areas where the special regional allowance is available, areas where the physical-planning allowance is on offer and areas where the SIR levy is applied. What is more, these various areas overlap at least to some extent. As a result, regional-incentive policy in the Netherlands must be amongst the most spatially discriminatory in the European Community at the present time. We return to this, and also pick up other features of comparative interest in the final concluding section. Before that, we wish in the section which follows to devote our attention to the investment premium. Despite the presence of a regional element to the WIR, this remains the most important regional incentive on offer in the Netherlands.

The Investment Premium

We have already noted the various changes to the investment premium which have taken place since its introduction in 1967. In this section, only the latest version of the scheme, dating from June 1977, is considered. For the most part, the section concentrates on two central aspects of the premium — eligibility conditions and award levels.

As we have seen, the investment premium is a capital grant available both to industrial projects and to service projects of a regionally exporting character, where such projects involve setting-up or expanding in designated development nuclei in the Northern Development Area and in the Reconversion Area of South Limburg, as well as in a limited number of municipalities outside these main problem areas. The standard award is a fixed 25 per cent of eligible fixed-capital costs up to a maximum grant of Fl 4 million (with associated fixed-capital costs of Fl 16 million), except in a few specified municipalities where it is a fixed 15 per cent up to a maximum grant of Fl 2.4 million (giving, again, associated fixed-capital costs of Fl 16 million). The *maximum* additional award is 25 per cent of the *extra* investment (except in the few specified municipalities noted above, where it is 15 per cent) but in practice, and as already noted, the discretionary extra award made to large projects averages well below the possible maximum.

As an alternative to the standard 25 per cent award (but not, it must be stressed, the 15 per cent award), there is also available a so-called 'mixed premium', based on job creation as well as capital expenditure. Under this version of the investment-premium scheme (introduced in September 1975 but, in the event, little used since then) a grant of 15 per cent of eligible fixed investment up to a maximum of Fl 2.4 million is coupled with a premium of Fl 12,500 for every permanent job created (as verified by the local labour office). In this case the maximum 'automatic' award is Fl 5 million (as against Fl 4 million under the standard scheme). As under the standard scheme, there is discretion to make further awards beyond the 'automatic' maximum. This alternative scheme has, however, been so little used up until now that we do not consider it further.

The administration of the investment premium is straightforward. Application is made to the appropriate Regional Development Company (or, in those areas where no such company exists, to the relevant provincial government) before the project starts, and only investment undertaken after the submission of the application is eligible for aid. The Regional Development Company and both provincial and local government – the latter being particularly concerned with possible environmental or physical-planning objections – then submit recommendations on the application to the Ministry of Economic Affairs. The Ministry then decides whether to make an award (in practice, a more or less automatic decision dependent solely on whether the conditions of award are met) and – for large projects – the value of the award. The Ministry is also responsible for the payment of the grant.

Since its introduction, and up until July 1977,[12] 287 industrial setting-up projects (eligible for investment-premium aid since 1967) had received awards to the total value of almost Fl 495 million; 993 industrial extension projects (eligible since 1969) had received awards to the total value of Fl 656 million; 16 service setting-up projects (also eligible since 1969) had received awards of over Fl 21 million; and 38 service extensions (eligible only since 1975) had received just over Fl 22 million worth of awards. In total, then, 1,334 awards had been made by July 1977 to the value of over Fl 1,194 million. Annual average expenditure has therefore been in the region of Fl 100 million, although in recent years, and reflecting both higher rates of award and wider coverage, expenditure has certainly been higher than this (being over Fl 150 million in 1976/7 and almost Fl 240 million in 1977/8). Associated with this expenditure, there has been fixed-capital investment of over Fl 8,700 million since the inception of the scheme and, according to official estimates, the creation of about 60,000 jobs.

Eligibility Conditions

From our description of the investment premium so far, it will be clear that eligibility for an award is determined, amongst other things, by project location, project activity and project type. In this section we wish, first, to consider these eligibility conditions in more detail before setting out some other, no less important, conditions of award.

Beginning with activity coverage, the investment premium is, as we have seen, limited to industrial projects and service projects of a regionally exporting character. Manufacturing is therefore eligible, but both the primary and tourist sectors are not. Nor do local building contractors or local services qualify for the premium, although firms producing building materials (including pre-fabricated housing) are eligible, as are potentially mobile service activities (i.e. those of more than local importance). Finally, it should be noted that laboratories and similar research departments also qualify where it can be shown that they are essential to industrial development.

Turning now to project-type coverage, both setting-up projects and extensions are eligible insofar as they result in an (unspecified) increase in employment or productive capacity. Transfers within the investment-premium area are not eligible, but firms coming from the SIR area to an investment-premium locality do qualify, as long as they do not come from one of the 'growth nuclei' in the SIR area. Moreover, the book value of machinery transferred with a firm making such a move is regarded as fixed-investment costs for investment-premium purposes. All other project types are generally ineligible, though there is provision for a normally ineligible project to be aided if employment is maintained, if the project is of special regional significance and if the investment is in line with industrial restructuring or sectoral policy.

Finally, regarding spatial coverage, industrial setting-up projects are eligible on government-prepared industrial sites in the 28 designated development nuclei in the Northern Development Area; on 'appropriate' industrial sites — generally government-prepared — throughout the Reconversion Area of South Limburg (although in two South Limburg municipalities — Roermond and Melick en Herkenbosch — only the 15 per cent investment premium is available) and on government-prepared industrial sites in a further 18 development nuclei in Overijssel, North-Brabant, Gelderland and Limburg (though in half of these municipalities only the 15 per cent premium is available). The same areas are appropriate for industrial extensions, with the addition of the entire Twente region. Moreover, for industrial extensions, there is no requirement that the project be located either in a development nucleus or on an industrial site.[13] For service setting-up projects and extensions, the Northern Development Area, South Limburg and a further seven municipalities in Overijssel, North-Brabant and Gelderland (all of which are also eligible for the 25 per cent investment premium on industrial projects) are eligible, although once again it should be noted that in Roermond and Melick en Herkenbosch in South Limburg only the 15 per cent premium is available. It should also be mentioned that, while service setting-up projects are bound to the designated development nuclei in the Northern Development Area, service extensions are eligible throughout the area.

Among other eligibility conditions, the most important are that a minimum of Fl 200,000 investment is undertaken (previously Fl 400,000, and before that Fl 500,000); that at least 35 per cent of the fixed-capital costs of the project are 'own-financed'; that after completion of the project there is an acceptable relationship of equity to liabilities (this is evaluated with regard to both the nature of the firm and its return on earnings); that the project involves a permanent new building (either constructed for the project or bought as part of the project); and that the project is consistent both with the regional labour-market situation and with sectoral requirements. As a result of the whole range of eligibility conditions, some 19 per cent of industrial setting-up applications and just over 8 per cent of industrial extensions have been turned down since the start of the investment-premium scheme, together with 13 service projects (from 67 service applications by July 1977). For setting-up projects, turndown is mainly because the financial conditions of award, noted above, are not fulfilled or because the sector concerned is suffering from overcapacity. For extensions, turndown is due, rather, to the fact that applicant projects are often too small and marginal and, as such, do not lead to a sufficient increase in employment or productive capacity.

Award Levels

Leaving the little-used mixed premium to one side, the basic nominal award under the investment-premium scheme is, as we have seen, a fixed 25 per cent of eligible fixed-capital costs where such costs amount to less than Fl 16 million, except in a few specified municipalities in Overijssel, North-Brabant and Limburg,[14] where the basic award is a fixed 15 per cent. On top of this base there is then a discretionary award available for all fixed-capital investment beyond the Fl 16 million limit at rates of up to 25 per cent in the standard case and up to 15 per cent in those few municipalities where 15 per cent is the basic fixed award.

Unfortunately there is no comprehensive information available on annual average award levels over time. We do, however, know the cumulative position up until July 1977. Up until that time the average award for industrial setting-up projects was 16 per cent, reflecting the fact that a significant proportion of these projects were bigger than the upper limit for 'automatic' awards (of Fl 12 million, it will be recalled, in the period up until September 1975, and Fl 14 million between September 1975 and June 1977). For industrial extensions the average was even lower, at 12.1 per cent. This, however, is less a reflection of the size of the extensions undertaken than of the fact that, for most of the period 1969-77, the maximum rate of award for such projects was 15 per cent — and indeed was only 10 per cent between January 1970 and October 1972. For their part, service projects tend on the whole to be relatively small, with the result that the average award was 21.3 per cent and 24.7 per cent for setting-up projects and extensions, respectively.

We noted above that there is no year-by-year information on annual award levels over time, the only long-run data being on a cumulative basis. Since July 1976, however, this cumulative data has been complemented by information on annual awards. This shows that, between July 1976 and July 1978, 38 awards (averaging 18.3 per cent of eligible investment) were made to industrial setting-up projects, 326 awards (averaging 18.9 per cent of eligible investment) went to industrial extension projects and 55 awards (averaging 24.9 per cent of eligible investment) were received by service projects — seven going to service creations. Clearly these percentage figures are very much in line with those in the previous paragraph, the higher industrial-extension percentage in recent years being a direct consequence of the fact that only since May 1975 have such projects qualified for 25 per cent awards in respect of the initial investment quota.

Although actual awards are more representative of what applicant firms actually do receive than the nominal rates of award noted earlier, they are not a measure of the *effective* value of the investment premium to recipient firms. In considering effective value, there are three main factors to be taken into account: the tax treatment of the incentive; the timing and phasing of its award; and both eligible items and eligible forms of expenditure. These are now dealt with in turn.

The tax treatment of the investment premium is relatively straightforward. For tax purposes, aided investment is depreciated net of any premium received. The result is that tax-deductible depreciation allowances are less than they would have been had no investment premium been awarded. In consequence, more tax is paid wherever profits are being made. In effect, therefore, the premium is taxed through the depreciation system. In this, it contrasts with the new WIR scheme. As already noted, the WIR is taken in the form of reduced tax payments when profits are made and negative tax payments when there are losses. It is obviously not, therefore, subject to tax.

Moving on to the timing and phasing of premium payment, awards can in theory only be paid out when the project, or a major part thereof, is operating. In practice, however, advance payments are available on request for blocks of at least 25 per cent of the total fixed-investment costs (the minimum advance being Fl 100,000) — up to a maximum of 75 per cent of the total agreed premium. These advances relate to expenditure already made by the applicant (as verified by an accountant), and obviously significantly reduce possible delays in the payment of award. Indeed, the average delay is probably of the order of only three months or so.

Finally, in the context of effective values, eligible items and forms of expenditure must be considered. For the investment premium, eligible items are restricted basically to fixed-capital expenditure — the purchase costs of land (inclusive of transfer taxes and transfer costs), the construction costs of permanent buildings (inclusive of capital provisions like water, gas, electricity and drainage) and the purchase price of plant and equipment (including second-hand machinery). Tools and implements are not eligible, nor are vehicles or (obviously) working capital — and expenditure on feasibility studies is also excluded. Regarding eligible forms of expenditure, land acquired on a long lease from government authorities — local, regional, provincial — can be aided through subsidising the leasing authorities where they agree to pass the benefits on to the leaseholder in twenty equal instalments. This, however, is the one instance where leased assets are eligible for investment-premium assistance. Hire purchase, too, is a generally ineligible form of expenditure unless the transaction involves a government institution.[15] In contrast, phased payments are allowed if they are limited to three or four instalments and represent an integral part of the delivery arrangements.

Comparative Conclusions

Perhaps the most obvious point to arise from our review of Dutch regional incentives is that there are so few on offer, far fewer than in most other European Community countries. Even taking the regional element of the WIR scheme as a separate incentive, there are nominally only four regional incentives available in the Netherlands. However, because of its limited spatial coverage, the Lelystad employment premium must be viewed as more local than regional (and it is, anyway, due to remain in force only until 1980), while the municipal-industrial-site subsidy has been little used. In addition, as already mentioned, the advantage to be gained from the regional component of the new WIR scheme is considerably reduced by the requirement that total project assistance be less than the aid ceiling specified as part of the European Commission's co-ordination solution. This ceiling, it will be recalled, is set at 20 per cent of fixed-investment costs after tax in the Dutch problem regions. But, after tax, the maximum 25 per cent investment premium reduces to only 19.2 per cent of the fixed-investment costs of a 'standard' project,[16] i.e. just under the co-ordination-solution ceiling. The regional component of the WIR scheme is therefore of no great value to projects already in receipt of a 25 per cent award (which, of course, includes all suitably located projects of less than Fl 16 million). Only for larger projects, projects in receipt of nominal awards of less than 25 per cent, is the WIR regional element likely to have a significant impact.

Clearly, the investment premium is far and away the most important regional incentive in the Netherlands. It is also of considerable comparative interest. Of particular note is the form of the premium — a more or less automatic fixed-rate award on project costs up to a given level (currently Fl 16 million), plus a discretionary topping-up facility for project costs beyond that level. No other capital grant in the European Community takes quite this form, although the idea of a fixed base plus discretionary topping-up is found elsewhere (for example, as part of both the British and German incentive packages).

Also of interest is the fact that there is a mixed premium (consisting of a capital grant and a fixed labour subsidy for every new job created) available to more labour-intensive projects as an alternative to the standard premium, even though this alternative has in practice been rarely taken up. The offer of such an alternative — particularly where the choice lies with the firm and not with the administering authorities — is rare in the Community countries, as indeed is the availability of a labour subsidy, even such a partial one. But if the investment-premium scheme is generous in its offer of an alternative in the form of the mixed premium, it is less than generous in the fact that basically only setting-up projects and extensions are eligible for aid. In most other Community countries (the most prominent exception is France) aid is available, too, towards modernisation, rationalisation and re-organisation.

A final interesting feature of the investment premium is its value to those firms which receive it. We have already noted that, apart from in a few municipalities, the maximum rate of award for large projects (and the fixed rate of award for small projects) is 25 per cent — well below the maxima for capital grants in Italy, Ireland and Northern Ireland, but standard for most of the rest of the Community. In effective-value terms, too, the investment premium is in the middle of the capital-grant range — which is not surprising, since in terms of tax treatment, timing and phasing and eligible items of expenditure it hardly departs from Community norms. Of course, as we have seen, average awards for large projects are considerably below the possible maximum. For such projects the Dutch investment premium is very much less attractive on average, and indeed is at the low end of the Community range.

One last point to be made about the Dutch system relates to its spatial complexity. Not only is spatial coverage under the investment-premium scheme complicated (with the identification of growth areas on which to concentrate assistance, some lying outside the broadly defined problem regions while some qualify for lesser awards) but on top of this, as we have seen, there are areas where the special WIR regional allowance is available, areas where the WIR physical-planning allowance is on offer and areas where the SIR levy is applied. While it will not be possible to judge the workings of the new WIR-SIR system until it has had time to settle down, what can be said is that it has certainly resulted in one of the most spatially discriminatory incentive packages in the European Community.

Notes

1. Central Planning Agency and National Spatial Planning Agency, *The West and the Rest of the Netherlands* (1956).
2. A.J. Hendriks, 'Regional Policy in the Netherlands' in N.M. Hansen (ed.), *Public Policy and Regional Economic Development* (Ballinger, Cambridge, Mass., 1974), p. 193.
3. See, for example, F.J. Gay, 'Benelux' in H.D. Clout (ed.), *Regional Development in Western Europe* (John Wiley and Sons, London, 1975); and J.L. Sundquist, *Dispersing Population: What America Can Learn from Europe* (Brookings, Washington DC, 1975), Ch. 5.
4. South-West Groningen; Eastern Groningen; Eastern Friesland; South-East Drenthe; North-East Overijssel; Eastern West-Friesland (in the province of North

Holland); South-West North-Brabant; North-East North-Brabant; and Northern Limburg.

5. 'Owing to political pressure from lower governmental levels, too many growth poles (or development nuclei) were at first selected' – Hendriks, 'Regional Policy in the Netherlands', p. 196.

6. Ibid., p. 194.

7. Quoted in Sundquist, *Dispersing Population*, p. 201.

8. Ibid., p. 199.

9. The five 'growth cities' are Groningen, Zwolle, Helmond, Breda and Leeuwarden. *Either* Bergen op Zoom *or* Rosendaal may soon be added to the list.

10. For more details, see Ch. 11.

11. A numerical example should make the point clear. With investment costs of Fl 100 and a SIR levy of Fl 15, a 23 per cent WIR amounts to Fl 26.45 (i.e. 23 per cent of Fl 115), giving a net subsidy of Fl 11.45, after subtracting the SIR levy.

12. Until recently, the only information obtainable on investment-premium awards was produced on a cumulative basis. Information on an annual basis is not available prior to July 1976.

13. The industrial-site condition may also be dropped for industrial setting-up projects where the building in which the project is housed is bought rather than self-constructed.

14. The municipalities of Deventer, Kampen and Zwolle in Overijssel; Bergen op Zoom, Cuyk, Oss and Uden in North-Brabant; and Roermond, Melick en Herkenbosch, Venlo and Venray in Limburg.

15. In Limburg, for example, an intermunicipal institution, the *Industrieschap Oostelijke Mijnstreek*, finances the construction of industrial buildings which are then placed at the disposal of entrepreneurs on a hire-purchase basis.

16. The standard nominal rate of tax is 48 per cent. However, as already noted, the investment premium is taxed only 'indirectly' by reducing the value of aided assets by the value of the premium for depreciation purposes. This results in an effective tax rate of only 23.2 per cent. For more details, see K.J. Allen *et al., Regional Incentives in the European Community: A Comparative Study* (European Commission, Brussels, 1979).

10 REGIONAL INCENTIVES IN THE UNITED KINGDOM

The Nature of the Problem

The existence of a regional problem in the United Kingdom has long been recognised. Attention was first drawn to it in the 1920s as certain areas experienced exceptionally high levels of unemployment in the Depression years and thereafter. Broadly speaking, the main problem areas, then as now, were the peripheral areas of the country, Northern Ireland, Scotland, the north of England and South Wales — areas which had been very much at the heart of the Industrial Revolution and which then had to pay the price for their heavy reliance on ship building, coal mining, iron and steel and textiles as these industries went into decline (in employment terms at least) or developed other locational requirements. 'The regional imbalance in the United Kingdom was therefore essentially a reflection of the changes in the structure of the national economy'.[1] Unlike the position in many other European countries, there was no agricultural element to the problem and indeed at present only about three per cent of the national labour force is found in agriculture and forestry — a very small proportion by international standards.

Although the problem first came to light in the 1920s, regional problem areas were not designated until 1934. These so-called 'Special Areas' were centred on the depressed coal-mining areas of South Wales, the north-east of England, West Cumberland in the north-west of England, and Clydeside/North Lanarkshire in Scotland. They were perhaps most notable for the fact that they excluded the major towns in these areas (since unemployment was somewhat less severe in the main population centres). Immediately after the war, 'Development Areas' were identified, with much the same broad coverage as the previous Special Areas but, this time, including the major towns. This made them 'continuous and compact regions . . . suitable economic and social units for development as a whole'.[2]

After some minor additions between 1946 and 1948 these Development Areas remained unchanged for the next ten years. This was, as we shall see, a dormant period for regional policy; the reawakening coming in response to the high levels of unemployment associated with the recession of 1958-9. The immediate government reaction included the designation of 'Development Places' (where unemployment was especially severe) in addition to the existing Development Areas. This emphasis on unemployment as a problem indicator was carried even further in the Local Employment Act of 1960. As part of this Act, Development Areas were abolished and so-called 'Development Districts' introduced in their place. These Districts were designated on the basis of actual and expected unemployment rates – in practice, the line between designation and non-designation was drawn at an unemployment rate of about 4.5 per cent. Areas with higher unemployment usually found themselves on the list of Development Districts, while those with lower unemployment were normally not designated. As a result of this system, and in line with general cyclical movements, the coverage of the Development Districts varied considerably over time. Holding some 12.5 per cent of the national insured population in 1961, they declined to 7.2 per cent in 1962 and reached a maximum coverage of 16.8 per cent in 1966.

The disadvantages of the Development District system were soon recognised. The frequent spatial-coverage changes created an atmosphere of uncertainty for businessmen and public planners alike and thus led to an obvious dilution of the impact of regional-policy measures on investment and location decisions. Moreover, the concentration on areas of need rather than areas of potential was also felt to be undesirable. Indeed, as in other European countries at this time, there was strong pressure to move towards a growth-area strategy. This pressure was, however, short-lived, so that when the Development District approach came to be abandoned in 1966 it was replaced by a system of 'broad-banding' of problem areas.

Broad assisted areas were seen to have three main advantages over the 'pepper-potting' approach of the Development Districts. First, with broad areas designated, changes of designation tend to be less frequent, thus allowing incentives to be more effective in influencing location decisions. Second, since broad areas include both declining localities and localities of potential growth they leave more scope for natural economic forces to operate, as well as giving firms moving to the assisted areas a wider locational choice. Finally, broad-banding means that there are fewer boundary difficulties – a direct consequence of the fact that 'fewer lines need to be drawn'.

Despite the advantages claimed for a simple system of broadly-drawn problem regions, economic and political pressures have combined to complicate the assisted-area map. The Development Areas designated in 1966 (and covering about 20 per cent of the British population) survived in their initial form only until November 1967, when colliery closures and the resultant (or anticipated) high localised levels of unemployment caused areas heavily dependent on coal mining to be designated as 'Special Development Areas'. In 1970, following representations from areas just outside the designated problem regions (and the report of the Hunt Committee), so-called 'Intermediate Areas' were designated bordering the Development Areas.[3]

The three-tier system of Special Development Area (SDA), Development Area (DA) and Intermediate Area (IA) remains in force in Britain. Continual extension over the years meant, however, that, by mid-1979, these areas held more than 43 per cent of the employed British population, just over half being located in the IAs and the remainder being spread fairly evenly between the DAs and the SDAs. With the addition of Northern Ireland well over 45 per cent of the United Kingdom workforce was located in the designated UK problem regions as at mid-1979 (see Figure 10.1), a percentage considerably higher than that found in most other European Community countries. However, in July 1979 major area changes were announced, following a review of regional policy by the new Conservative Government, in an attempt to cut back on public expenditure and make policy more effective by concentrating on the areas of greatest need. These changes involved a phased reduction in the coverage of the SDAs, DAs and IAs such that, by August 1982, they will be limited to those parts of the country with the most severe unemployment problems and will hold just 25 per cent of the employed British population. Even after the addition of Northern Ireland, fewer than 30 per cent of the United Kingdom workforce will then be located in designated problem regions, a percentage lower than the current European Community average.

Clearly this is a very significant reduction in assisted-area coverage. In recognition of this and of the damaging effect of sudden policy changes the new map of the assisted area is, as already noted, to be phased in over three years. Moreover, where former SDAs or DAs are due to be descheduled, a special review will take place before they are actually taken off the assisted-area list. As the first stage in redrawing the assisted-area map, thirteen labour-market areas were upgraded with immediate effect (i.e. as from 18 July 1979) — three previously non-assisted areas becoming IAs, five IAs being upgraded to DAs and 5 DAs becoming SDAs. The second stage is then due in August 1980 when some SDAs will become DAs while many more DAs will be downgraded to IAs. At that stage, the coverage of the assisted areas will be illustrated in Figure 10.2. The third and final stage will then take place in August 1982 when a very large number of IAs (including many which before

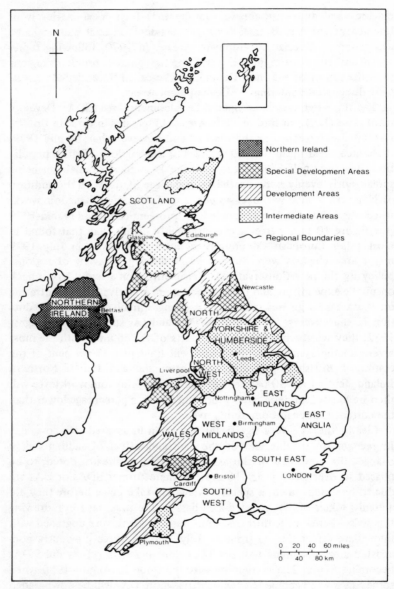

Figure 10.1: Designated Areas in the United Kingdom: June 1979

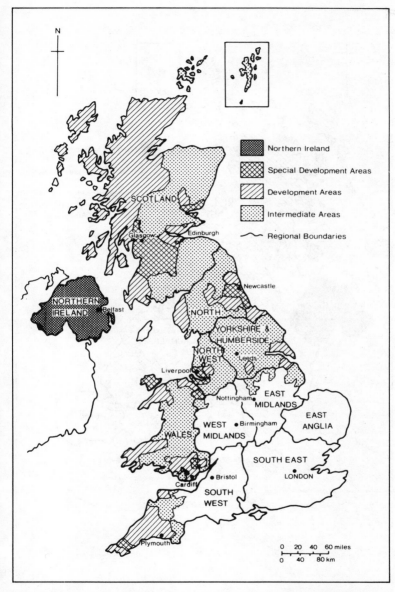

Figure 10.2: Designated Areas in the United Kingdom: August 1980

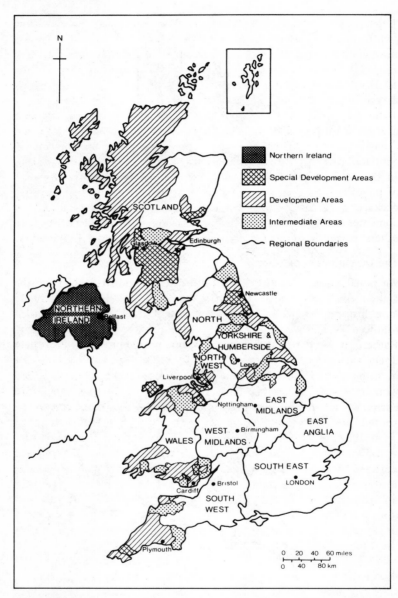

Figure 10.3: Designated Areas in the United Kingdom: August 1982

August 1980 were DAs) are due to be descheduled. At the same time two former SDAs, downgraded in August 1980 to DAs, will be further downgraded to IAs while one former SDA (Haltwhistle in the north of England) is due to become non-assisted. The resulting map (Figure 10.3) will then come into force, subject of course to any changes which may arise from the special reviews mentioned earlier.

So far, we have traced out what have been quite considerable changes in the spatial coverage of regional policy over the years (even though the main problem regions have always been the west of Scotland, the north-east of England, Merseyside and South Wales). In the next section we wish to look more closely at the development of policy before turning to consider, first, the current regional-incentive package and, then, the main incentives in detail. A final section compares and contrasts the United Kingdom regional incentives with others currently on offer elsewhere in the European Community.

The Development of Policy

We noted earlier that the identification of a regional problem in the United Kingdom goes back to the 1920s. Regional policy has an equally long history. The first policy measure differed from those which followed in not being based on a 'work-to-the-workers' philosophy. Rather, an Industrial Transference Board was set up in 1928 to help direct unemployed workers in the problem regions to unfilled vacancies in other areas. The scheme aided the moves of an average 28,000 workers a year and lasted until 1938, since which time policies to encourage worker mobility have never played a significant role in the United Kingdom regional-policy package.

In 1934, as we have seen, the Special Areas were designated and, at the same time, a start was made with 'work-to-the-workers' policies. Between then and 1938 a significant range of policy instruments was introduced, including loans to private industry, the provision of factories on industrial estates, and subsidies to offset firms' tax, rent and rates (local-tax) liabilities. Expenditure was, however, modest and there was in any event little time for the measures to have a major impact before the outbreak of the war when, due to nation-wide pressures on resources of all kinds, regional policy became superfluous.

All the above measures, with the exception of the tax concessions, were retained in the immediate post-war package. This package included government factory building in the Development Areas, the award of loans to industrial-estate companies and the offer of grants or loans to commercially viable projects (provided that finance could not

be raised from any other source), on the advice of DATAC (the
Development Areas Treasury Advisory Committee). In addition, in
1948 a stick was added to these incentive carrots, the system of Industrial Development Certificate (IDC) control. By controlling development
in the more pressured regions, the aim of IDC control was to prevent
'overheating' in those regions and, at the same time, attempt to divert
'mobile' industrial projects (i.e. those with a genuine choice of location)
into the assisted areas. It did this by requiring that firms expanding
beyond specified size levels obtain IDC approval as a legal prerequisite
for application for local-authority planning permission. Without IDC
approval, firms could not expand as desired. Even so, IDC control
probably did not have a major impact in its initial phase, and this for
two main reasons. In the first place, at that time there were other, more
powerful, factors diverting firms to the problem regions – in particular
the availability of factory space there and its non-availability, in these
the early post-war years, in the pressured regions. But, in addition,
an external balance-of-payments crisis soon forced the government to
downgrade both IDCs and regional policy in general within its list of
priorities. 'Regional policy was quietly moved to a back burner where it
was to simmer until being brought to the boil again in the Sixties.'[4]

Between 1960 and 1972 (when the basic framework of the current
incentive package was laid down) there was almost continuous change
on the regional-incentive front. Rather than go through the details
here,[5] we want to simply pick out some of the more radical changes of
direction, before going on to discuss some key features of the period.

As we have seen, the most important change introduced by the
Local Employment Act of 1960 was the designation of Development
Districts. On the incentive front, this Act both extended and strengthened the financial incentives of the immediate post-war period, as well
as introducing a building grant calculated on the basis of the difference
between the cost of construction and the estimated market value of the
completed property. This complex measure was replaced by a straightforward grant of 25 per cent of building costs (conditional on the
creation of employment) in the Local Employment Act of 1963. The
same Act also introduced a grant of 10 per cent of plant and machinery
costs (again employment-related) while the Finance Act of July 1963
brought in free depreciation for industrial plant and machinery in
Development Districts – measures which, together, greatly increased
the value of the regional-incentive package.

A major change of direction occurred with the Industrial Development Act of 1966. Under this Act, as already noted, the Development

Districts were dropped in favour of more broadly defined Development Areas, while the combination of ten per cent grant plus free depreciation for plant and machinery investment was replaced by a system of largely automatic grants. These so-called 'investment grants' were nationally available on plant and machinery investment in 'qualifying processes', but had a strong regional differential (of 20 per cent of eligible expenditure) which was meant to be broadly equivalent in value to the previous mix of ten per cent grant plus free depreciation.

Yet another important innovation occurred in 1967 with the introduction of the regional-employment premium (REP) — a labour subsidy paid to employers in respect of manufacturing establishments located in DAs and SDAs. Viewed as a way of giving the poorer regions a labour-cost advantage and also of offsetting the standard capital orientation of regional incentives, the rate of weekly REP subsidy was initially £1.50 for full-time men, £0.75 for women and boys and £0.475 for girls, half these rates being payable on part-time workers. At the time of its introduction REP was estimated to account for between seven and eight per cent of aided firms' labour costs, and was to last for a trial period of at least seven years.

In 1970 a new Conservative Government took office, committed to cutting back on government intervention (and not only in the regions). In line with this philosophy it was announced that REP would indeed be phased out (albeit in an unspecified manner), starting in 1974. In the same vein, investment grants were dropped in favour of fiscal measures — a 100 per cent first-year allowance on new machinery and plants in DAs and SDAs and a 60 per cent initial allowance elsewhere. This change of direction lasted, however, only a very short time. Deteriorating economic conditions, particularly in the problem regions, soon caused the government to extend the 100 per cent first-year allowance on to a nation-wide basis, to introduce a national 40 per cent initial allowance on buildings, and to complement these national fiscal measures with a financial-incentive package in the problem regions. The main elements of this March 1972 package — virtually automatic regional-development grants on both new plant and machinery and building expenditure, and discretionary, project-related, selective financial assistance — remain the key components of the British regional-incentive package.

A number of interesting features arise from the above review of the changes made between 1960 and March 1972. First, there was a frequent switching of emphasis between fiscal and financial aids. As we have seen, depreciation allowances first introduced on a regional basis in 1963 were then withdrawn in 1966 on the grounds that their bene-fits 'were not understood (and, moreover, did not exist in the case of a firm that was making no profit, as is the fate of many firms in their earliest years)';[6] they were then reintroduced as the key regional ele-ment of the incentive package in 1970, and extended to cover the entire country in 1972 (thus being taken out of the regional-incentive arena).

Second, despite the continuous switching between fiscal and finan-cial measures, there was one relatively steady underlying trend — namely, the growing importance of automatic over discretionary aids. Although discretionary building grants were available throughout the period, all the fiscal concessions were 'automatic',[7] as were the invest-ment grant, the regional-development grant, and of course the regional-employment premium.

Reflecting this trend, and reflecting too both the increasing number of incentives on offer and their increasing spatial coverage, expenditure on the regional-incentive package rose dramatically — from less than £12 million in 1960/1 to over £30 million in 1964/5, almost £160 million in 1967/8, and over £300 million in 1970/1.[8] The changes in policy in the early 1970s damped down expenditure somewhat but it soon began to move upwards again with the introduction of the regional-development grant (expenditure on this incentive alone reach-ing over £400 million in 1976/7) and with the doubling of the regional-employment-premium rates in 1974 (thus re-establishing its initial value as a percentage of labour costs).

This trend towards rapidly increasing regional-incentive expenditure came to an end in July 1976 with the first of a series of public-expendi-ture cuts. As part of the July 1976 measures new rates of award for the regional-employment premium were announced of £2 for adults (both men and women) and £1.20 for boys and girls. As well as reducing overall REP expenditure, these new rates took cognisance of criticism that the premium discriminated between the sexes. However, before the new rates came into force, REP was abolished completely in further public-expenditure cuts in December 1976. Also as part of the July 1976 measures, it was announced that regional-development-grant assistance would be withdrawn from both mining and construction and, in addition, an extra three-month administrative delay was imposed on regional-development-grant payments. This imposed delay was then removed in December 1977 only to be reintroduced (this time as a four-month delay) in June 1979, again on public-expenditure-saving grounds.

Even more dramatic than these cutbacks, however, were the changes announced on 17 July 1979 following the new Conservative Government's review of regional policy — as already noted, an attempt to reduce public expenditure, to concentrate on the areas of greatest need and, generally, to increase the cost-effectiveness of policy. One aspect of the July 1979 changes has already been discussed — the reduced coverage of the SDAs, DAs and IAs. Of equal import, notice was given that the regional-development grant would be reduced from 20 to 15 per cent of eligible investment in the DAs and would be withdrawn completely from the IAs (where previously it had been available towards building expenditure only) in respect of assets provided (i.e. supplied or constructed and ready for use) on or after 1 August 1980, except where expenditure had been defrayed before 18 July 1979.[9] At the same time, minimum eligible asset sizes under the regional-development-grant scheme were increased from £100 to £500 for plant and machinery and from £1,000 to £5,000 for buildings and works in respect of expenditure defrayed on or after 18 July 1979. As a final change to the regional-incentive package it was stated that selective financial assistance would, in future, be available only where it was *necessary* to enable a project to go ahead. Previously there had been no such 'criteria of need'. While it is not, as yet, clear just what effect this change will have in practice, it can be expected that the number of successful applicants will be significantly reduced, that assistance will now largely go to inward-investment cases and projects with a genuine choice of location, and that small projects and minor extensions will now find it very much more difficult to obtain aid.

In addition to these changes to the regional incentives on offer changes were announced in respect of two other traditional components of British regional policy — the government factory-building programme and the system of Industrial Development Certificate control. The former has long been recognised as a useful and relatively inexpensive means of attracting mobile projects to particular problem locations. It was therefore decided to continue the policy but, at the same time, to take steps to increase the element of self-financing within it. Regarding the latter, it has for some time been clear that the control function of IDCs is of little relevance in periods of low investment and widespread unemployment and, in fact, very few IDC applications have been refused in recent years. The Secretary of State nevertheless decided to retain IDCs, arguing their usefulness as a means for bringing large, potentially mobile, projects to the attention of the Department of Industry. At the same time he raised the exemption limit significantly (to 50,000 square feet outside the assisted areas as from

6 August 1979)[10] and withdrew IDC control from the IAs.

No changes were, however, foreseen in the regional-policy functions of either the Scottish or the Welsh Development Agencies, creations of the previous Labour administration. They will continue to complement the regional-incentive system by offering commercial loans and equity finance and by being actively involved in promotional activities and environmental-improvement schemes. Their role outside the designated assisted areas is however to be the subject of a review, a review which, given the massive cutback in the coverage of these areas in Scotland and Wales (see Figure 10.3), is likely markedly to reduce their action radius.

Taken together, it is anticipated that these various July 1979 measures will save some £233 million annually by 1982/3 — representing almost two-fifths of current expenditure on regional-development grants, selective financial assistance and government factory building. They therefore clearly amount to a quite major change of policy. The adverse consequences of the change have, however, been minimised, as we have seen, by phasing the various cutbacks over a three-year period and by maintaining the basic incentive framework established initially in March 1972. It is to the role of the current incentive package within this framework that we turn in the next section.

The Current Incentive Package

The main element of the regional-incentive package in Britain is, without doubt, the regional-development grant, an automatic item-related grant on fixed-capital expenditure. At the present time regional-development grants are available on new plant, machinery, buildings and works in the Special Development Areas and the Development Areas at rates of 22 per cent and 20 per cent, respectively. In the Intermediate Areas only buildings and works are eligible, the rate of subsidy being, as in the Development Areas, 20 per cent. For assets provided after August 1980 the Development Area rate will be reduced to 15 per cent and regional-development grants will no longer be available in the Intermediate Areas. These changes, combined with the cutback in the coverage of the assisted areas noted earlier, will reduce regional-development-grant expenditure by almost £200 million, from its peak of over £400 million in 1976/7. Even so, the regional-development grant will remain far and away the most important British regional incentive in expenditure terms.

A key feature of the regional-development-grant scheme is that the payment of the grant is virtually automatic to eligible items of investment on qualifying premises. In contrast, selective financial assistance under Section 7 of the Industry Act 1972 – in cost terms the second most important source of regional aid in Britain, with assistance totalling over £160 million in 1977/8 – is both project-related and discretionary. Although selective financial assistance is, in theory, very wide-ranging, it has in practice tended to be mainly in the form either of a soft loan or – and this has increasingly been the case – an interest-relief grant (calculated in relation to the notional loan which would have been awarded had a soft-loan offer been made). Like the regional-development grant, selective financial assistance was cut back as part of the July 1979 measures (it now being limited to projects which would not otherwise be able to go ahead) and, like the regional-development grant, it will be covered in more detail in the next section.

Although soft loans and interest-relief grants are the main forms of Section 7 assistance, other selective aids are worth mentioning. Removal grants, for example, are available on up to 80 per cent of the 'reasonable' costs of moving both plant and stocks to an assisted-area location, as well as on the net redundancy payment arising from the move. In 1977/8 assistance to the value of over £2.2 million was approved under the removal-grants programme. In addition, loans from the European Investment Bank, previously unattractive despite their relatively low (7.5 per cent) rate of interest because of the exchange risk involved, have been made far more acceptable by a government guarantee against the risk of exchange losses where the loans are in respect of employment-creating projects in DAs, SDAs and Northern Ireland. In return for this guarantee an extra one per cent interest is payable, giving a rate of interest of 8.5 per cent – still well below the current UK market rates.

A further selective measure of considerable interest (since it is one of the very few schemes in the European Community directed at, and specifically designed for, the service sector) is the service-industry-grant scheme which aims to encourage the development of mobile services – services with a genuine choice of location – in the problem regions. As part of this scheme (which, it must be emphasised, is restricted to job-creating service projects), grants (of up to £6,000 per job in the SDAs, up to £4,000 per job in the DAs and up to £2,000 per job in the IAs) are paid in respect of each job provided within three years of a firm moving to or setting up in an assisted-area location. In addition, £1,500 is paid to essential staff moving with their work (as long as their removal expenditure exceeds this amount) up to a limit of 30 per cent of the jobs provided in the new location. These grants are just the latest version of a scheme initially introduced in June 1973, extended and considerably increased in value in October 1976, and much simplified in March 1979. However, despite continuing efforts to tailor the scheme closely to the needs of the service sector, its impact has not been great. In 1977/8, for example only 67 offers of assistance were approved under the service-industry-grant scheme, to the value of just £7.7 million.

Moving away from Section 7 aid, another traditionally important component of the regional-incentive package in Britain, as noted earlier, is the government factory-building programme. Over the last ten years or so, expenditure on this programme has averaged some £15 million annually, although in the mid-1970s the figure was considerably higher than this. New factories are built in advance of demand in areas of high unemployment and then rented or sold to industrialists. In addition, custom-built extensions are undertaken. Although rents are levied at the 'current market value' as set by the local District Valuer, these have, in the past, tended to be below the full commercial rent in the assisted areas and have certainly been below equivalent rent levels in the more pressured regions. It remains to be seen whether rent levels will rise once the steps envisaged within the July 1979 measures to increase the element of self-financing within the factory-building programme have been taken. In addition to relatively low rents, rent-free periods (of up to two years in the DAs and up to five years in the SDAs) are available, albeit subject to a (not very onerous) cost-per-job constraint. Despite these rent concessions, the 'incentive' element of the factory-building programme probably lies as much in the fact that the factories are ready for almost immediate entry as in any rent advantages there might be.

The remaining regional incentives in Britain are of minor importance compared with those reviewed so far in this section. Certain training services are provided free to firms in the assisted areas; labour mobility grants are available to aid the movement of both 'key workers' and 'nucleus labour forces'; and there is also a contracts-preference scheme whereby the government favours assisted-area producers in its purchasing arrangements. In addition (and regional only as far as service employment is concerned, manufacturing being eligible throughout the country), there is a labour subsidy of £20 a week for up to 26 weeks, available up until 31 March 1980, to firms employing less than 200 workers, for each extra job they provide. However, even taken together, these minor regional aids represent an insignificant proportion of the total regional-incentive bill.

So far, we have concentrated very much on the British regional-incentive package. There are, however, special incentives available in Northern Ireland which must be mentioned. The Northern Ireland package differs from its Great Britain equivalent in two major respects. First, it contains a greater variety of incentive measures, and second, even where the type of incentive is the same, the rate paid tends to be higher.

Turning to the details of current Northern Ireland assistance, all firms (both existing and incoming) which establish new factories in the region are eligible for one of two alternative programmes, both of which are broadly aimed at offsetting capital costs. One programme is more or less automatic, and is therefore attractive to firms which are averse to becoming too involved with government departments, while the other is a negotiated package dependent on employment being created or safeguarded.

There are two basic elements to the automatic programme. The prime component is the Northern Ireland equivalent of the regional-development grant but in this case the rate of grant is 30 per cent of approved capital expenditure and not 22 per cent, as in the British SDAs. On top of this standard grant, loans or interest-relief grants are available up to a limit of 75 per cent of fixed-capital costs − net, of course, of the 30 per cent standard grant. These loans/interest-relief grants are, however, only rarely taken up.

The alternative to this programme, the negotiated package, is some-what more complex. On condition that employment will be created or preserved there are four main incentives available: a capital grant of between 40 and 50 per cent of approved capital expenditure on build-ings and new plant and equipment, the actual award being dependent on the location of the project; soft loans or interest-relief grants along the lines of the British selective-financial-assistance scheme, but with higher public-sector-contribution and cost-per-job limits; removal grants covering up to 100 per cent of the costs of moving existing machinery and equipment from outside Northern Ireland to the province, and up to 75 per cent of removal costs for moves within the province; and employment grants, offered over a number of years (normally three or four) on proof of employment being created. These last are particularly interesting since they are normally used to 'top up' assistance to the maximum set by the public-sector-contribution/cost-per-job limits. It is therefore valid to view them as a form of capital rather than labour aid. They help to compensate labour-intensive projects (particularly where male jobs are involved), which may face serious setting-up costs and yet, because of their labour intensity, tend to 'miss out' on the other grants available.

In addition to these two major capital-assistance programmes, Northern Ireland has a number of other important weapons in its incentive armoury. Among the most significant are government factories (generally on more favourable terms than in Britain), a £15 per week training grant for training carried out on employers' premises, and a key worker scheme along very much the same lines as its British counterpart.[11]

Quite clearly the Northern Irish package is more extensive and valuable than that on offer in the British problem regions. In a final section we compare and contrast both British and Northern Irish incentives with those available elsewhere in the European Community. But before that, we wish to concentrate in the next section on the main British aids — the regional-development grant and selective-financial-assistance soft loans and interest-relief grants — laying particular emphasis on eligibility conditions and award levels.

The Main Incentives

The Regional Development Grant

An important objective of the regional-development-grant scheme is that the grant be 'simple, direct, and predictable'.[12] To this end, the payment of the grant is virtually automatic once certain conditions of award (to be specified in more detail below) are met. Grant administration is further simplified by the fact that the original legislation (Part I of the Industry Act 1972) is not detailed, but rather gives the responsible Minister discretion to amplify the provisions of the Statute. This discretion has been used to develop highly detailed administrative guidelines — rules which the four Regional Development Grant Offices of the Department of Industry (located in Glasgow, Cardiff, Bootle and Billingham) then follow in administering the scheme. These detailed guidelines are applied uniformly between cases. In this way the administration of the regional-development grant is standardised even though the Act itself contains no detailed provisions and despite the fact that the administrative system is regionally devolved. Moreover, the detailed guidelines mean that most of those administering the scheme are at a relatively low administrative grade, with the result that administrative costs per £ of assistance are extremely low.

Unlike all other regional capital grants in the European Community countries, the regional-development grant is item-related, and not project-related (as we shall see, a further important element in keeping the scheme simple). Grant is payable in respect of specified expenditure on plant, machinery, buildings and works in both the Special Development and Development Areas, but is restricted to buildings and works expenditure in the Intermediate Areas (and will be withdrawn from the Intermediate Areas on assets provided after 1 August 1980). Eligible fixed-capital investment is aided at the rate of 22 per cent in the SDAs, at 20 per cent in the DAs (post-August 1980, 15 per cent), and at 20 per cent in the IAs (post-August 1980, zero). Since its introduction in 1972 expenditure on the regional-development grant has grown rapidly — from £107 million in 1973/4 to £213 million in 1974/5, £325 million in 1975/6 and £407 million in 1976/7, before falling slightly to £393 million in 1977/8 — mainly as a result of the exclusion of mining and construction from the list of eligible activities as from April 1977. It is anticipated that the July 1979 measures will lead to regional-development-grant savings of more than £200 million annually at the end of the three-year transition period.

Eligibility Conditions. We have already noted that payment of the grant is more or less automatic once certain conditions of award are met. Prime among these, the capital expenditure to which the grant relates must be carried out on *qualifying premises*. In addition, these premises must be located in the designated assisted areas. As we have seen, the grant favours SDAs over both DAs and IAs in terms of rates of award, and both SDAs and DAs over IAs in terms of grant coverage. Indeed, as already noted, for assets provided on or after 1 August 1980 the regional-development grant will no longer be available in the IAs.

According to the Industry Act 1972, qualifying premises are 'premises which are for the time being used wholly or mainly for qualifying activities'[13] — basically production activities (as opposed to office work, storage, sales and distribution). In practice, qualifying premises are limited almost exclusively to the manufacturing sector, although certain repair activities, the processing of scrap and waste materials and both scientific research and staff training also qualify if carried out in connection with qualifying activities. The identification of qualifying premises is particularly important within the regional-development-grant scheme because once premises are classed as qualifying then *all* capital expenditure carried out on those premises — whether or not it is in respect of a qualifying activity — is eligible for grant. On the other side of the coin, all capital expenditure carried out on non-qualifying premises — even that relating to qualifying activities — is ineligible for grant. This 'all-or-nothing' rule has an element of rough justice about it, but it has proved highly effective in simplifying the administration of the scheme.

A further major simplification, already noted, is that the regional-development grant is item- and not project-related. Consequently, there is no requirement to establish the existence of a 'project', nor to prove the commercial, financial and technical viability of that project, nor to show that it has a favourable impact on the problem regions and will create at least X jobs and £Y-million-worth of capital investment — conditions normally 'part and parcel' of project-related schemes. As a result, a wider range of investment qualities for regional-development-grant aid than would be eligible for assistance under most project-related grant schemes.

Award Levels. We saw earlier that the nominal rate of award of the regional-development grant is 22 per cent of eligible capital expenditure on plant, machinery, buildings and works expenditure in the SDAs, 20 per cent of eligible plant, machinery, buildings and works expenditure in the DAs and 20 per cent of eligible buildings and works expenditure in the IAs, in respect of expenditure defrayed before 18 July 1979 or assets provided before 1 August 1980; and that thereafter the rate of award is 22 per cent in the SDAs, 15 per cent in the DAs and zero in the IAs. But just how valuable is the regional-development grant in practice? How does its *effective* value compare with its nominal value? There are three main factors to be taken into account in moving from nominal to effective rates of award — the tax treatment of the grant, delays in the payment of the grant and eligible items of expenditure.

The first of these factors is easy to deal with since regional-development grants are not treated for tax purposes as income receipts, nor must they be deducted from the cost of aided assets for tax-depreciation purposes. In short, they are not taxed. This again is a consequence of the aim to make the regional-development-grant scheme 'simple, direct and predictable' and is one of the features distinguishing the regional-development grant from its predecessor, the investment grant. It also distinguishes regional-development grants from all other capital grants in the European Community (with the exception of the investment allowance in Germany), since these are all liable for tax to some degree.

As far as delays are concerned, the standard *processing* delay is three months, although as might be expected, the variation around this average is significant. At the one extreme, where the applicant takes the trouble to prepare the ground and where the application is straight-forward, grant can be paid within a couple of weeks; while at the other extreme certain cases (normally where information is lacking in some respect) can drag on for months or even years. This processing delay, incidentally, is calculated from the date of grant application, which can be any time after asset *provision* (broadly speaking, any time after the asset is ready for use). In this respect, too, the regional-development-grant scheme has an advantage over many project-related grant schemes since these tend not to accept claims for grant payment until project construction, or a significant proportion thereof, is complete. But against this an extra delay has recently (June 1979) been introduced into the regional-development-grant scheme in the form of a four-month waiting period between the completion of processing and the payment of grant. This public-expenditure-saving measure means that the average delay between grant claim and grant payment is now of the order of seven months.

The final factor affecting nominal values of award is grant coverage. Which items of expenditure are eligible for assistance and which are not? As already noted, the regional-development grant is item-related and is restricted to plant, machinery, buildings and works. Working capital is therefore ineligible. To be eligible, the plant and machinery must be new, must have a minimum value of £500, and must have a life of not less than two years. Vehicles are ineligible (except for on-premise vehicles), as are items of furniture, recreational equipment and most pipelines. Buildings and works, too, must be new (buildings must have been previously unoccupied), although the cost of adapting old build-ings is ineligible. They must, moreover, have a minimum value of £5,000. Finally, it should be noted that all forms of asset 'purchase' — cash and phased payments, hire purchase and leasing — are eligible for regional-development-grant aid. In the case of hire purchase, however, it is the cash price and not the hire-purchase price which is of relevance; while, where leasing is involved, it is the leasing company which receives the grant (again, on the cash price) and not the user of the equipment.

Selective Financial Assistance

As mentioned earlier, there are two main forms of selective financial assistance under Section 7 of the Industry Act 1972 — soft loans and interest-relief grants. They are treated together here because they are direct alternatives. No project (selective financial assistance, it will be recalled, is project-related) can receive both. Initially, most awards were

in the form of a soft loan but now the preference of both administrators and industrialists is for interest-relief-grant assistance. Indeed, the
position has been reached where soft loans are awarded only where
project finance is not available from any other source. In 1977/8 only
30 soft-loan offers were made compared with 866 interest-relief grants.

Selective-financial-assistance soft loans are medium-term loans
(normally of between five and seven years' duration) and are available
towards any of the normal capital requirements of an undertaking,
including working capital. Rates of interest are three percentage points
below what is viewed by the Department of Industry as the 'broadly
commercial' rate. Interest-free periods and (concurrent with these)
principal-repayment holidays are available for up to three years in the
SDAs and up to two years in the DAs and IAs.

As an alternative to these loans a project may be offered an interest-
relief grant. This grant is based on the notional loan award which the
Department of Industry would have been prepared to offer the project
under the above soft-loan scheme, and is normally paid at the annual
rate of three per cent of the notional loan for up to four years. In
addition, where it would have been appropriate to allow an interest-
free period on the loan, then, for that period, the grant is at what is
known as the 'higher interest-relief-grant' rate — a rate roughly in line
with the previously mentioned 'broadly commercial' rate — before
reverting to three per cent of the notional loan for up to a further four
years. Broadly speaking, therefore, the interest-relief grant amounts to
the concessionary element present in the soft loan scheme.[14]

As an incentive type, interest-relief grants were completely new to
the 1972 legislation. But also new were many of the administrative
aspects of the selective-financial-assistance scheme. While there had
been some discretion within the incentive system between 1960 and
1972 (particularly in respect of building grants), this discretion was
administered very much from the centre. In contrast, selective financial
assistance exhibits a relatively high degree of regional devolution. For
example, Ministerial responsibility for regional selective assistance in
Scotland and Wales lies with the Secretaries of State for Scotland and
Wales, respectively, while the major English regions have freedom to
deal with all but the largest of cases (those involving more than £2
million) without reference to headquarters.

Given this, it might be asked if there remains any real standardisation between regions within the scheme. The answer is that there is
indeed standardisation, and that it is achieved by regional offices of the
Department of Industry,[15] following joint Treasury/Department of

Industry guidelines on the administration of the scheme. These guidelines are not, however, as tightly drawn as in the regional-development-grant scheme where Regional Development Grant Offices have virtually no administrative discretion. Rather, the selective-financial-assistance guidelines give the Department of Industry's regional offices a certain degree of independence, in particular with respect to the award of interest-free periods and principal-repayment holidays. The guidelines therefore aim to allow the advantages of regional devolution (cases being 'dealt with quickly and by people who are familiar with the region and can take account of the region's needs, as well as the circumstances of the application, in reaching decisions'[16]) to be reaped without the attendant dangers of inconsistency of treatment and even competition between regions. One official has described the system in the following terms:

> We lay down policy guidelines from headquarters and within those guidelines we allow regions to operate with a certain amount of independence. I do not think, however, that we would conclude from this that at the end of the day in terms of assistance actually available and offered there is substantial difference between the regions.[17]

A further administrative feature, new to the 1972 Act, was the creation of so-called 'Regional Industrial Development Boards' (RIDBs). There is one of these Boards in each region, made up of experienced local industrialists, trade unionists, commercial and professional people. Project recommendations are submitted to the RIDBs by the regional offices of the Department of Industry and, although their approval is not mandatory, 'in practice their view is rarely set aside'.[18] The Boards are therefore a further factor making for consistency of treatment between cases. In particular, they look critically on the question of viability and are viewed as being especially helpful in marginal cases and in identifying features of general importance within any given project.

Eligibility Conditions. As far as eligibility is concerned, the key point to be determined with regard to any application is whether or not the project in question is viable. Under the Section 7 guidelines, viability refers 'to a company's ability after receiving selective assistance on a once-for-all basis . . . to achieve and maintain profitability without continuing subsidies other than those available to all eligible enterprises,

in particular regional development grants . . .'[19] Moreover, profitability
— and, hence, viability — must be achieved within a relatively short
timespan. A project will not in normal circumstances be viewed as
potentially viable 'if forecasts based on reasonable assumptions do not
show profits and positive cash flow within three years'.[20] From this,
it should be clear that the assessment of viability is primarily an
'arithmetic' exercise — it is 'a matter of facts, figures and commercial
judgement, in which wider economic and social factors have no part to
play'.[21] If discretion has a role to play within the selective-financial
assistance scheme, then it is far more in respect of award levels than
eligibility conditions.

Apart from viability, the only other major pre-condition of award
until recently was that the project either create or (less often) safeguard
jobs. This job condition has meant that in the past only setting-up
projects and extensions (i.e. employment-creating projects) and
modernisations and rationalisations (i.e. employment-safeguarding
projects) have been assisted, with most awards being in respect of the
former project types. As part of the July 1979 measures a new
condition was introduced: namely, that Section 7 assistance must be
necessary for the project to go ahead. While it will obviously take time
before the full impact of this change becomes apparent, it would seem
to suggest that there will be a quite significant decrease in the number
of successful applicants (since in comparatively few instances up until
now has selective financial assistance turned 'no go' into 'go' projects)
and might also lead to more serious attempts to make awards marginal,
i.e. to award the minimum necessary for the project to go ahead. We
would further suspect that, if the intentions of the government are
fulfilled, selective financial assistance will in future be limited to
inward-investment cases and projects with a genuine choice of location,
basically large setting-up projects.

Finally, we should mention the industrial coverage of the scheme.
Although, in principle, this is not a limiting factor, in practice awards
tend to be very much concentrated on the manufacturing sector.
Mining, construction and mobile services (i.e. services with a genuine
choice of location and able to create at least ten new jobs by moving to
the assisted areas or 25 new jobs by expanding in the assisted areas)
do, however, also qualify.

Award Levels. We have already noted that the concessionary element
of a selective-financial-assistance soft-loan award is broadly equivalent
in value to an interest-relief grant. In 1977/8 the higher interest-relief-

grant rate (roughly equivalent to the 'broadly commercial' rate of interest) varied between 10 per cent and 13.5 per cent. Given the former rate, the maximum interest-relief grant in the SDAs is 42 per cent of the notional loan which would have been offered had a soft-loan award been made, while in the DAs and IAs the equivalent maximum percentage is 32 per cent.[22] Given the latter rate, the corresponding maxima are 52.5 per cent in the SDAs and 39 per cent in the DAs and IAs. Whatever the maxima (and the maximum award, it will be recalled, is determined by the higher interest-relief-grant rate which, in turn, is dependent on the market rate of interest), the actual award made (which is, of course, directly related to the length of interest-free period granted) is at the discretion of the regional offices of the Department of Industry, and is normally determined by the cash-flow position of the recipient project. In 1977/8 all soft loans carried with them an interest-free period (not surprising since, as already noted, projects in receipt of a soft loan would normally be in a relatively weak cash-flow position), as did four-fifths of the interest-relief-grant offers.

In the award of soft loans and interest-relief grants regional-office discretion enters primarily in the decision whether or not to offer an interest-free period. But there is also scope for discretion in the determination of the loan/notional loan offered. Once viability has been determined and eligible project costs have been identified (and we return to this below), two conditions limit the amount of loan/notional-loan assistance which can be made available. First, 'applicants are normally expected to ensure that the greater part of the cost is provided from outside the public sector'.[23] As well as selective financial assistance, both regional-development grants and the occupation of a government factory are taken account of in this public-sector-contribution limit. Secondly, a cost-per-job limit sets the maximum loan/notional loan at £X times the number of jobs created. This limit is confidential but is known to 'bite' only in relatively capital-intensive cases. Normally it is the public-sector-contribution limit which sets the upper limit to the loan/notional-loan award.

So far the discussion has been in terms of the lower of the maxima set by the public-sector-contribution and cost-per-job limits determining the maximum available assistance. In fact, in practice, the lower maximum is often the *actual* loan/notional loan adopted. Although discretion could enter in at this stage, it tends not to be important. The average loan/notional-loan award is normally within five percentage points of the maximum possible.

We mentioned earlier that eligible project costs must be identified before the appropriate loan/notional loan can be estimated. These costs are defined in a negative way. Basically, they exclude all revenue payments, apart from the cost of plant and machinery leased for a minimum of four years. Such favourable treatment of leasing is not always found amongst European regional incentives; and the fact that working capital is an eligible item of expenditure further distinguishes British selective financial assistance from most other European regional-aid schemes.

Apart from eligible items of expenditure, there are two additional factors which can reduce the effective value of any award made — tax treatment and delays in payment. By reducing debt-servicing charges, the concessionary element of the soft loan is taxed in as far as it increases taxable profits. Since the interest-relief grant is regarded as income, it is also taxed to the extent that it leads to increased profits. As for delays, these are insignificant in the case of the soft loan since it can be drawn down on proof of need. For the interest-relief grant, delays in payment are, however, important. The grant is paid annually over anything up to seven years (depending on the length of interest-free period awarded). Payment of the first instalment can normally be claimed when one-third of project fixed-asset expenditure has been defrayed, with subsequent instalments being made on the anniversary date of the first grant payment.

Comparative Conclusions

To a greater extent than in many other European Community countries, the United Kingdom has adopted an explicit package approach to regional-incentive policy — the main elements of the package being an automatic, predictable and highly visible base, the regional-development grant, and a discretionary flexible upper tier, selective financial assistance. Both elements are of considerable international comparative interest, but most especially the regional-development grant.

Alone among the regional capital grants in the European Community countries, the regional-development grant is item-related. As a result, far fewer conditions are attached to its award than to the award of most project-related grants. Associated with this point, regional-development grants are more certain in their award than most other grants (it normally being 'obvious' whether an applicant is eligible or not) and are also more certain as regards the nominal rate of award, this being fixed (in contrast to the majority of capital-grant schemes in the Community countries, which are couched in 'up to' terms).

Moreover, and unlike all other capital grants with the exception of the investment allowance in Germany, the regional-development grant is tax-free — adding certainty to its effective value, too.

Because it is so different in so many respects from the 'standard' project-related grant schemes, but in particular because, being item-related, it cannot readily be incorporated within the European Commission's co-ordination methodology (see Chapter 11), there have been considerable pressures put upon the regional-development grant from Brussels and elsewhere. However, any significant modification of the scheme in the direction of making the regional-development grant project-related would rob the scheme of its central virtue — the fact that, as the base of the British regional-incentive package, it is 'simple, direct and predictable'.

The regional-development-grant scheme is both highly visible and administratively straightforward. The role that selective financial assistance plays within the British regional-incentive package is very different. Not only does it involve fairly complex administration, but it also sacrifices visibility and predictability to the attempt to tailor the package as a whole to the needs of both the applicant firm and the recipient region. To this end, selective-financial-assistance soft loans and interest-relief grants are project-related — like all other interest-related subsidies in the European Community. But even though similar in this respect to other Community schemes, they exhibit a number of significant differences in other respects. For example, in no other Community country are interest-free periods available; in no other Community country is working capital eligible to the same extent (although, as we saw in Chapter 7, stocks do qualify for assistance under the national soft-loan scheme in Italy); in no other Community country is leased equipment treated so favourably; and in no other Community country is there an equivalent degree of regional devolution within what is basically a discretionary scheme.

As a result, in particular, of the availability of interest-free periods and the eligibility of working capital, selective financial assistance is more valuable than all other interest-related subsidies in the European Community in effective-value terms, with the exception of the Italian national soft loan — and this despite the fact that the interest-rate concession (at three per cent) is no better than 'average', while the length of subsidy (at between five and seven years) is shorter than in most other schemes (subsidised loans normally being of 15 to 20 years' duration). With the regional-development grant being at least as valuable as most other capital grants in the Community in effective-value terms (apart from the grants on offer in Ireland, Italy and Northern Ireland, all of which have a maximum nominal value of 50 per cent or more of eligible investment), the combination of regional-development grant and selective financial assistance compares favourably with most other incentive packages in the Community (again, with the exception of the incentive packages on offer in Ireland, Italy and Northern Ireland).

But, of course, there are other interesting comparative features of the British regional-incentive package beyond regional-development grants and selective financial assistance. In particular, the service-industry-grant scheme is worthy of mention, as it is one of the few schemes in the Community countries designed specifically for the service sector. The system of government advance factory building (found only in Ireland of the other Community countries) and the IDC control system (one of the very few location controls in the Community which have been effective) are also worth highlighting, as is the fact that both of these measures originated in the immediate post-war period. Regional policy in Britain has a much longer history than in the remaining Community countries and has encompassed a greater variety of policy measures than any other regional-policy package in the Community.

Finally, and moving away from the British mainland, it must be stressed once more that there is a separate incentive package in Northern Ireland. As already noted, this differs from its British counterpart by being both more extensive and more valuable. More than this, with capital grants of from 40 to 50 per cent of eligible investment, and with interest-relief grants, removal and employment grants on top of this — not to mention government factories and training grants — the Northern Irish package is one of the most valuable, if not *the* most valuable, in the European Community. But this is only to be expected. Even with incentives on this scale, and notwithstanding an improving security situation, it remains a major task to break down the huge barriers currently facing inward investment to Northern Ireland.

Notes

1. OECD, *Re-appraisal of Regional Policies in OECD Countries* (OECD, Paris, 1975), p. 1.

2. Cmd 7540 (HMSO, London, 1948), quoted in G. McCrone, *Regional Policy in Britain* (Allen and Unwin, London, 1969), p. 109.

3. *Industry Act 1972*, Section 1 (4).

4. J.D. McCallum, 'A History of British Regional Policy to 1964' University of Glasgow Discussion Papers in Planning No. 5, March 1976, p. 14.

5. For details, see, amongst others, A.J. Brown, *The Framework of Regional Economics in the United Kingdom* (Cambridge University Press, Cambridge, 1972); OCED, *Regional Problems and Policies in OECD Countries* (OECD, Paris, 1976), vol. 2, Ch. 1; and McCrone, *Regional Policy*.

6. Brown, *Framework of Regional Economics*, p. 290.

7. That is, 'administered within standard rules of procedure to determine the eligibility of applicants and within these rules available to all comers' – G.M. Field and P.V. Hills, 'The Administration of Industrial Subsidies' in A. Whiting (ed.), *The Economics of Industrial Subsidies* (HMSO, London, 1976), p. 8.

8. Figures taken from H.M. Begg *et al.*, 'Expenditure on Regional Assistance to Industry 1960/1 – 1972/3' in *Economic Journal*, vol. 85 (December 1975), pp. 884-7.

9. This in effect means that the new rates will not have a major impact on RDG expenditure until after 1 August 1980. For more details of the transitional arrangements, see *Trade and Industry*, 20 July 1979, pp. 99-102.

10. Prior to 6 August 1979, IDCs were necessary for developments over 12,500 square feet in the South-East and over 15,000 square feet elsewhere outside the SDAs and DAs. It is perhaps worth noting that, when the system of IDC control was at its most stringent (in the mid-1960s), the exemption limit was a mere 1,000 square feet in the Midlands, the South-East and East Anglia and was only 5,000 square feet elsewhere.

11. In addition, there are a number of schemes aiming to compensate firms for any additional costs (including, for example, higher insurance premia) resulting from the current situation in Northern Ireland.

12. *Third Report from the Committee of Public Accounts* (HMSO, London, 1974), HC 303, Appendix 1, para. 12.

13. *Industry Act 1972*, Section 2 (1).

14. In fact, in net-grant-equivalent terms, the concessionary element of a soft loan is worth slightly less than the equivalent interest-relief grant.

15. To simplify the discussion, we use the term 'regional offices of the Department of Industry' in this and subsequent paragraphs. However, as a result of an administrative change in July 1975, the Scottish Economic Planning Department is in fact the responsible department in Scotland, while the Welsh Office plays the same role in Wales. Both these departments liaise very closely with the Department of Industry in the administration of the scheme.

16. Field and Hills, 'The Administration of Industrial Subsidies', p. 12.

17. *Third Report from the Committee of Public Accounts*, Minutes of Evidence, para. 39.

18. Field and Hills, 'The Administration of Industrial Subsidies', p. 12.

19. Department of Industry, 'Criteria for Assistance to Industry' in *Industry Act 1972: Annual Report for the Year ended 31 March 1976* (HMSO, London, 1976), HC 619, p. 36.

20. Ibid., p. 37.

21. Ibid., p. 36.

22. That is: in SDA: $(3 \times 10) + (4 \times 3) = 42$; in DA/IA: $(2 \times 10) + (4 \times 3) = 32$.

23. Department of Industry, *Incentives for Industry in the Areas for Expansion* (HMSO, London, 1978), p. 13.

11 CONCLUSIONS

So far in this book we have been concerned with regional-incentive policy in the various countries of the European Community. The aim of this, the final, chapter is to draw together, compare and contrast the information contained in the individual-country chapters. To this end, the chapter starts with a brief review of the regional problem in the different Community countries, before moving on to trace out the development of policy in the post-war period. The role of the European Commission in the regional-policy sphere is then briefly discussed before concentrating, in the second half of the chapter, on a detailed comparison of the incentives currently on offer in the various Community countries. In a final brief section the chapter returns to the theme of the development of policy, consideration being given to likely future policy trends.

The Regional Problem

We have seen that all countries in the European Community have regional problems. We have seen, too, that these problems vary considerably from one country to another. While in every case the basic problem is a lack of job opportunities, in some instances this can be attributed to overconcentration on the rapidly declining agricultural sector, whereas in others it is due to poor industrial structure with an excess of slow-growth and/or dying industry. With almost one-quarter of its working population employed in agriculture, the Republic of Ireland is perhaps the best example of the former type of problem, but the Italian south and parts of Denmark and France exhibit a similar over-reliance on agriculture. As far as poor industrial structure is concerned, the United Kingdom Development and Special Development Areas, the Lorraine region of France and much of the Walloon part of Belgium are good examples. On the other hand, in almost all Community countries, areas with an industrial concentration on declining sectors like coal mining, iron and steel, textiles or ship building tend to be problem regions.

As well as there being differences in the basic cause of the problem between countries and between regions within countries there are also differences in the intensity of the problem. The problem is undoubtedly at its most extreme in the Italian south (where, as we saw in Chapter 7,

214

unemployment in 1977 was almost double the centre-north average, and this despite the emigration of four million people between 1951 and 1976, well over half of these moving to the centre-north), in the Irish Republic (where the nation *as a whole* has unemployment rates twice the Community average and where a region like the north-west has unemployment more than 60 per cent above the national average) and, for completely different reasons, in Northern Ireland. In more central parts of the Community, however, regional differentials are far less severe, and indeed the problem is not one of large areas being disadvantaged in any major sense. Rather, as in the case of Germany, the problem is concentrated in a limited number of sub-regions distributed throughout the country.

Given what are fairly wide differences between countries in terms of problem intensity, it is perhaps surprising that there is in fact a reasonable element of uniformity in terms of the proportion of the population in the different countries included within those areas designated for regional-policy purposes, as Table 11.1 shows.

Although the range is from 17 per cent in the Netherlands to 45 per cent in the United Kingdom, a figure of about 35 per cent is very much the norm. There would, moreover, seem to be no strong correlation between problem intensity and the proportion of the national population contained within the designated areas. But broad uniformity in terms of area coverage is probably only to be expected, given the political pressures which seem inevitably to arise whenever area designation is considered. Nowhere in the Community has it proved possible to come up with an 'objective' measure of the problem (either in the form of a single indicator or weighted combination of indicators) – not even in Germany where, as we saw in Chapter 5, considerable effort has been devoted to the development of designation methodologies. At the end of the day, political pressures have everywhere played an important role in the designation process and, therefore, in the determination of the areas finally designated.

The Development of Policy

We noted above that the basic problem facing the designated problem areas in the European Community is that of insufficient job opportunities. This problem need not, however, have led to a policy of taking work to the workers (i.e. regional policy in the conventional sense) but could rather have been met by assisting out-migration to more prosperous areas. True, some countries (e.g. the Netherlands) have schemes which compensate labour for inter-regional movement but

Table 11.1: Proportion of Population in Designated Problem Regions
by Community Country, 1978

Country	Designated problem regions[a]	Percentage of national population
Belgium	Development Zones	42
Denmark	Development Regions	27
France	Regional-development-grant Award Zones	35
Germany	G.A. Areas	36
Ireland	Designated Areas	33
Italy	Mezzogiorno	35
Luxembourg	No designated areas	
Netherlands	Investment-premium areas	17
United Kingdom	Assisted areas plus Northern Ireland	45

Note: (a) These regions are described in detail in the individual-country chapters.
It should be noted that, in July 1979, it was announced that the British assisted
areas would be cut back over a three-year period such that, by August 1982, the
United Kingdom assisted areas plus Northern Ireland will hold just under 30
per cent of the UK working population.

nowhere, in the post-war period, have such incentives ever been on an
even remotely comparable scale to those measures aimed at encouraging the movement of firms — even though it must be recorded that the
movement of labour has in fact probably done more to balance regional
demand and supply than has the movement of jobs.

Like the causes of the problem and the intensity of the problem the
rationale for adopting a 'work-to-the-workers' policy in response to the
problem varies between countries and indeed between problem areas
within countries. In a few instances it reflects military considerations
and, more specifically, the desire to avoid depopulating sensitive border
areas; in others it is based on the raw political power of the affected
areas; in some it can be traced to a social concern for disadvantaged
communities and in particular to a desire to minimise the many social
problems created by large migratory flows and by the selective nature
of migration; and in others it is the outcome of regional-planning priorities and the desire to maintain a 'preferred' distribution of population
throughout the country.

In addition, a strong economic case has been made over the years in
favour of the work-to-the-workers approach. Above all, proponents of
the policy have argued that it permits the utilisation of resources

(and, in particular, human capital resources) which might otherwise remain redundant, since it is often the case that people prefer to be unemployed in their home environment than gainfully employed in totally unfamiliar surroundings. Further, so the argument has run, a work-to-the-workers policy helps to take the economic heat out of the more pressured parts of the country, and thus allows the national economy to be run at a higher level of activity than would otherwise have been the case — in contrast to a policy of encouraging migration, which tends to increase the problems and pressures facing the more prosperous regions.

These, then, have been the various reasons put forward for adopting a policy of taking the work to the workers. But, as already noted, no single factor can be picked out as being of over-riding importance, either in any given country or at any point in time. Rather, it has been a combination of the various factors listed above — military, political, social, planning and economic — which has led to consensus on the need for action.

Whatever the rationale of the work-to-the-workers policy in the different Community countries, the stage has now been reached where all member states have such a policy. If one was to attempt to trace out the development of policy on a Community-wide basis, one could perhaps identify three broad phases of policy in the post-war years — a first phase lasting until the latter half of the 1950s, a second phase covering the 1960s and taking in, too, the start of the 1970s, and a third, current phase.

In most countries, the first decade or so after the war was a period of recovery and reconstruction, with a concentration on *national* growth and development. At this stage, regional policy was not a key issue, an increase in the national cake being viewed as far more important than questions of how the cake might be spatially distributed. Regional problems were, in any case, far less pressing than they were later to become, in that most of the future problem industries were experiencing buoyant demand and growth in a general situation of shortages. Certainly, this first policy phase was a period during which regional financial incentives were either non-existent or were playing only a very minor role. If there was a regional policy at all — and policy was evident in only a few countries — then, with the possible exception of the United Kingdom, it was a policy based overwhelmingly on infrastructure provision. This, for example, was the approach adopted in the Italian south in the period up until 1957, the belief being that if only southern infrastructure levels could be brought up to those found in the more prosperous parts of the country then industrial development would take place spontaneously.

Towards the end of the 1950s, a new phase was to begin, a phase which in most countries spanned the 1960s and lasted into the oil-crisis years of the early 1970s. In many ways, this second phase was an extremely exciting period throughout Europe, and not only in respect of regional policy. It was a period of great political consciousness, a period where equality (and not only spatial equality) was very much to the fore. Indeed, distributional questions were seen to be as important as growth in many quarters, particularly towards the end of the period. A related factor was that it was a time during which both local and regional aspirations rose, and pressure was put on central government to move towards meeting those aspirations. For its part, central government was confident that just about any problem could be solved, given appropriate planning and policy. Finally, it was during this period that the *need* for a regional policy became almost self-evident as a result of the major (but, for the most part, localised) structural changes taking place in, for example, the mining, ship building, textile and iron and steel industries.

Obviously, different factors had a different force in different countries at different times but, taking the period as a whole, the general flow was in the same direction throughout Europe — towards more active regional policy. It was a flow, moreover, which drew in countries not themselves under mainstream pressures, such that by the late 1960s all the (current) Community countries — even those with no major regional problem — had an incentive package on offer in their problem regions. In addition, some countries (Britain, France and, by the early 1970s, Italy and the Netherlands) had control policies in operation in their pressured regions. Moreover, there was in some countries, Italy being the prime example, a heavy use of state industry to further regional-development objectives, and in a number of others (Denmark, the Netherlands, the United Kingdom) the dispersal of government offices towards the designated areas was being planned or had taken place. Infrastructure spending, too, continued to be important in many countries, even though it more and more came to be viewed only as a 'permissive' element of policy — not sufficient in itself to encourage the development of the problem regions. But the main concentration, as already noted, was on incentives. Not only did all countries have them by the late 1960s but, as the individual-country chapters show, they had them on a scale and at a level of intensity markedly greater than ever before.

In Belgium, for example, the minor interest subsidy in favour of the problem regions in the 1959 legislation was increased in 1966 and complemented by an alternative capital grant. In Denmark, a package based primarily on loan guarantees was transformed by the introduction of a capital grant in 1969 and by the replacement of the loan guarantees by concessionary loans in 1972. In France, a period in which great administrative discretion was exercised in respect of both incentive awards and the designation of the problem areas gave way, in 1964, to explicit designation of the problem regions and to a more automatic approach to the administration of incentives — with the result that the overall policy became far more visible than previously. In Germany, the late 1960s saw a shift of emphasis away from the promotion of infrastructure investment and towards incentive policy (with the incentives on offer increasing dramatically in importance); and at the same time a start was made on what was to become a continuing attempt to harmonise Federal and *Land* aids. In Ireland, after almost two decades during which there was some form of shared responsibility in the regional-development field, the system was re-organised in 1969 so as to give the Industrial Development Agency almost exclusive responsibility for grant awards and for the promotion of industrial investment. Also in 1969, the Irish incentive package was increased in value to make it one of the most attractive in Europe. In Italy, financial incentives were first introduced into southern policy in 1957, were extended in 1965 and were then further strengthened in 1968 with the introduction of a social-security concession, one of the few existing regional labour subsidies in the Community. In Luxembourg, incentive innovations in neighbouring states led to the offer of incentives (basically concessionary loans) in 1962, and culminated in the introduction of a capital grant in the early 1970s. In the Netherlands the late 1960s saw a crucial move away from awards linked to floorspace and to employment created and towards a less constrained and more valuable incentive, the investment premium. And in the United Kingdom there was a rapid increase in incentive expenditure in the course of the 1960s, despite frequent switches of emphasis between financial and fiscal measures. Moreover, in 1967, a labour subsidy was brought into the package, in the shape of the regional-employment premium.

In sum, the second phase of policy — what could be termed the 'heyday' of regional policy — saw the introduction of increasingly valuable incentives and of a wider range of incentive types. It was, moreover, a period of great innovation and experimentation, reflected not only in the constant chopping and changing found in many countries, but also in attempts to target policy in a very specific manner through highly discriminatory schemes (e.g. Italy) and to link policy closely to the general planning process (e.g. France). The widespread atmosphere of experimentation and innovation permeated, too, the sphere of area designation. In particular, there was a strong interest in growth-area policy in many countries, an interest taken perhaps to the extreme in Italy with, as mentioned in Chapter 7, the planning of a fully blown inter-related-industry complex at Bari Taranto. However, probably because of the serious political (and technical) difficulties of operationalising policy, the growth-area approach has not proven durable, being found to any notable degree only in the Dutch and German incentive packages at the present time. But even in the Netherlands and Germany, the number of such areas identified is such as seriously to reduce the value of the policy. Indeed, it could be argued that there is currently no true growth-area policy in operation, at least as far as incentives are concerned. Certainly those areas at present designated in most countries cover a large proportion of the land mass and, as we have seen, contain a considerable percentage of the national population.

That this second regional-policy phase was the heyday of regional policy should come as no surprise. The general environment in which policy was operating — economic, social, political — was after all, as we have seen, highly favourable to regional policy. Indeed, given the overall national pressure of demand, given the strains imposed by overheating in the more prosperous regions, and given the political fears generated in certain countries by potentially large migratory flows to the tight labour-market areas and major urban centres, the case for regional policy was 'obvious' in most European countries — and any policy effort was therefore viewed, almost by definition, as 'successful' and 'worth while'.

This situation changed dramatically with the oil crisis of 1973-4, an event which heralded the third, and current, policy phase. Throughout this phase, policy has been operating in a far more hostile environment. The environment has been hostile, most obviously, because present economic conditions — conditions of widespread high levels of unemployment, inflation, industrial overcapacity, low levels of investment, increasing competition from low-labour-cost countries and public-expenditure curtailment — are clearly not at all favourable to policy, even though the regional problem as such is still very much a problem. Related to this general economic *misère*, the earlier fears of huge migratory waves engulfing the major urban centres have receded. Indeed, by the mid-1970s, the flow was in the reverse direction in many countries, and a large number of major cities were suffering migratory losses. As a result of this trend it has become less fashionable to voice worries about present and/or possible future congestion. On the contrary, there has been a serious concern in some countries about the lack of activity in the inner areas of large cities. Moreover, at least in the British context, this problem, and the more general problem of a lack of growth in what previously were among the most dynamic parts of the economy, has actually been attributed by some observers to regional policy itself — the view being that policy has helped to 'drain' the prosperous areas of their potential. But even in the problem regions there have been feelings of discontent arising from what some see as the negative effects of policy; for instance, worries have been expressed about the increasingly branch-factory nature of the problem-region economies. Of course, some would argue that these negative reactions to policy are simply part of a more general disillusionment with the ability of government to solve problems. They do, however, mean that no longer is the need for, and success and effectiveness of, regional policy taken for granted.

Given this dramatic change in the environment within which regional policy operates, it is only natural that many of the features which characterised policy during its heyday soon disappeared from the scene. Whereas previously incentive expenditure had risen rapidly in most countries, in the years after 1973 it tended to level out, at least in real terms. Whereas previously the range of incentive types had widened considerably, the post-1973 period saw the main regional incentives remaining very much as they were, although there was undoubtedly above-average growth of what might be called the 'small end' of the incentive market (key-worker mobility schemes, schemes to aid product development, schemes to provide venture capital, etc.) as countries facing increasingly severe expenditure constraints tried both to plug gaps in their incentive programmes and to exploit potential opportunities not covered by their main incentive schemes. And whereas previously there had been much experimentation in the regional-incentive arena, there was considerably less innovation after 1973.

In short, for regional-incentive policy, the post-1973 period has been very much one of consolidation in a hostile environment. To suggest that there has been consolidation is not, however, to say that policy has not changed at all. In fact, there have been a number of quite significant shifts of emphasis as a result of the new situation.

First, recognising the current shortage of potentially mobile manufacturing industry, there have been attempts in a few countries (and perhaps above all in France and the United Kingdom) to encourage service-industry mobility. We discuss such attempts in more detail below but for the present it is worth mentioning that they have not up until now been noted for their success. Second, controls have fallen into relative disuse in those countries where they are part of the policy package. It has just not proven politically feasible to operate such policies in conditions of high national unemployment, and anyway the lack of expansion by manufacturing industry has meant that controls have currently very little leverage. Third, as mentioned earlier, plans to disperse government offices have also tended to be put into abeyance, a reflection both of the general economic situation and of the particular problems facing the major conurbations. Finally, there has been a tendency in a number of countries (France, Italy, the United Kingdom and Ireland are the main examples) to devolve the administration of policy, at least as far as the day-to-day details are concerned. In part, this move can be attributed to a desire for increased administrative efficiency (since important elements of project vetting and monitoring can only be done on site, i.e. locally) and perhaps to a felt need to make more use of local knowledge in the administrative process, but it can also be put down to an attempt to meet (if not defuse) some of the political aspirations of the problem regions. As already noted, such aspirations grew considerably during the 1960s and early 1970s and, in many countries of the Community, are still at a very high level.

Despite these shifts of emphasis in a number of countries, there have been no *major regional*-incentive initiatives during the current policy phase – or at least this was the case until the significant changes announced in the United Kingdom by the incoming Conservative Government in July 1979. As stated in Chapter 10, over the next three years the map of the United Kingdom assisted areas is to be redrawn such that, by August 1982, they will contain less than 30 per cent of the UK workforce, whereas previously they had held over 45 per cent; the main incentive weapon, the regional-development grant, is to be reduced in value in the Development Areas (from 20 per cent to 15 per cent) and is to be withdrawn completely from the Intermediate Areas; and selective financial assistance, an important discretionary component of the United Kingdom incentive package, is to be limited to cases which *need* aid to enable them to go ahead. Through these changes it is hoped to reduce regional-incentive expenditure by almost two-fifths (i.e. some £230 million) while at the same time making that expenditure which remains more cost-effective by concentrating it on the areas of greatest need.

Apart from this very recent UK exception – an exception which perhaps heralds the next policy phase – there have been no *major* changes to the regional incentives on offer in the Community countries in the past few years. On the other hand, there have been important changes in the *national*-incentive sphere, changes which have had a serious impact on the effectiveness of regional policy — namely, the very rapid growth in national and sectoral aids. The WIR scheme in the Netherlands, the national 'twin' of the 1976 *Mezzogiorno* Law in Italy, and the selective-investment scheme and a whole host of industry schemes under Section 8 of the Industry Act in Britain are the most obvious examples; but in almost every Community country there have been similar developments. To some extent this trend reflects the view that such micro-policies are the best instruments for encouraging investment and employment. However, it also stems from a reluctance to use conventional macro-economic policies under current economic conditions (and especially the combination of high unemployment and rapid inflation) and from a recognition that alternative policies (like, for example, the introduction of import restrictions) are not politically feasible in the present international climate.

Whatever the reason for the trend, micro-policies at the national level have had the effect of cutting down on the net advantage conferred by regional incentives. In some instances this has been intentional (as an approach, it is politically more acceptable than the explicit reduction of differentials by cutting back on the available regional aids or the extension of already very widely drawn problem-area boundaries) but in others it is simply an unfortunate side effect. Whether intentional or not, the trend must clearly be of grave concern to the regional policy-maker since, in effect it is undermining the ability of regional policy to divert investment to the problem regions, an important aspect of policy. His concern must, moreover, be intensified by the knowledge that those micro-policies which have been introduced will not readily be withdrawn, certainly not if the current national economic conditions continue. In view of this, many would argue that there is a strong case for actively examining the extent to which a regional element can be added to national aids to offset any negative side effects such aids may be having on the problem regions. In some countries this is already being done. In Belgium, for example, a cyclical 'premium', recently added to the nationally available soft-loan scheme to help counteract the impact of the current recession, was in fact biased in favour of the designated problem regions.

If one were to attempt to sum up the third phase one would have to say that, while regional incentives themselves have consolidated their position in a generally hostile environment, they have been weakened by related developments, and in particular by the rapid growth of very similar national (or at least non-problem-region) incentive schemes. But regional-incentive policy in this third policy phase has not only been affected — some would say undermined — by related national developments; it has also been influenced by international events and, above all, by the interventions of the European Commission in the regional-incentive field.

The Role of the European Commission

At the present time there are two major arms to the Commission's involvement in regional policy. On the one side, the Competition Directorate (DG IV) has the remit to control, amongst other things, regional aids which might distort trade, while, on the other, the Regional Policy Directorate (DC XVI) is concerned with the fortunes of the Community problem regions.

DG IV's interest in regional incentives (and state aids generally) arises from Article 92 of the Treaty of Rome. Under this article:

> Any aid granted by a member state or through state resources in any form whatsoever which distorts or threatens to distort competition by favouring certain undertakings or the production of certain goods shall, insofar as it affects trade between member states, be incompatible with the Common Market.

While Article 92 would appear, in principle, to call into question all state aids of a potentially trade-distorting character, including regional ones, in practice — and in line with later provisions of the Rome treaty — regional incentives are permitted, even though subject to regulation. This regulation takes the form of the so-called 'co-ordination solution', under which ceilings of aid are set for projects locating in different parts of the Community. Up until the end of 1978 these ceilings were in terms of project fixed-capital costs but, in response to political pressures from countries with labour-related regional measures, to worries that the fixed-capital-cost denominator might impose a bias in favour of capital-incentive projects and to a general increase in interest in the creation of jobs within incentive schemes (not surprising given the employment situation in most member states), an *alternative* labour denominator has recently been developed. Current aid ceilings in terms of the new twin denominators are shown in Table 11.2.

A number of criticisms can be levied at this form of co-ordination. Most important, the development of the approach by DG IV has been

Table 11.2: Co-ordination Solution Aid Ceilings, 1979

Country	Problem region	Maximum aid as a net-grant-equivalent percentage of initial investment		Maximum aid in European units of account per job created by initial investment
1) Ireland Italy UK Germany France	Whole country Mezzogiorno Northern Ireland Berlin (West) Overseas Departments	75%	*or*	13,000 EUA
2) France Italy UK	RDG Areas Aided centre-north Development Areas	30%	*or*	5,500 EUA *up to* 40%
3) Germany Denmark	Zonal Border Area Special Development Regions	25%	*or*	4,500 EUA *up to* 30%
4) All other	Community regions[a]	20%	*or*	3,500 EUA *up to* 25%

Note: (a) Excluding Greenland, where there are, in fact, no aid ceilings.

Source: Commission of the European Communities, COM (78) 636 final, Brussels, 21 December 1978.

largely divorced from the regional problem and from policy attempts to solve that problem. While the ceilings in Table 11.2 do vary between problem regions, their level has been determined by the level of assistance available in those regions at the time the ceilings were first introduced and not by any analysis of the severity of the problem in the various regions. Similarly, aids are judged by DG IV not on how effective or worthwhile they are (or even on the extent to which they actually distort trade) but rather mainly with respect to their ease of measurement. As a result, a number of incentives which do not fit readily into the arithmetic of the co-ordination solution but which are viewed within their own countries as central to the regional-development effort (the Irish export-profits-relief scheme and the British regional-development grant are just two of the more prominent examples) have been called into question. In turn this has led to considerable time and effort being spent by member states in the defence of existing aids. But, even more significant, it has meant the creation of a general atmosphere which almost certainly has had a stifling effect on new incentive initiatives. As if it were not enough for regional-policy designers to be faced with the delicate and difficult problems created by a generally hostile economic environment at home, they have also had to look over their shoulders continually in the direction of Brussels.

A second major criticism of DG IV's co-ordination work is of a more technical nature, and relates to the control denominators chosen. While these may have a role to play in the prevention of competitive outbidding between countries for mobile projects, many would doubt whether they are appropriate to the control of trade distortion. A more relevant denominator for this purpose would surely be value added. But if the aim of control is to stop competitive outbidding for mobile projects (which seems to be how DG IV has interpreted its remit), then it is necessary to ask whether it is appropriate to include *all* projects within the control mechanism, as the current elaborate procedure apparently does. After all, there can only be a relatively limited number of projects which are internationally mobile. Moreover, if the prevention of competitive outbidding to the detriment of the problem regions is the objective, then one wonders whether the Regional Policy Directorate should not be concerning itself with this, rather than DG IV.

A third major criticism of the current co-ordination solution is perhaps even more fundamental, since it relates to the effectiveness of the current system. There seems to have been a failure on the part of Brussels to recognise that control in such a sensitive and political area of policy can only be effective given the goodwill of the participants. DG IV has, however, been governed by rigid views about the primacy of competition policy and, by emphasising rigid arithmetical solutions, has been prepared to put goodwill at risk. But without goodwill, considerable pressure is set up to search for means of circumventing the regulations — a waste of the intelligence and energy of everyone involved.

The role of DG XVI, the Regional Policy Directorate, is quite different from that of DG IV. Basically, DG XVI is concerned with making sure that regional policy in the various countries is consistent with development priorities in the different problem regions of the Community, as viewed from the Community perspective. To this end, DG XVI has, amongst other things, responsibility for the European Regional Development Fund — the main direct source of aid for regional development at the Community level. The Fund has, however, been disappointing in its impact, and this for three main reasons: it has too few resources at its disposal; it has spread those resources too widely; and, of key importance, it has been used by member states to substitute for national awards in the problem regions rather than to supplement them. As a result, the influence of DG XVI on regional development has not been great.

A Comparison of Current Incentive Policy

We have so far taken the reader through the various phases of regional policy in the post-war period, dwelling in particular on a variety of key features and issues of the present policy phase. We now want to look in more detail at the current position and at how the various Community countries compare with one another, not only in terms of the type and form of the incentives on offer but also with regard to their value and availability. We begin by considering incentive type and form.

Incentive Type and Form

In the individual-country chapters we identified 25 major regional incentives, major in the context of each country in terms of both expenditure and the number of awards made. Broadly speaking, these incentives fall into five different types — capital grants, interest-related subsidies, tax concessions, depreciation allowances and labour subsidies. In Table 11.3 the distribution of the main incentives is shown by the incentive type and by country.

From the table, it can be seen that, throughout the Community, capital grants are the mainstay of most regional-incentive packages. Indeed, only in Belgium is there no *direct* capital grant on offer. It might appear from Table 11.3 that interest-related subsidies run capital grants a close second in the incentive league, there being eight of them compared with ten capital grants. However, the table tends to give an exaggerated impression of the importance of interest-related subsidies since in both Belgium and the United Kingdom what are noted in the table as two separate measures are in practice alternative versions of a single incentive scheme, interest-related grants being available as an alternative to interest subsidies when firms choose to self-finance their projects. For their part, fiscal concessions are less popular than financial measures, four countries having regional tax concessions on offer while two have regionally differentiated depreciation allowances. Finally, following the withdrawal of the regional-employment premium in Britain (and the selective employment premium in Northern Ireland) Italy alone has a *major* labour subsidy within its regional-incentive package.

That capital grants have been the most utilised incentive type up until now within regional-incentive packages is hardly surprising. They are more flexible than the other incentive types in that they can be item- or project-related, automatic or discretionary, and can be readily targeted to favour particular activities, areas, project types,

Table 11.3: Main Regional Incentives by Country and Type

Country	Incentive name	CG	IRS	TC	DA	LS
		Incentive type[a]				
Belgium	Interest subsidy		√			
	Capital grant		√/b			
	Accelerated depreciation				√	
Denmark	Company soft loan		√			
	Municipality soft loan		√			
	Investment grant	√				
France	Regional-development grant	√				
	Local-business-tax concession			√		
Germany	Investment allowance	√				
	Investment grant	√				
	ERP soft loan		√			
	Special depreciation				√	
Ireland	Capital grant — new	√				
	Capital grant — re-equipment	√				
	Export-profit tax relief			√		
Italy	Capital grant	√				
	National soft loan		√			
	Social-security concession					√
	Tax concessions			√		
Luxembourg	Capital grant	√				
	Tax concession			√		
Netherlands	Investment premium	√				
United Kingdom	Regional-development grant	√				
	Soft loan		√			
	Interest-relief grant		√/b			

Notes:

(a) Abbreviations: CG, capital grant; IRS, interest-related subsidy; TC, tax concession; DA, depreciation allowance; LS, labour subsidy.

(b) These incentives are calculated in terms of the interest concessions which would have been awarded had a soft-loan award been made. Because of this, they have been allocated to the interest-related-subsidy column although they are in effect capital grants.

and project-size groupings, both in terms of award conditions and the level of award made. Even more advantageous, they are highly visible to applicant firms and can be pushed to high values both in terms of nominal/advertised rates of award and effective award values (i.e. rates of award after incentive tax treatment, timing and phasing and item coverage have been taken into account). For these various reasons, capital grants are the prime components of most regional-incentive packages in the Community. The exceptions are in Belgium, where, as we have seen, there is no direct capital grant on offer, and in Denmark, where the investment grant is limited to the Special Development Regions and is used there to 'top up' the company soft loan in especially deserving circumstances.

In both the Belgian and Danish cases interest-related subsidies form the base element of the incentives on offer. But in the three remaining countries where they are available, interest-related subsidies are far less central to the incentive package, especially in Britain, where they are used selectively to 'top up' the automatic regional-development grant, and in Germany, where they are confined to local services. There are, however, very obvious reasons why interest-related measures have been used less than capital grants within regional-incentive packages. In the first place it is difficult to push the concessionary element of interest subsidies to high levels, most obviously because the size of subsidy is limited by the amount of interest paid but also because, in practice, very much less than the maximum possible subsidy is normally offered. Certainly, with the modest percentage subsidies on offer in most countries (three to five percentage points per annum) and with interest-free periods limited to British selective financial assistance, the current interest-related incentives fall far short of capital grants in grant-equivalent terms. Only where the applicant project is not considered an acceptable commercial risk, and would not therefore normally have received loan assistance, does the appeal of concessionary loans to firms increase (since, in effect, the receipt of the loan itself represents a subsidy). From the administrative viewpoint, too, loans have certain disadvantages *vis-à-vis* grants. Since for the duration of the loan public money will be 'at risk', they involve detailed investigation of applicants before award and demand close monitoring after award. This normally means that they only go to viable projects, the very projects which could anyway expect to receive loan assistance on the open market. A further problem is that where the loan itself comes from public funds this gives rise to a marked increase in public expenditure — especially unwelcome in current economic conditions. Capital grants offer administrators far more leverage in respect of expenditure made.

From Table 11.3 it can be seen that a majority of countries have a fiscal incentive of one form or another amongst their main regional measures. Even those countries without such incentives regionally have national fiscal aids, some of which are very generous. Thus, although neither Britain nor the Netherlands have major fiscal measures restricted to the problem regions, the British have a comprehensive set of capital allowances at the national level while, as noted in Chapter 9, the

Dutch have just introduced the WIR, a fiscally based incentive available nationally, but with differentiation in favour of the problem regions. Of the remaining Community countries, only Belgium and Germany have special depreciation allowances on offer among their main regional incentives. Despite being relatively minor in expenditure terms, it is often claimed that these allowances have an impact greater than their monetary value would suggest as a result of the almost pathological distaste of businessmen in all countries for paying tax and the fact that, since depreciation allowances represent only a postponement of tax payment, they encourage further investment with a view to putting off the payment of tax as long as possible. Tax concessions, too, have a significant psychological impact, suggesting, as they do, that awarding bodies take an especially positive stance to recipient firms. Such concessions are available in France, Italy, Ireland and Luxembourg, the Irish concession being viewed as particularly valuable in increasing the attractiveness of that country to incoming business.

But the fact that fiscal concessions can be attractive to firms should not obscure a number of serious disadvantages attached to them. There are, for example, occasions when industrialists cannot make full use of them — be it during the project build-up phase when losses, even at the firm level, may be the order of the day or in generally depressed economic conditions when taxable profits are not anyway being made. Moreover, they carry with them certain administrative drawbacks, the main one being that they are normally administered by the tax authorities. As a result, it is not always possible for them to be finely tuned to the needs of the problem regions. Rather, they are constrained, often severely, by the demands for administrative simplicity imposed by the tax system and tax authorities. They do, however, have one administrative advantage which may be useful under conditions of exchequer stringency — namely, that they involve revenue foregone rather than positive expenditure. For this reason, there may be times when they are more acceptable to government than, for example, capital grants.

Beyond the financial and fiscal measures discussed so far there is one other major regional incentive in the Community — the Italian social-security concession. It is perhaps surprising that this is the sole major labour subsidy limited to the problem regions, especially since the emphasis is on job creation in so many incentive schemes. Given this emphasis, and bearing in mind that labour is, after all, the main spare resource in the designated areas, one might expect policy to be more directly related to labour costs and employment. However, it would seem that labour subsidies have to be wide-ranging to be effective and that they have to be operated over a reasonably long time period. They are, as a result, an expensive form of policy, and it is no coincidence that the British regional-employment premium (the only other major labour subsidy operated in recent years) was withdrawn as part of public-expenditure cuts in December 1976.

From the above review it can be seen that all incentive types have both advantages and disadvantages. The flexibility and visibility of capital grants must be set against their expense; the very real value of soft loans to firms starved on the capital market must be weighed against their administrative complexity and lack of leverage; the possible psychological benefits of fiscal aids must be measured against not only their monetary cost but also their general inflexibility; and the advantages gained from lowering labour costs through labour subsidies must be matched against the seeming wastefulness of such blanket measures. In recognition of these points most countries (the Netherlands with its investment premium is the exception) have concentrated not on any single aid but rather on developing incentive 'packages'. Notwithstanding the obvious 'visibility' benefits attached to automatic measures, most countries have also tended to favour an element of administrative discretion within the available incentive packages, in an attempt to tailor the incentives to the needs of both recipient regions and applicant firms. There have, however, been significant differences in the degree of discretion in the various incentive packages on offer in the Community, as Table 11.4 makes clear.

The table shows that, while incentive type does have a bearing on whether an incentive is administered in an automatic or discretionary fashion (fiscal measures, for example, tend to be less discretionary than financial aids – which is not surprising since, as already noted, their day-to-day administration is in the hands of the tax authorities), a far more important determinant of the form of any given incentive policy is the country in which the incentive is operated. In Belgium, Denmark and Luxembourg the incentive package is basically discretionary, in Italy it is basically automatic and in the remaining Community countries certain measures are automatic, others are discretionary, and some are a mixture (the Dutch investment premium, for instance, is automatic for investment up to Fl 16 million and discretionary for investment beyond this level).

A number of factors help to explain the picture illustrated in Table 11.4, most obviously country size. The table shows clearly that it is the small countries of the Community which have the most discretionary

232 *Conclusions*

Table 11.4: Main Regional-incentive Discretion[a] by Country and Type

Country	Incentive name	CG	IRS	TC	DA	LS
		Incentive type[b]				
Belgium	Interest subsidy		D			
	Capital grant		D			
	Accelerated depreciation				D	
Denmark	Company soft loan		D			
	Municipality soft loan		D			
	Investment grant	D				
France	Regional-development grant	A/D				
	Local-business-tax concession			A		
Germany	Investment allowance	A				
	Investment grant	D				
	ERP soft loan		A			
	Special depreciation				A	
Ireland	Capital grant — new	D				
	Capital grant — re-equipment	D				
	Export-profit tax relief			A		
Italy	Capital grant	A				
	National soft loan		A			
	Social-security concession					A
	Tax concessions			A		
Luxembourg	Capital grant	D				
	Tax concession			D		
Netherlands	Investment premium	A/D				
United Kingdom	Regional-development grant	A				
	Soft loan		D			
	Interest-relief grant		D			

Notes:

(a) Abbreviations of discretion categories: D, administrative discretion in award, rates *up to* a maximum; A, little or no administrative discretion in award, rates *fixed*; A/D, basically automatic, but with an element of discretion for large projects.

(b) Abbreviations of incentive types: CG, capital grant; IRS, interest-related subsidy; TC, tax concession; DA, depreciation allowance; LS, labour subsidy.

incentive packages, perhaps primarily because they have fewer applications with which to deal, making discretion more feasible. But, of course, discretionary elements are found, too, among certain incentive schemes in the larger Community countries. In Germany, the discretionary nature of the investment grant is a direct consequence of the federal structure of the country. Federalism, and in particular the need to maximise *Länder* flexibility, has also meant that the main fixed element in the system — the Federally administered investment allowance — has a relatively low value, while the discretionary investment grant has at least the scope to reach very high levels, albeit within the overall maximum-preferential-rate ceiling. Britain also has adopted a two-tier approach to incentive policy but, in contrast to the position in Germany, the automatic base, the regional-development grant, is the more important component. Like Britain and Germany, France has both discretionary and automatic elements within its regional-incentive system. However, at least as far as the main incentives are concerned, there is very much less of a package approach to the French scheme, the administration of the regional-development grant being largely divorced from that of the local-business-tax concession. Finally, we should mention the position in Italy, where there is virtually no discretion in the administration of the incentives on offer — a reflection of the severity of the problem in the *Mezzogiorno* and perhaps also of the shortcomings of Italian administration.

Having described the type of incentives on offer in the Community countries and their form, we turn in the next section to consider their value.

Incentive Values

In the previous section we saw that capital grants are the most common of all incentive types. They are also generally the most valuable incentives on offer, nominal/advertised rates of award ranging from a maximum 15 per cent of eligible investment in Luxembourg to maxima of 50 per cent or more in Ireland, Italy and Northern Ireland. In all other Community countries the maximum nominal/advertised rates of award lie at or around 25 per cent of eligible investment, except in Belgium where, as we have seen, there is no *direct* capital grant within the regional-incentive package.

While these figures are not without interest, representing what can be an important first impression of the generosity of any given incentive package, it is of course dangerous to draw any strong conclusions from them. In the first place, they relate to only one incentive type — an incentive type, moreover, of varying importance in the different regional-incentive schemes. Second, they are in terms of award maxima. Where the grant is discretionary actual awards may be much lower, and again there may be great differences between schemes in the extent to which average awards fall below the maximum. Finally, the figures take no account of incentive tax treatment, the timing and phasing of incentive award or eligible items and forms of expenditure, factors which obviously influence the real or effective value of the grants to recipient firms. We shall return to the issue of effective value later.

Moving on now to interest-related subsidies, it is potentially even more difficult to compare values since nominal/advertised rates of award do not consist of a single figure but rather depend on a number of factors: level of interest subsidy, loan and subsidy duration, repayment provisions (and in particular the availability of principal-repayment holidays) and the award of interest-free periods. On the other hand, there is in practice a great deal of similarity between the interest-related subsidies on offer in the member states in respect of these factors. Most schemes (and it will be recalled that interest-related aids are available in Belgium, Denmark, Germany, Italy and the United Kingdom) have an interest subsidy of around three percentage points per annum, a principal-repayment holiday of up to two years, no interest-free concession and a loan/subsidy duration of between 10 and 15 years. Only two exceptions are worthy of comment — the Italian case, where the interest subsidy can be as high as 70 per cent of the market rate of interest (currently giving an annual concession of over 10 percentage points for the duration of the loan), and the British case, with the availability of interest-free periods coincident with principal-repayment holidays. The British loan is, however, of relatively short duration — 5–7 years — with the result that the overall British concessionary element is not markedly in advance of that available in Belgium, Denmark and Germany. In contrast, the Italian subsidy is worth more than double the Belgian, Danish and German measures, and indeed ranks alongside many of the capital grants available in the Community in net-grant-equivalent terms.

For fiscal aids, more significant differences are found between countries, especially in respect of profit-tax concessions, as the individual-country chapters make clear. Whereas Irish export-profits tax relief is a full concession for 15 years and a partial concession for a further five years (or until 1990, whichever is the earlier), the Italian concessions last for only 10 years and cover all of the ILOR tax but only half of the IRPEG liability, the Luxembourg concession amounts to 25 per cent relief on taxable profits for just eight years, and the French concession is for a maximum of only five years and relates not to the national profits tax but to the local business tax. It is, however, once more the countries with the most serious regional problems — Ireland and Italy — which offer the highest nominal/advertised awards.

Indeed, if one were to sum up the position for all the main regional incentives in terms of nominal/advertised award maxima, it would be to say that there is in fact much similarity between countries, those countries that offer above the 'going rate' for any given incentive type normally being those recognised to have the most demanding regional problems.

However, while maximum nominal rates of award can be important as a first indication of the value of an incentive (and may be crucial in attracting firms where the system is discretionary), even more significant for firms making investment/location decisions is the effective value of any award made (i.e. the net-grant equivalent of the concession after taking incentive tax treatment, delays in payment and item coverage into account). This, after all, is the value that the firm would (or should) insert into any discounted cash-flow appraisal of the project under study. Let us briefly have a look at the various factors which determine effective value.

Beginning with incentive tax treatment, the position is that, largely for technical reasons, an almost identical approach is adopted everywhere with regard to interest subsidies (these normally being taxed in as far as they increase taxable profits by reducing debt-servicing charges) and fiscal aids (usually not taxed). More variety is, however, found in respect of capital grants – at least on the surface. Two capital-grant schemes (the British regional-development grant and the German investment allowance) are explicitly free of tax; a further five (the Luxembourg capital grant, the Dutch investment premium, the German investment grant and grants available under both the new-industry and re-equipment programmes in Ireland) are taxed indirectly, in the sense that the value of the assets aided is reduced by the value of the grant for depreciation purposes, thus indirectly increasing income and hence taxable profits; and the remaining three (the Danish, French and Italian grants) are regarded as income and hence pass directly into taxable profits.

In practice, however, the differences are less marked. For example, although regarded as income, the Danish grant, as we saw in Chapter 3, need not be brought into income for ten years, thus significantly reducing the impact of taxation. The Italian grant, too, is only minimally taxed in practice, there being provision for its allocation to a tax reserve, while the French grant, although treated as income, is taxed according to rules akin to those applicable to indirectly taxed grants. Where grants are taxed indirectly the impact of taxation is greatly reduced, since tax payments are spread over time. More than this, profits-tax concessions in Italy, Ireland and Luxembourg may mean that little or no taxable profits are anyway being made in those countries, a situation found, too, elsewhere in the Community in times of economic recession. Quite clearly, the differences between countries in the tax treatment of capital grants are very much less in practice than they at first sight appear.

Delays in the payment of incentives – the second factor to be taken into account in any effective-value calculation – are also relatively standard between countries) although there are obvious differences between incentive types, with fiscal measures normally being 'paid' with relatively long delays due to their attachment to the tax system). Generally speaking, for financial aids, claim-processing delays tend to be less than three months, claims normally being submitted in line with expenditure. The most notable exception is the German investment allowance, claims for which cannot be submitted until the first three months of the calendar year after the financial year in which the expenditure to be aided took place (reflecting the fiscal origins of this incentive).

The final step in calculating the effective value of any given incentive scheme involves adjusting for eligible items and forms of expenditure. As far as eligible items are concerned, plant and buildings are standard for almost all incentives, and land is also normally eligible for capital-grant assistance. The British regional-development grant, the German investment allowance and the Italian capital grant are, however, excep-tions to the rule and are not available towards the costs of land. While fixed-capital costs are usually eligible, working capital is normally excluded from eligibility. The exceptions in this regard are the British and Italian interest-related subsidies, both of which aid working capital. Turning to eligible forms of expenditure, it is leasing in particular which is normally closely scrutinised. At the end of the day, however, most countries tend to aid at least some form of leasing. Only in the Nether-lands and Denmark is leasing not aided at all as part of the regional-incentive system.

As far as incentive tax treatment, payment delays and eligible items and forms of expenditure are concerned, then, it can be seen that there are significant similarities between countries, even if there is always the one or other exception to prove the rule. However, those exceptions which we have identified are very often of a 'swings and roundabouts' character. An incentive which is generous in one respect is frequently miserly in another. As a result, the ranking of regional-incentive packages in the Community by effective value is very much in line with what one would expect given the nominal/advertised rates of award identified earlier. Italy, Ireland and Northern Ireland form the top group, well in advance of the remaining Community countries, which

are reasonably well grouped together but with Britain somewhat in the
lead and Luxembourg lagging behind.[1]

Incentive Availability

While a comparison of regional-incentive values has obvious attractions
for those interested in compiling international league tables, it by no
means tells the whole story. When considering the potential impact of
an incentive, those factors which determine its availability are at least
as important as those which determine its value — nominal or effective.
A 10 per cent capital grant payable automatically to manufacturing
industry throughout the problem regions is likely to do more towards
solving the problem than a 50 or 100 per cent grant restricted to setting-
up projects which create at least one thousand jobs in a growth pole
and are put forward by a managing director with one blue and one
green eye! Within this section we wish to compare those factors which
influence the availability of the incentives on offer in the Community
countries — and in particular their spatial, industrial and project coverage.

Spatial Coverage. We saw in Table 11.1 that the designated problem
regions in four of the nine Community countries contain between 33
and 36 per cent of the national population. Since in a fifth country
(Luxembourg) no areas are designated, this means that half of the
Community countries are remarkably similar in terms of the spatial
coverage of their designated areas. Of the remaining countries, the
Netherlands (with 17 per cent of the national population in designated
regions) and Denmark (27 per cent) fall below the 'norm' while
Belgium (42 per cent) and the United Kingdom (45 per cent) lie above
it — but, with the exception of the Dutch case, the range around the
norm is not great, particuarly when it is recalled that the United Kingdom assisted areas are about to be cut back and will hold fewer than 30
per cent of the national population by August 1982. As a result, and
bearing in mind that most of the 25 main regional incentives which we
have identified are available throughout their countries' designated
problem regions, it is tempting to draw the conclusion that there is a
great deal of similarity between incentive schemes in terms of their
spatial availability. Such a conclusion is, however, difficult to sustain in
practice, and this for three main reasons.

First, a number of important incentives are on offer only in parts of
the designated areas. In particular, the British regional-development
grant is at present available towards both plant and building expenditure
only in the British Special Development and Development Areas

(currently holding about 23 per cent of the national population but due to be cut back significantly over the next three years — see Figure 10.3) and from August 1980 will be withdrawn completely from the Intermediate Areas; the German special depreciation allowance and that part of the investment allowance relating to re-organisation and basic rationalisation projects can both be obtained only in the Zonal Border Area (containing about 12 per cent of the German population); and the Danish investment grant is limited to that country's Special Development Regions (holding 17 per cent of the Danish population). This last example is especially noteworthy since, as we saw in Chapter 3, the investment grant is far and away the most valuable Danish regional-incentive. While within the Special Development Regions the Danish regional-incentive package stands comparison with most others in the Community, outside these regions it is very much less valuable. In addition to the above cases, it should be noted that, while not limited to a particular type of problem region, the Dutch investment premium and German investment grant are available only to projects located in designated growth areas. This is not, however, a very restrictive condition in practice since in both countries a large number of growth areas have been identified — over 40 in the Netherlands and well over 300 in Germany.

Second, and in contrast to the above limitations on coverage, a number of incentives are available not only in the designated areas but also outside them. Most significantly, the Irish package — as made clear in Chapter 6 — is a national-incentive package, while in Italy the soft loan is also national (although with marked differentiation in rates of award) and the ten-year ILOR concession is on offer in the depressed parts of the centre-north as well as in the south. In the Netherlands the investment premium is available in selected nuclei outside the designated regions (i.e. the Northern Development Area and the Reconversion Area of South Limburg), even though often at a reduced rate, and in France the regions designated for local-business-tax-concession purposes are far more widely drawn than those for the regional-development grant.

Finally, in addition to these coverage differences, a distinction is often made between different problem-region types when determining rates of award — with the result that the maximum award is frequently available in only a limited part of the problem areas. In fact, almost all countries have some element of spatial discrimination in award rates. In Belgium, for example, the maximum interest subsidy/capital grant is available only in the Category I Development Zones; in Category II

Zones the maximum subsidy is one percentage point less. In France a distinction is drawn between three separate award zones for regional-development-grant purposes, the maximum award being 25 per cent in Award Zone I, 17 per cent in Award Zone II and 12 per cent in Award Zone III. In Germany different types of Growth Point face different maximum preferential rates, ranging from 10 to 25 per cent. In Ireland, the Designated Areas are favoured, with award maxima of 50 per cent for setting-up projects and major extensions and 35 per cent for minor extensions and re-equipment, compared with Non-designated Area maxima of 35 per cent and 25 per cent, respectively. In Italy, priority-area projects receive a 20 per cent premium on the basic grant awarded. In the Netherlands, the basic investment premium is 25 per cent in the main development nuclei and 15 per cent in a number of other nuclei. And in Britain the regional-development grant is available at 22 per cent in the Special Development Areas, at 20 per cent in Development Areas (post-August 1980, 15 per cent) and at 20 per cent in the Intermediate Areas but only in respect of building expenditure (post-August 1980, zero); while selective financial assistance also distinguishes between the different types of problem region in terms of award maxima.

Given these various points, it is clear that a comparison of the spatial availability of the main regional incentives in the Community countries is far more complex than a simple comparison of designated-area coverage would suggest. Certainly there is no way in which one could draw up a clean and clear league table of spatial coverage. Even an attempt to indicate areas where maximum awards are available would be misleading. It would mean, for example, that only Special Development Areas would be covered in Great Britain — but, as we saw in Chapter 10, the difference between these areas and the Development Areas is minimal (even though the recently announced changes in the Development Area rate of regional-development-grant award will increase the differential between these areas and the Special Development Areas to seven percentage points as from 1 August 1980). Given this, the picture thrown up by concentrating on maximum-award areas would obviously give a distorted impression of the overall position in practice. Really all that one can do with any degree of confidence is to try to identify the extremes — those incentive packages which are especially generous and those which are not at all generous as regards spatial coverage. Within the former category one would almost certainly include the Irish and Italian packages, and within the latter the Danish package and perhaps also those on offer in the Netherlands and Germany.

Industrial Coverage. We have seen that, in respect of spatial coverage, a situation which at first sight appears to be relatively simple and straight-forward is, in fact, highly complex. For industrial coverage the reverse holds. While the position seems complicated (there being scope within most incentive schemes to offer assistance to a wide and varied range of activities) there is in practice considerable uniformity between incentive packages. Although there is usually the possibility to award incentives outside the manufacturing sector, and in particular to aid potentially mobile services (i.e. those with a choice of location, like banking, consultancy, data processing and research and development), most incentive schemes tend to draw a practical distinction between manufacturing and services and to concentrate assistance on the former. Certainly the vast majority of awards in the Community countries go to manufacturing projects.

The difficulties of encouraging service-industry development through general incentive schemes have been increasingly recognised. Such schemes are, for example, primarily capital-oriented and are thus less directly relevant to the service sector — a basically labour-intensive sector and a sector, moreover, dominated by rented buildings and leased equipment. But there has also been a growing consciousness of the potential role of service employment in the problem regions. The relative importance of service employment in the economy at large is, after all, rising rapidly and, at the same time, many would argue that the supply of potentially mobile manufacturing industry may be beginning to dry up. More than this, service activities meet many of the needs of the problem regions to the extent that they provide stable, high-quality jobs and also female jobs (very attractive to regions with low activity rates). For these reasons, a number of countries have tried to design regional-aid schemes aimed specifically at the service sector. The idea has probably been taken furthest in France and Britain.

In France, service-industry schemes have a long history, the first having been introduced in 1967. Currently there are two schemes in operation — one is intended to encourage the setting-up, extension, and transfer from the Paris region of management, administration, consultancy and data-research activities, while the other is aimed at research activities. Both depend crucially on a significant number of jobs being created. In Britain, too, service-industry aid is very closely related to job creation, and indeed takes the form of a grant (of up to £6,000 in the Special Development Areas, up to £4,000 in the Development Areas and up to £2,000 in the Intermediate Areas) per job provided. But even with the emphasis on job creation rather than capital investment (the standard focus of attention for manufacturing) it is clear that in neither country has the impact on the service sector been major. What is less clear is whether this relative lack of success is because the schemes are still not sufficiently tailored to service needs or because there are serious barriers to service-industry mobility (like, for example, the importance of key personnel and the fact that growth takes place gradually rather than in discrete jumps as in manufacturing) which incentives alone cannot overcome.

But away from these specific service-industry schemes, the general point is that industrial coverage tends, as we have seen, to be broadly uniform between countries, and is certainly more uniform than spatial coverage. Similarly, there is far less discrimination in terms of rates of award between eligible industries than there is between eligible areas. Indeed, in only two countries is there *explicit* rate discrimination along industrial lines — in Belgium, where lists of priority industries have been drawn up for the purposes of determining award levels (with, for example, only priority 1 industries qualifying for the maximum rate of award), and in Italy, where priority-industry projects receive a 20 per cent premium on the basic *Cassa* grant. On the whole, however, inter-industry differences are slight — a reflection, no doubt, of both the administrative and political problems of introducing discrimination along industrial lines.

Project Coverage. To complete our discussion of the availability of the main incentive types in the Community countries we now turn to project coverage. In practice, most Community assistance is project-related, i.e. is tied to identifiable projects. Of the main financial incentives, only the British regional-development grant is item-related, being paid on individual items of expenditure irrespective of whether or not they are part of a given project. As a result, this grant tends to be available to a wider range of investment than the typical project-related grant, although the difference between the two in practice does, of course, depend very much on the conditions attached to the project-related assistance. If there are very few conditions of award then, for all practical purposes, the difference may not be great. However, where, for example, projects must be viable, must create a specified level of employment, must involve a minimum amount of investment and must be to the long-term benefit of the recipient region (and we consider these and related conditions in detail shortly), then certainly a narrower range of investment is likely to be declared eligible for the project-related grant than would be aided under an item-related grant scheme.

Moreover, less investment will tend to be put forward for project-related incentives, since firms will almost certainly be put off by the need for detailed (and often time-consuming) administrative contact with government departments which project-related assistance normally demands.

Of the project-related aids on offer in the Community, most are available to a wide range of project types — setting-up, extension, transfer, modernisation, rationalisation and re-organisation. A few, however, are restricted to job-creating projects (i.e. setting-up projects, extensions and also transfers in as far as they involve moves *into* the designated problem areas). This is true of the Dutch investment premium, is largely true of the French regional-development grant and is true, outside the Zonal Border Area, of the German investment allowance.

In a number of packages, moreover, there is overt rate discrimination between eligible project types. In Germany, for example, the maximum preferential rate is up to 25 per cent of eligible investment for setting-up projects and extensions but, except in extreme border locations, is only up to 15 per cent for re-organisations and basic rationalisations (and then only if the project in question has a high structural effect). Elements of the British and Irish packages similarly favour job creation over job maintenance with, for example, the Irish capital grant having administrative maxima of 50 per cent for setting-up projects and major extensions and 35 per cent for re-equipment projects. Finally, in France a distinction is drawn between setting-up projects and extensions, and the former qualify for slightly higher rates of regional-development-grant award (FF 25,000 per job created in Award Zone I, FF 20,000 in Award Zone II and FF 15,000 in Award Zone III, as compared with awards of FF 22,000, FF 17,000 and FF 12,000, respectively, per job created for extension projects).

Summing up the position as regards project-type coverage and discrimination, it would appear that the Dutch and French packages and, to a more limited extent, the German package, tend to be restrictive, while the British package is generous, the regional-development grant being item-related. However, as already noted, the extent to which there are indeed differences between incentives and countries depends very much on the conditions attached to the available aid. We now consider these briefly.

A number of conditions are common to all project-related incentive schemes. It is, for example, a standard condition of award that the project to be aided be viable. A related condition found in most schemes is that a certain proportion of project funds — usually about one-third — be in the form of 'own finance'. Two exceptions to this rule are the Belgian case, where a minimum of 50 per cent own finance is demanded of capital-grant-aided projects and, at the other extreme, the Italian case, where only 14 per cent own finance is necessary for a small priority-industry project locating in a priority area (since, as we saw in Chapter 7, the area and industry premia attached to the Italian capital grant are not taken into account for the purposes of the public-sector-contribution limit). Further common conditions are that the project have a favourable impact on the recipient region (such a condition is mentioned explicitly as part of the Danish, German, Luxembourg and Dutch schemes) and that it be in line with both environmental and physical-planning regulations (specifically referred to in Belgium, Germany, Luxembourg, the Netherlands and Italy; the Italian condition is especially wide-ranging, ensuring conformity not only with environmental and physical plans but also with economic planning). Less common conditions are that the project must be in need of aid (mentioned in Ireland, and as part of the German ERP soft-loan scheme and recently given emphasis with the British selective-financial-assistance scheme), that it have a favourable sectoral impact (referred to in Belgium, Germany and the Netherlands), that aided assets be used on given premises for a specified time period (five years in Italy, four years as part of the British regional-development-grant scheme) and that the project must be located on a government industrial site (the Netherlands).

Of the above conditions, those relating to the viability of the applicant project are far and away the most significant, although the extent to which they are in fact restrictive certainly varies from scheme to scheme and from country to country, depending on administrative interpretation. But often even more limiting than viability conditions are two important conditions not yet referred to – job conditions (i.e. a minimum number of jobs to be created or safeguarded) and size conditions (i.e. a minimum level of investment to be undertaken). In Belgium, projects must involve investment of at least FB 500,000 (£8,500) and must create employment (specified in the case of the accelerated-depreciation allowance as a minimum 20 jobs). In Denmark, the minimum project size is DKr 0.5 million (£48,000) for the company soft loan and DKr 1 million for the investment grant and, again, there must be an (unspecified) impact on jobs. In France, there is a whole matrix of job and investment minima ranging, for example, for setting-up projects within the standard designated areas from six jobs and FF 300,000 (£35,000) to 30 jobs and FF 800,000 (£95,000). Moreover, as part of the French system, job and investment targets are laid down and have to be met within three years. In Germany, minimum job conditions are specified for extensions (e.g. 150 jobs or a 20 per cent increase within the investment-allowance scheme), and there is also an investment-cost ceiling of DM 3.6 million (almost £1 million) per job created or secured. In Ireland, no specific job targets are laid down, but the distinction between jobs created and jobs maintained is crucial in determining under which grant scheme an award can be made and, hence, the level of that award. In Luxembourg, too, there are no explicit job conditions although, with the down-turn in the steel industry, more attention than previously is beginning to be focused on the jobs issue. In the Netherlands there is again no specific target but only setting-up and extension projects of over Fl 0.2 million (£50,000) are aided, and then, in the case of extensions, only when they result in a 'sufficient' increase of employment or productive capacity. And in the United Kingdom, job creation has always been an important element of the selective-financial-assistance scheme (a cost-per-job limit being one of the determinants of award levels) even though, recently, increasing emphasis has been placed on job maintenance – although, in this instance, a 'substantial' number of jobs must be involved.

With such a varied list of job and investment conditions, and with the jobs to be created very often being unspecified, it is extremely difficult to rank incentive packages in terms of the severity of the conditions imposed – especially since this depends not only on the minima set but also on the extent to which the system is 'policed' to see that these minima are indeed met in practice. One country which does stand out, however, is France, not only because of the matrix of job and investment conditions which operates there but also because industrialists are actually held to the targets which they promise to meet – to such an extent that, as noted in Chapter 4, regional-development-grant clawback in France in any one year has recently been as high as 10 per cent of the total value of grants awarded in the same year.

Future Developments

So far in this chapter, we have commented on the scale and intensity of the regional problem in the various Community countries, have examined and analysed the stages through which regional policy has evolved over the post-war period and have compared and contrasted the regional incentives on offer in terms of their type and form, their value and their availability.

As we have seen, the current picture is one of considerable similarity but, at the same time, there are certain features in certain countries which differ markedly from the 'norm'. For example, while capital grants form the base element of most regional-incentive packages, there is no direct capital grant on offer in Belgium, and in Denmark the investment grant is used to 'top-up' the basic company soft loan in the Special Development Regions. While most countries do not have a major labour subsidy on offer, the social-security concession in Italy is far and away the most expensive of the Italian incentive measures. While administrative discretion plays a role in most incentive schemes, in Italy the system is virtually wholly automatic. While most capital grants are taxed, the British regional-development grant and German investment allowance are tax-free. While most schemes are limited to fixed-capital costs, in both Britain and Italy interest-related subsidies are available on working capital. While most countries aid at least some form of leasing, it is wholly ineligible within the Dutch and Danish schemes. While, in terms of effective values, most country packages are fairly closely grouped together, the Italian, Irish and Northern Irish packages have an especially high value, and the Luxembourg package a relatively low value. While in most schemes the designated areas are broadly defined, the schemes in both Germany and the Netherlands identify growth areas on which to concentrate assistance. While most incentives are limited in practice to the manufacturing sector, in Britain and France specific schemes have been developed to encourage service mobility. While most incentive schemes are project-related, the British regional-development grant is item-related. And while conditions of award would not seem to bite too harshly in most incentive packages, there is a very high clawback of the French regional-development grant.

How long these inter-country differences will remain is difficult to say, given current pressures at the Community level to harmonise the incentives on offer. It is also not easy to judge just what new developments there are likely to be in the regional-incentive field, especially at this juncture. Some would argue that little or no change can be expected. There has, after all, been no major *regional*-policy reaction up until now to the changed economic conditions of the latter half of the 1970s. Rather, as noted earlier, the incentives on offer at the end of the regional-policy heyday in the early 1970s have by and large remained in force, even though the increasing award of national and sectoral measures have tended to cut back on their relative advantage. On the other hand, the longer adverse economic conditions persist nationally then obviously the greater the likelihood that regional-policy measures spawned in the 1960s (and designed to tackle the problems of that decade) will come up for reappraisal. As we have seen, reappraisal has already taken place in the United Kingdom (encouraged by a change of government) and led to a considerable reduction in regional-incentive expenditure achieved primarily through a cutback in the coverage of the assisted areas and a concentration of aid on those areas facing the severest problems.

It will be interesting to see whether other countries follow the United Kingdom lead. Certainly, a number of questions are ripe for discussion, given the new economic situation facing most Community countries. If, for example, the new situation is to be one of very large labour reserves nationally, is it sensible for capital-oriented aids to be the main incentive instrument? If it is to be one of low taxable profits, is there not a case for concentrating less on fiscal measures and more on financial aids? If it is to be one where the current trend towards leasing in industry continues, are there not grounds for taking a more generous view towards leased equipment when considering eligible forms of expenditure? If it is to be one of little mobile manufacturing investment (both because of the relative decline of manufacturing and because push factors are likely to be less powerful), is it not desirable to shift the policy emphasis towards potentially more fruitful targets — the service sector or indigenous small firms, for instance? If it is to be one of public-expenditure curtailment, is there not a case to be made for the introduction of more discretionary (and less costly) measures, or does discretion invariably lead to the adoption of administrative precedents such that the advantages which could have been gained from making an incentive both visible and certain in award would be sacrificed to what was no more than the charade of discretion? If it is to be one of harsh competition for a few internationally mobile projects, is there not a real need for effective co-ordination at a European level, so as to prevent competitive outbidding for such projects, or does such a goal fly in the face of the realities of the situation? And if it is to be one of increasing micro-intervention at the national level, is it not essential to ensure a permanent regional bias to such measures, so that the advantage currently enjoyed by the problem regions is not more seriously eroded away?

But an even more fundamental issue for reappraisal concerns the extent to which regional policy itself is relevant and in general worthwhile. It will be recalled that, at the outset of this chapter, five possible justifications were put forward for the adoption of a 'work-to-the-workers' regional policy — military, political, social, planning and economic. Of these, the military, the planning and, in part, the social justifications are related to the existence of migratory outflows from the depressed areas into the more pressured regions. To the extent that such flows tend to decline as unemployment spreads throughout the country, then these justifications, too, will decline in strength. The economic justification for policy action is also less convincing than it perhaps was (at least to the extent that it relied on overheating in the more pressured regions), although an economic case for policy can certainly still be made based on the differing opportunity costs of labour in the problem and non-problem regions. Finally, there is the political justification to consider. As mentioned earlier, regional aspirations, ignited during the 1960s, are still at a high level, and indeed continue to grow in some Community countries. Added to this, the political will for a united Europe and, with it, a common European currency — still a potent force in some countries — mean that an effective regional policy on a Community-wide basis is viewed in certain quarters as essential.

But, if the justification for policy action still appears strong, the need for reappraisal as regards the most appropriate form of policy is even stronger. Current policy is very much the child of the 1960s. We are now, however, entering the 1980s. A reappraisal of incentive weapons, incentive targets and incentive targeting systems could do much to improve the design of policy such as to make it more suited to the new environment in which it must operate. Without reappraisal, and without appropriate policy adjustments, there is a very real danger that the expectations generated in earlier policy phases will be frustrated, with perhaps severe political consequences both for the individual member states and for the Community as a whole.

Notes

1. For a more detailed discussion of effective values, and a comparison of these between countries, see K.J. Allen *et al.*, *Regional Incentives in the European Community: A Comparative Study* (European Commission, Brussels, 1979).

NOTES ON CONTRIBUTORS

Kevin Allen: former Research Fellow at the International Institute of Management, Berlin, and currently Co-Director of the Centre for the Study of Public Policy at the University of Strathclyde

Lotty Boersma: University of Delft

Ullrich Casper: Research Fellow, International Institute of Management, Berlin

Professor Rik Donckels: Department of Economics at the University of Leuven

James Eustace: Department of Town Planning, Trinity College, Dublin

Chris Hull: Research Fellow, International Institute of Management, Berlin

Silvio Ronzani: formerly a Research Fellow at the International Institute of Management, Berlin, and currently a Research Fellow at the Centre for the Study of Public Policy in the University of Strathclyde

Jean Paul Schmit: member of the staff of Arbed, Luxembourg

Gert Strande-Sørensen: Institute for Future Studies, Copenhagen

Professor Paul Van Rompuy: Department of Economics, University of Leuven

Douglas Yuill: formerly a Research Fellow at the International Institute of Management, Berlin, and currently a Research Fellow at the Centre for the Study of Public Policy in the University of Strathclyde

INDEX